TIME FOR A CHANGE

Donal Dorr

Time for a Change

A FRESH LOOK AT SPIRITUALITY, SEXUALITY,
GLOBALISATION AND THE CHURCH

the columba press

First published in 2004 by
the columba press
55A Spruce Avenue, Stillorgan Industrial Park,
Blackrock, Co Dublin

Cover by Bill Bolger
Origination by The Columba Press
Printed in Ireland by ColourBooks Ltd, Dublin

ISBN 1 85607 444 7

Table of Contents

Introduction

There is a real hunger for spirituality in our time. Many people who have become disillusioned with formal religions are still looking for a meaning in life and a source of hope and spiritual energy. They seek peace of mind, harmony with their neighbours, healing and reconciliation for wounded relationships, justice in society, and a sense of communion with nature. They are interested not so much in doctrines or moral regulations but in a wisdom which is rooted in the heart and appeals to the heart. They do not want to hear people talking 'at' them about God; they want to experience God directly, to feel the Spirit moving in their heart and guiding their lives. They want to experience community, to feel warm with people, to love and be loved, to celebrate. They want a spirituality which is earthy, of the body, but which at the same time finds an echo in their souls.

Christianity should be meeting this hunger for an experiential and authentic spirituality. But many people are becoming disillusioned with the church as a place where they can find a spirituality which touches their hearts and is in tune with their deepest moral convictions. I have written this book as an attempt to bridge this widening gap. I began it in some frustration because it is not easy to be a member of the Catholic Church at the present time. On many occasions church authorities have said or done things which seem to me to be out of harmony with the fullness of the Christian faith as I understand it. The tone of several recent documents or statements – for instance, about other Christian churches or other religions, or about various issues related to sexuality – left me disappointed and at times quite angry.

Writing the book has strengthened and deepened my faith. I have become more convinced than ever that, despite all its failures and inadequacies, our church still has a rich heritage to draw on and a message which is relevant to the people of today's world. I have tried to communicate some of this richness to readers who may be struggling with doubts about the church as a 'carrier' of spirituality.

My choice of the title *Time for a Change* reflects both my impatience with much of what is going on in the Catholic Church today and my renewed faith that things can be different. Throughout the book I have tried to ensure that any criticisms I make are balanced with positive material. What I understand by 'positive material' is not just proposals for change, since there is no shortage of such proposals or of people to make them. As my subtitle indicates, what I have tried to offer is a fresh and positive look at four key areas of faith today: firstly, the nature of spirituality and how it relates to religion; secondly, sexuality as a key component in spirituality; thirdly, a spirituality which can be a response to the damaging effects of globalisation; and finally, how the church can be a more effective 'carrier' and promoter of genuine spirituality.

My ideal has been to write a book that is radical – by which I mean one that goes back to our roots in the Christian tradition, while at the same time being open to the movement of the Spirit in our world today. I must leave the reader to decide whether I have succeeded in living up to that ideal.

I am aiming for a broad readership, many of whom will be people who are interested in spirituality but who are unlikely to read books of academic or technical theology, economics, philosophy, or psychology. I believe, however, that a spirituality which fails to take account of the findings of these sciences is likely to be superficial and sentimental. So I have incorporated elements from them in what I hope is a 'digestible' form, concentrating on the practical implications from the point of view of spirituality.

In the book I have tried to draw together, in a popular and

manageable form, ideas from a wide range of sources. Spirituality is understood in a variety of different ways. Some people see it as primarily their relationship with God. Others scarcely advert to God at all when talking about what spirituality means to them. For them it is about values such as justice, or ecology, or about the practice of meditation and mindfulness. I believe that all of these elements are important. So in this book I have tried to present a coherent picture which can include them all.

There are four main parts in the book. In the first part there are three chapters under the general heading, 'What is Spirituality?' The first chapter gives an outline of spirituality as a relationship with God. I think our Christian faith becomes impoverished if we think only in terms of a relationship with God in general. We need to take seriously the fact that God is experienced by Christians as a Trinity. So I have given some account of what it means to relate to God as the provident Creator, and to have a personal relationship with Jesus, and with the Holy Spirit.

In chapter 2, I consider the more 'worldly' side of spirituality – that is, the aspect which overlaps with ethical behaviour. I give a short account of each of twelve different items ranging from ecology and justice to interpersonal respect and personal integrity.

In the third chapter I try first to clarify the relationship between spirituality and religion. Then I go on to examine how well the Catholic Church measures up at present in witnessing to, and promoting, the various aspects of spirituality which I listed in chapter 2.

The second part of the book is devoted to a topic which is important and rather problematic at this time, namely, a spirituality of sexuality. Chapter 4 offers a general account of how sexual love 'unfolds' and develops. Chapter 5 examines some of the major problems in the development of a balanced and authentic spirituality of sexuality. And Chapter 6 is devoted to the topic of a spirituality of celibacy.

The third part of the book consists of two chapters in which I

address another very important and difficult topic – globalisation. In chapter 7, I give a general account of the problems
caused by the present model of globalisation; then I go on to
write briefly about a spirituality of liberation as a 'Third World'
response to globalisation. Chapter 8 is devoted to an examin-
ation of how people in the Western world may develop a spirituality which can offer an alternative to the destructive style of
globalisation which is affecting all of our lives.

In the final part of the book I turn again to the church, looking
this time at its mission to be a 'carrier' of integral spirituality. I
begin chapter 9 by recalling the opening lines of the Vatican
Council document on *The Church in the Modern World*. This document commits us as Christians to taking on 'the joys and hopes,
the griefs and anxieties' of the people of our time. So I give a
rather extensive account of many different aspects of human
experience and try to evaluate how effectively the church is responding to the challenge.

In the tenth chapter I look at the issue of pastoral priorities
and strategies which we in the church should adopt in order to
help people in the wider world to develop and live by a balanced
and integral spirituality. This is spelled out further in Chapter
11, where I focus particular attention on how we in the church
can help to build up a sense of community and solidarity among
people, even those who do not normally come to church; I pay
particular attention to the issue of how the eucharist can become
a means of reaching out to people and perhaps drawing them
into community.

In the final chapter I move on to address the challenging
issue of the need for significant structural changes in the church
if it is to become a truly effective instrument for promoting and
nourishing people's spirituality. I focus on three main issues –
the need to dismantle clericalism, the need to adopt a more
collaborative way of exercising authority, and the need for a
considerable amount of decentralisation. This leads on to the
suggestion at the end of the book that it may be better to see the
church more as a movement than as an organisation.

Some parts of the book cover ground on which I had previously done a lot of research and reflection. Other parts deal with topics which I had not previously studied in depth. This is particularly the case in the three chapters which deal with sexuality. So in these chapters I have relied heavily on the writings of people whom I consider to be good guides in this difficult area. On the issue of celibacy I have drawn on the work of Richard Sipe, a recognised expert on the topic. In writing about shame and intimacy I have used the highly respected psychiatrist Donald Nathanson as my principal source. On the issue of the development of sexual love, the most valuable source I could find was Ben Kimmerling, who happens to be my sister. I decided that I should not allow this to prevent me drawing heavily on her reflections – particularly as they were published some years ago in periodicals which are no longer easily accessible to the general reader.

In parts of chapters 5, 10 and 11, I have incorporated revised versions of passages taken from articles which I wrote for *The Furrow*. In chapters 8 and 9, I have included a revised version of some material drawn from a contribution I made to the book *Work as the Key to the Social Question*, published in 2002 by the Pontifical Council for Justice and Peace.

I have included in the bibliography only the books and articles which I have referred to in the text of the book. If I were to list even a small proportion of the books which are relevant to this vast topic, the bibliography would have become unduly long. I see the bibliography simply as way of avoiding the need for cumbersome footnotes. Page references to the books and articles listed in the bibliography are incorporated within the text of the various chapters.

My special thanks go to my sister, Ben Kimmerling, who not only generously allowed me to share her best insights about sexuality, but also read drafts of this book and made helpful comments and suggestions. Also to my good friends Pádraig Ó Máile and Sister Jean Eason MMM for their critical reading and valuable suggestions.

Donal Dorr
January 2004

CHAPTER 1

Christian Spirituality

If we ask a number of people what the word 'spirituality' means to them we are likely to get two kinds of answer. Some answers will be similar to that of Patricia Higgins who says, 'I understand spirituality as "my relationship with God"' (Higgins 123). But others will probably describe it in more 'worldly' terms, such as being nourished by Nature (e.g. walking the hills or by the sea), or their relationship with friends or family, or their commitment to the poor, or to the struggle for justice for women, or for the victims of racism or exploitation.

So we find that there are two apparently different conceptions of spirituality. The first of these is a very traditional one, namely, a personal relationship with God. The other is one which has come to the fore in the Western world in recent times. It seems not to focus at all on a personal relationship with God. Instead it is concerned with one or more of a whole variety of 'worldly' values which are ethical and political, or purely personal, rather than religious. These values range from personal integrity and mindfulness, to interpersonal respect, and from fervent concern for human rights and justice in society to a passionate commitment to preserving the integrity of the world of nature.

For me, both of these understandings of spirituality are valid. I know individuals whose view is the more traditional one, and other people whose spirituality takes little or no account of God. In my own life, however, as in the lives of many other Christians, the two approaches come together and are fully integrated with each other. If I were asked which of the two views is central for me I would have to reply that it does not make sense to me to try to choose between them. This is because my relationship with God permeates my commitment to justice, my interpersonal relationships, and the other 'worldly' aspects of my spirituality. In the next chapter I shall give a systematic account of the various 'worldly' aspects of spirituality. But before that, I propose in the present chapter to give an account of spirituality as a relationship with God – more specifically a relationship with each of the persons of the Trinity.

SECTION ONE: JESUS, THE HUMAN ONE

In attempting to give an account of Christian spirituality I begin with Jesus since he is the origin and centre of our faith. What is most important for me about Jesus is that he provides a key link between spirituality as a personal relationship with God and the more 'worldly' ingredients or aspects of spirituality. At the heart of this link is the title which Jesus gave to himself. On dozens of occasions in the gospels Jesus calls himself 'the Human One' (cf. Brown 91). The usual translation is 'the Son of Man'; but – as I have spelled out elsewhere – this is a misleading and sexist translation; a more accurate translation is 'the Human One' (cf. Dorr 1996).

What does it mean for Jesus to call himself 'the Human One'? It means first of all that he is saying that he is one of us, in solidarity with all other humans in the world. Secondly, it implies that Jesus is in some way a model for what it means to be human. Thirdly, it suggests that his main concern was to help people to live a fully human life.

The fact that Jesus called himself 'the Human One' tells us that the way to come close to God is not to try to escape from this world or to run away from everyday human issues and problems but rather to live fully authentic human lives. By taking this title Jesus is inviting us to avoid the mistake which many Christians (and Muslims too) have made in the past and which many still make today. They undervalue all aspects of our life here on earth by seeing this present life simply as a kind of test to see whether we deserve to be rewarded by getting to heaven.

If Jesus the Human One is inviting us to live a fully human life as he did, this means that to be his followers we can and should commit ourselves wholeheartedly, alongside 'humanistic' people, to the values of justice, respect, personal integrity, ecology, and so on. For these are key ways of living an authentically human life. What is interesting for us as Christians is that we can live out each of these values in conscious dialogue with Jesus. We can explore how he lived out these aspects of spirituality and see how we ourselves can imitate him – while at the same time taking account of the major differences between his culture and ours, and the gap of 2,000 years between us. So the 'worldly' and the transcendent aspects of spirituality come together. The living out of ethical and political values is fully integrated into our personal relationship with Jesus.

There is an on-going dialogue among theologians about whether the Christian faith reveals new moral values and obligations, or whether on the other hand the content of morality is the same whether or not one is a Christian. I agree with those who hold that Christianity does not add on any specific new moral obligations (cf. MacNamara 1994: 647-9; and 1998: 157-9). But I have no doubt at all that reflection on the life of Jesus, and prayer to and through Jesus, throws a great deal of new light on how to live morally. Such prayer and reflection brings out aspects and nuances that we find exciting and challenging – and sometimes quite new. In the following pages I shall give some examples of the fresh light thrown by Jesus on different aspects of the ingredients of 'worldly' spirituality.

Jesus and Nature

Jesus lived mainly in a rural situation where he was in close touch with the rhythms and cycles of nature. It is not surprising that most of his images and parables were drawn from the daily life of the farmers and fishermen around him. But it is significant that in the midst of his very busy public life he felt the need at times to 'get away from it all' by going into the wilderness or up on the hills. This is very encouraging for those of us who find spiritual nourishment through contact with nature, especially in its 'wilder' aspects. It reminds us that this does not involve some far-out nature-worship but brings out the fact that in the creation we can make contact with the Creator. It provides a corrective for a conception of God which is one-sidedly transcendent and helps us realise that Christian spirituality includes an ecological dimension.

The gospel accounts of the nature miracles of Jesus raise a very interesting question for me. Could it be that Jesus was so fully in accord with the natural world that he could influence the weather? Could it be that in calming the storm which was threatening to swamp his boat, or in foreseeing a very large catch of fish for his friends, he was exercising neither a magical nor a divine power but rather a power that is strictly human but rarely attained? Jesus, the Human One, may perhaps be inviting us to stretch our human powers beyond what we would have thought possible. Perhaps he wants us to imitate him by becoming so fully in rapport with nature that we too can at times work such 'wonders'.

This approach offers a framework in which we can accept and understand the well-authenticated accounts we hear of exceptionally holy Hindu men or women who perform actions, such as levitation, which seem to be beyond ordinary human powers. We can see them as people who have learned to exercise 'spiritual' powers which are part of our human potential but are developed only by exceptionally spiritual people. If we follow this line we can give a very practical meaning to the remarks which the gospels attribute to Jesus, when he criticises his followers for the weakness of their faith (Mt 8:26). The faith he has in mind may be not just a general trust in God's care but also a trust that they could ride out the storm or even calm it as Jesus did; and that much more specific trust would be based on being fully in tune with the rhythms of nature.

Power and Powerlessness
One of the most striking things about the public life of Jesus was

his attitude to power. What we find in him is a delicate balance. He never used his power abusively. This becomes evident especially in the accounts of his temptations, where we see his determination not to overwhelm or captivate people by an exercise of spiritual power (cf. Dorr 1996: 61; Dorr 2000: 170).

But on the other hand it is clear from the gospels that he did not go to the opposite extreme of relinquishing his personal power and authority. When people were inspired by his personality and his preaching, he had no hesitation in inviting some of them to leave everything and follow him. The life of Jesus is a model which helps us to develop a healthy and respectful lifestyle and spirituality in which we exercise our power and are not afraid to use our charm. But, if we are following Jesus, our life will be one where we avoid all abuse of power and do not allow charm to take on an aura of falseness, or to be tainted by attempts to manipulate others.

Jesus was particularly uncompromising in his challenge to religious forms of domination, authoritarianism, and legalism. He saw that the religious authorities of his time had distorted the fundamental purpose of the Jewish Law. The Law was intended to be an instrument for the protection of the poor and the marginalised. But in the time of Jesus it was being used by self-proclaimed 'experts' (the Scribes) to oppress 'ordinary people'. Looking at our own church, it has to be admitted that in recent centuries church leaders and theologians frequently exercised a quite oppressive power over members of the church. We must repudiate this abuse of power and ensure that it is not repeated.

The gospel accounts of the passion and death of Jesus bring out another aspect of his attitude to power, namely, his ability to discern when it is right to hold on and when to let go. When exercising his public ministry he was quite strategic, at times using his power to confront his enemies strongly and in public, at other times withdrawing from the public arena to devote his energy to coaching his small group of close followers. But then, while he was still in the prime of his life, there came a total change. He knew that 'his hour' had come. This meant that he had reached a stage where ordinary human power was no longer efficacious. The only authentically human response to this new situation was to give up his long struggle and to accept that, from a purely human point of view, his mission had failed. So his task now was to relinquish his human powers and resign himself to death. After his struggle in the garden of Gethsemane he was able to do this – but in doing so he entrusted himself utterly into the hands of God (Mk 14:36: '… not my will but yours be done').

There may be times when we find ourselves helpless before the bitter hostility or shameful indifference of those who have power over us. That was the situation faced by Jesus when he was arrested and condemned. He, whose aim was to share our life to the full and to bring us the fullness of human life, now found himself faced with the sheer perversity of a hatred and rejection which was determined to frustrate his purpose and bring his life to a meaningless end. Faced with this intractable evil, Jesus did not deny it or run away. In accepting his crucifixion and death he taught us to have faith in a meaning beyond evil – and even, in the last resort, beyond death.

Helpless on the cross, Jesus made his supreme act of faith. In doing so he taught us that the only authentically human response to some rampant evil may be to entrust ourselves utterly into the hands of God as he did (Lk 23:46). When Jesus made that ulti-mate act of trust he actuated a totally different kind of power – a divine power which drew good out of human failure and powerlessness and which vindicated him when all human power had been defeated in a shameful death (cf. Dorr 2000: 181-2).

All this is very relevant for us in the development of our spirituality. In situations which are difficult or awkward – for instance where we find ourselves in conflict with others or oppressed by a system – we need to be able to discern when to continue the struggle and when it is best to give up and let go. 'Letting go' can mean a variety of different things. Sometimes it means walking away from a job which has become too stressful, or from a relationship which has become intractably abusive. At other times it means abandoning the attempt to control the response of one's colleagues, one's partner, or one's children. But eventually it involves facing death. At that point, 'letting go' means trusting that the darkness of death does not empty our lives of all meaning. In the last analysis, in situations where the whole project of my life has been frustrated and I am facing total failure from a human point of view, 'letting go' means following Jesus by entrusting myself to God in blind faith that God's love will triumph in ways which I cannot control, or predict, or even imagine.

Jesus' Option for Justice, Liberation and the Poor

It is easy to be *concerned* for justice and for the poor. Even people who are rich and powerful can be genuinely concerned about the plight of the poor and about structural injustice in society. But to make a really effective *option* for the poor is far more difficult. It means taking a stand on the side of the poor. And to do this with authenticity and credibility one must come into *solidarity* with the poor. This means sharing their life in some degree – and not just by living a simple lifestyle but also by experiencing some of their vulnerability, and their sense of being powerless and on the margins.

Jesus gives us a radical example of this kind of solidarity. He came from a despised village. His lifestyle was that of a traveller who had 'nowhere to lay his head' (Mt 8:20). He mixed with the common people, he made friends with outcasts who were seen as sinners, and he gave time to healing the sick who were seen as cursed by God.

In this experience of solidarity with poor and despised people Jesus made a clear option not merely to share life with them but to challenge those who were responsible for injustice and oppression – and those who claimed that riches are the mark of God's favour. By healing those who suffered from shameful diseases he showed that God has not cursed these despised ones, but cares for them with a special love.

Jesus spoke out strongly against those who held power in his country. Not content with condemning their abuse of wealth and power, he set about transforming society in a radical way. So he proposed a set of values which are in stark contrast to those of his time – and of ours: 'Blessed are you who are poor ... blessed are you who are hungry ... blessed are you ... when they exclude you, revile you, defame you ...' (Lk 6:20-22). Then he gathered a core-group of trusted followers whom he trained to carry on the message and the liberating action. He even dared to invite women into his inner circle of friends and followers.

The rich and the powerful – including the religious leaders – soon realised that, from their point of view, Jesus was a subversive. His words and actions and his whole life were a threat to the very fabric of the society in which they were dominant. Their hatred and opposition built up to the point where they determined to get rid of him. The different power-groups who felt threatened by him formed an alliance to destroy him. And so he paid the price of his option for the poor by being condemned to a criminal's death.

Even this sketchy account of the life and mission of Jesus shows quite clearly that those who take the side of the poor must expect to pay dearly for their choice. It also shows that it is a dangerous illusion to assume that religion can be kept separate from politics. More frightening still, it shows that religion can be used as an instrument of oppression and that some religious leaders may be very unjust or may be colluding with tyrannical political rulers.

And yet ...! The gospels and our Christian faith assure us that it is all worth while. Jesus was vindicated – at least for those who have faith. His witness and his message resound down through the centuries, frequently misunderstood and distorted but constantly re-discovered. They stand today for us as a beacon of hope and inspiration.

Jesus and Patriarchy
Jesus lived in a situation where patriarchy was rampant and

women were treated as second-class human beings. He challenged this patriarchy quite radically. He repudiated all claims to power and status based on fatherhood (cf. Schüssler Fiorenza 147–51). Jesus treated women as equal to men. For instance, having healed a sick women he put her in the middle of the synagogue (a place reserved for men); and he called her a 'daughter of Abraham', a phrase that is unique in the Bible since the Jews invariably spoke of the 'sons of Abraham' (Lk 13:12-6; cf. Wink 1992: 129-131). Furthermore, he praised Mary, the sister of Martha, when she took the position of a disciple – a role which, in the patriarchal system, only men could have (Lk 10:39-42). The only conclusion a faithful follower of Jesus can draw from all this is that a fundamental aspect of a Christian spirituality must be a repudiation of all traces of the patriarchal mindset.

The Vulnerable Jesus
The gospel of John puts a lot of emphasis on the love of Jesus for his friends. We see him as somebody who had really deep friendships – for instance, with Peter, with the disciple John, and with Mary, Martha and Lazarus. In interacting with them he was warm, forthright, compassionate, sensitive – and sometimes frustrated and irritated (e.g. Mt 17:17; Lk 13:34). By offering his love in such an unconditional and trusting way, Jesus left himself very vulnerable – open to be betrayed by Judas whom he had accepted as a friend (Mt 26:49–50), and to be denied by Peter, whom he had picked out for a leadership role (Mt 26:70–5).

Jesus was not content with a one-way relationship where he would be the one offering support and love. He wanted a two-way relationship in which he could call on his friends for support in times of difficulty. This became clear when he faced up to his death in the agony in the garden. He asked Peter, James and John to come with him into the garden and to 'watch with' him during those hours of struggle (Mt 26:38). The fact that he begged their support shows not only how vulnerable he was at that time but also how willing he was to let them see this human vulnerability.

This is relevant for us when we come to reflect on spirituality. It indicates that if we wish to live a fully Christian life we should not think in terms of mastery or independence, or rigid self-control. It suggests rather that a Christian spirituality is one which involves asking for support and a willingness to be hurt, to feel rejected and even betrayed. Vulnerability lies at the heart of any authentic spirituality.

Jesus the Celibate

I shall treat this topic in chapter 6, so at this point I will confine myself to a brief comment. The gospel accounts of Jesus give no indication that he got married or had an intimate sexual relationship with anybody. When we put that fact alongside the title 'The Human One' which Jesus gave himself, an important conclusion emerges. It is that it is not necessary to be sexually active in the genital sense in order to live a fully human life.

That is important, because it goes against the taken-for granted assumption of people of different cultures. In the present-day Western world it is widely assumed that a person cannot be humanly fulfilled without an intimate sexual relationship which is fully genital. And in most traditional African and other primal cultures it has been taken for granted that the human life of a man or woman remains incomplete, almost defective, until that person has a child. The lifestyle of Jesus as portrayed in the gospels calls both of these assumptions into question. It suggests that those who see celibacy as a truly human value and who wish to defend their option to live celibately may find it best to say simply: 'I am following Jesus and what was good enough for Jesus is good enough for me.'

Jesus the Healer

It is clear from the gospels that Jesus had an ability to heal those who were sick or disturbed: 'power was going out from him and healing them all' (Lk 6:19). But there is a restraint in these accounts which is in sharp contrast to the apocryphal gospels, which give the impression that the power of Jesus was magical. The way I read the gospels is that Jesus was in touch with a healing energy which is an intrinsic part of human life – a type of power or energy which has been used by deeply spiritual people in various religious traditions.

Jesus passed on this healing power to his followers (Lk 9:1–2; cf. Jn 14:12 and Mk 16:18). When Paul and Barnabas healed a lame man in Lystra, they insisted 'We are only human beings like yourselves' (Acts 14:15). They had learned from their own experience that they could be in touch with the same kind of healing power as Jesus used. The New Testament suggests that this power normally requires that the person being healed must co-operate by having 'faith' (Mt 13:58). The story of the man whose blindness was healed in stages (Mk 8:24) seems to imply that in these cases 'faith' involves a particular kind of trust – one which enables the healer to activate within the sick person that person's own healing power.

It is unfortunate that nowadays healing is associated mainly with exceptionally saintly people, or with wonder-working evangelists, or with people in the charismatic movement. Consequently it remains largely on the margins of Christian spirituality. But the New Testament teaches us that the healing ministry should have a central place in mainstream Christian spirituality and in the life of the church. This means being in touch with, and making use of, some degree of healing powers – whether they be in the spiritual and psychological sphere or more related to a healing of the body; and the gospels indicate that these different kinds of healings are all closely related to each other.

SECTION TWO: CREATION, PROVIDENCE, AND CO-CREATION

I have devoted several pages to an exploration of aspects of spirituality which are directly associated with Jesus. But in order to give a balanced account of Christian spirituality I want now to look also our relationships with the other two persons of the Trinity. I begin by saying something about the One whom Jesus called 'Abba', the One whom I think of mainly as the Creator, and whom I experience mainly in the form of Providence.

When I walk the hills in brilliant sunshine, or facing a wind which threatens to blow me away, I am sometimes lifted beyond my everyday concerns and suffused with a sense of gratitude and freedom – an admiration for the wonder of creation and the power and generosity of the Creator. In this way God becomes present and real to me. This can happen too when I look at the stars on a frosty or balmy night: 'The heavens reveal the glory of God, the skies proclaim God's handiwork!' (Psalm 19:1); or when I sit by the ocean and get a sense of its sheer power and beauty: 'Greater than the roar of mighty waters, more powerful than the waves of the sea, is our God' (Psalm 93:4). However, I'm not a very contemplative person, so for me these graced moments are occasional and transitory. But there are many people who have a much more placid temperament and who come close to being nature mystics. They are drawn to stay for long periods contemplating the wonder of creation, and communing with the Creator in and through the creation.

In my own case, the most frequent way in which I find myself in touch with the Creator is not in such contemplative moments but through God's answers to my prayers of petition. I experience God's Providence in my life almost all the time. For me, this is much more than just finding myself cared for in a rather passive way. I have what I call a 'strong' faith in Providence, by which I mean that it feels right to me to ask God to do me little favours. When something has become mislaid I ask God not to let me get hassled about it but to help me find it quickly and easily. I get a thrill of gratitude when this prayer is answered almost immediately. Several times a day I experience these little reminders of God's interest in me and God's willingness to be intimately involved in even the most minor details of my life.

Over the past couple of years I have come to see these answers to my prayers as instances of co-creation. By this I mean that I believe that God has made the world in such a way that my prayer of petition is not just a *request* for God to intervene. The petition also plays a part in *bringing the answer*. In other words, my prayer and God's answer together form an act of co-creation, in which I play an active part alongside God. God allows me to play a key part in shaping the world in such a way that my intention is fulfilled and my prayer is answered. My part is to turn my mind to what I am looking for and set my intention clearly and firmly in that direction as I make my request.

I frequently facilitate specialised workshops or retreats in which participants seek guidance and direction in their lives. A central feature of these processes is an emphasis on the *intention* or purpose of the participants. As the workshop or retreat progresses, I see very many examples of how effective an intention can be – provided it is 'taken on' clearly and with full commitment but also in freedom of spirit. Time after time I have found that when a person 'takes on' a firm intention, then what that person intends is what actually takes place. This is not explicable in terms of the kind of causality investigated by mainstream science. I find it closer to the phenomenon of synchronicity which Carl Jung explored (Jung 1973).

I now see my prayers of petition as fitting into this pattern. So I pray to God earnestly, really wanting and asking for something. But at the same time my aim is to make my request in freedom of spirit, convinced that God is looking after me all the time, wanting only what is best for me. So I want to leave God free – and this comes down to the same thing as being free myself. It means not being neurotically wedded to the thing I'm asking for, but open to accepting the answer 'no' to my prayer. My experience is that whenever I manage to achieve this freedom of spirit my prayer is answered. There's a paradox here – as there is in almost everything that is really significant in life. It is that God will give a positive answer to my earnest prayer so long as I leave God free to say 'no' as well as 'yes'. The paradox is summed up in the phrase from T. S. Eliot's poem 'Ash Wednesday': 'teach us to care and not to care'.

I have been saying that the focusing of one's attention on some desired outcome – through prayer, or in the context of a workshop, or in daily life – can become efficacious. I want now to add that this focusing of attention can have a creative effect on another person as well as on ourselves. Scientists have devised experiments to test the hypothesis that prayer for a sick person can help to bring about healing; and they have come up with some evidence that this is the case.

I have some reservations about any such attempt to fit the power of prayer into a scientific framework. It feels somewhat disrespectful – almost like an attempt by us to 'harness' God's energy and control it. But, without making any such 'scientific' attempt, we can easily find anecdotal evidence that prayer of petition is effective – that it produces results.

The evidence for the reality of spiritual energy as a power which can be applied to others is even more obvious when we think about the power of love for others. There are ample indications that love has a creative power which can help to bring about the healing, growth, and flourishing of the person on whom this love is focused. We see this quite clearly wherever parents lavish their love on young children. Again, it is not unusual to see a similar healing and creative effect on old people who are taken out of a very institutionalised life in an old folks' home and cared for lovingly by their family. Another striking example is the way in which two people who are deeply in love with each other can enable each other to come alive and flourish to a remarkable extent.

This leads me to believe that love for another person is an efficacious creative power – a crucial way in which we are enabled to share in God's own providential power and allowed to be co-creators. So my conception of Christian spirituality is not just one in which providence is central. It is one in which we are privileged to share in God's creative and providential power through prayer of petition, through a focusing of our intention, and perhaps especially through the power of the love which we have for others and they have for us.

Other Christians – and particularly other theologians – have a very different conception of divine providence. Their experience of God's care for them may be much less specific and detailed.

They often seem to have what Karl Rahner aptly called 'a winter experience of faith'. So I am not suggesting that all Christians have to agree with my attempt to explain how we become co-creators with God, and agents of divine providence. I am simply putting it forward as a possible approach to one aspect of Christian spirituality.

SECTION THREE: THE HOLY SPIRIT

In recent years the Holy Spirit has come to play a central role in my spirituality. This is partly because as a missionary I have been forced to take more account of the ways in which God works in the hearts of people who may know little or nothing about Jesus. I now realise that, if I focus only on the sending of Jesus into the world, I am neglecting a major part of Christian revelation. I need to put a new emphasis on the sending of the Spirit – and on the role of the Spirit, which is quite different from that of Jesus.

The incarnation means that Jesus came at a particular time and in a particular place. He is an historical figure, with all the advantages that brings. People saw him, heard him, wrote down the words he spoke and the actions he did. He lived a human life and died as we must die. But there are corresponding disadvantages to all this. Jesus lived 2000 years ago in a culture that is very different from ours. So we cannot find an easy answer to all moral issues of today by turning to the text of the gospels.

That is one limitation which comes from the fact that the incarnation took place at a particular time and place. A second limitation is that there were many people who never heard of Jesus (those who lived before his time) and many others who, even today, know little about him. We must assume that God has been, and still is, in active dialogue with these millions of people. The Holy Spirit provides a 'solution' for both of these necessary limitations of the incarnation.

I am not saying, however, that there are two distinct ways of being saved – one through Jesus and one through the Spirit. For the Spirit is the Spirit of Jesus and the work of the Spirit is to lead us to Jesus and to the God revealed by Jesus. Long before Jesus came on earth as the incarnate Word, the Word of God was act-ively present in the world (Jn 1:3: 'all things were made through him'; cf. Kavunkal 2001). So, from the beginning, the Word and the Spirit have been at work in the world in complementary ways – the Spirit bringing God's energy into our world and the Word providing concrete expressions and articulations of that divine life.

The Spirit, not being incarnate, has the advantage of being equally available to people of every age and every place: 'The Spirit blows where it chooses …' (Jn 3:8). The disadvantage of this (if disadvantage it be) is that the action of the Spirit remains elusive and mysterious '… you do not know where it comes from or where it goes' (Jn 3:8). Speaking and working in our hearts – sometimes 'with sighs too deep for words' (Rom 8:27) – the Spirit can be heard clearly only to the extent that we are in touch with the deepest and truest depths of our hearts. So we can never be quite sure that what we are hearing or sensing is an undiluted communication from the Spirit. The message may have become distorted or even corrupted by our lack of sensitiv-ity or our self-centred preoccupations.

It would be a serious mistake to imagine that once one knows about Jesus there is little need to think about the Spirit. Yet this is a mistake made by many Christians – not of course in theory but in practice. They have never learned to watch out for the Spirit, to invite the Spirit to speak and move in their hearts. And, equally, it never occurs to them to 'read the signs of the times' in the wider world and to interpret what is happening there as the work of the Spirit.

Love
When I try to articulate the role of the Spirit in the spirituality of the Christian, the two words which stand out for me are 'love' and 'guidance'. So I propose to look at each of these in turn. Our faith tells us that the Spirit is the love of God poured out into our hearts. This is a love which is utterly gratuitous, not based on or

proportionate to our efforts. Furthermore, it is a love which we can at times *experience* – it warms our hearts.

For much of the time in recent centuries most of the Christian churches were inclined to play down this 'felt' aspect of God's love. Mainstream Protestants did so because they were suspicious of what was called 'enthusiasm', that is, the excessive spiritual exuberance of some Protestant sects. Catholics did so because of a misguided theology of the supernatural which located grace in a sphere that was not accessible to our consciousness. Of course it is important to recognise that the Spirit can be at work in times of spiritual dryness and even in the experience of 'the dark night of the soul'. But we should normally expect to have some awareness of the Spirit's presence and work in us.

The 'fruits of the Spirit' should normally be experienced realities. These 'fruits' are certain qualities or spiritual feelings such as joy, inner peace, gentleness, and patience. Of course we often lose touch with these life-giving gifts. But even then we are not in dire straits so long as we are aware of missing them. Feeling their absence, we long to recover them and we examine our behaviour to see whether we have done something – or failed to do something – which caused us to lose them.

Because the gift of God's love, poured out in our hearts, is a purely unmerited and gratuitous gift, its whole tendency is to spread wider and carry that gratuity further. So it inclines us to be generous in return. It makes us want to give ourselves freely, first of all to God, but also to others. This kind of generous love is called *agape*. It is usually contrasted with *eros*, which is seen as the type of love which impels us to possess the object of our love. However, I think that theologians have done us a disservice by over-emphasising the distinction between *eros* as a rational, self-regarding, and even egoistic love and, on the other hand, *agape* as a love which is totally self-surrendering with no concern for one's own self-interest (e.g. D'Arcy: 1956, cf. Black 111)).

In chapter 4, on 'the unfolding of sexuality' I shall spell out in some detail how *eros* can develop into a very generous love. Here I need only to note that we can find many examples of love

which has elements of both *eros* and *agape*. For instance, the person
who falls in love with somebody else wants to be close to that
person but, hopefully, not to control the person. In fact those
who are deeply in love are usually willing to devote themselves
and sacrifice themselves for the sake of the beloved. I think
much the same applies in our love for God at its best. It calls us
to give ourselves generously, but at the same time it assures us
that it is precisely in the letting go of narrow self-interest that we
will find our fulfilment. We are not restricted to a choice between
self-sacrifice and fulfilment. God shows us a way of transcend-
ing selfishness and self-interest which nevertheless fulfils the
deepest desires of our hearts.

This has practical implications. Take the example of somebody who loves God very fervently and feels called to be utterly
generous in response to the Spirit's outpouring of love. This
person may also feel attracted to become, say, a journalist, or an
artist, or even a politician. There is a perverse type of spirituality
which suggests that such a person can show unselfish love for
God only by giving up all personal desire and 'ambition'. I shudder
when I recall how Gerard Manley Hopkins tore up his poems in
the belief that poetry was an obstacle to his love of God.

I think on the contrary that the Spirit works in and through
our human attractions. God is never in competition with any
created reality – unless we turn that reality into an idol. So we
should begin with a working assumption that the Spirit is inspiring each person to respond generously to God, precisely by
following the person's own strong attraction for some particular
vocation in life.

Having said that, I must add at once that there will be times
when that working assumption is no longer valid. There is need
for a careful discernment to ensure that one's attraction to a particular action or object or way of life is not merely a product of
self-interest, but springs from a deep part of one's heart which is
uncontaminated by selfishness. For it is only then that it is a vehicle
which can carry the call of the Spirit. It is at this point that we
must move on to consider the issue of guidance from the Spirit.

Guidance

People who are spiritually discerning often have a sense that their deepest movements of inspiration, challenge, or consolation come from some Power that is greater than themselves. It is not presumptuous to trust this inner sense and to believe that at times these movements which well up from the unconscious into our conscious awareness may be gifts from the Holy Spirit. St Paul assures us that the Spirit lives in us, guides us, and endows us with a wide variety of gifts including the gift of discernment. We are told too that the Spirit helps us in our weakness, prays in us, pleads with God on our behalf in sighs deeper than words, joins with our own spirit in declaring that we are God's children, and enables us to groan in expectation of a new creation (Rom 8:9-27; 1 Cor 12:3-11).

Of course the Spirit works also through our more rational faculties and through the advice of others and the guidance of wise authorities. But when we reflect on issues in a very rational mode we may have already decided that we know what is right for us; and so we may not be very open to hearing new and unexpected ideas or suggestions. There is perhaps more room for the Spirit to work in the deep 'unconscious room of our hearts' of which the poet Patrick Kavanagh speaks (256).

If all this is to happen for us, it is important that we expect that God's Spirit will touch us, move us, inspire us, and guide us frequently. Otherwise we are quite likely to miss the gentle movement of the Spirit when it comes. Furthermore, we need to dispose ourselves – for instance, by taking quiet time for prayer and reflection and also by developing the more intuitive non-rational aspects of our mind and heart, where there may be more room for the Spirit to do its work.

The gospels tell us that Jesus often spent the whole night in prayer. During those hours of meditation and contemplation he opened himself more fully to the inspiration and guidance of Spirit. It was the Spirit who enabled him to read 'the signs of the times'. So he was able to adapt his missionary approach in accordance with each new situation – to know, for instance, when it was right to go up to Jerusalem, and when 'his hour' had come.

Discernment

Following the example of Jesus, we too need to spend quiet and prayerful time so as to be open to, and able to get in touch with, the voice and guidance of the Spirit (cf. Dorr 2000, 175-6). At the *individual* level each of us is expected to engage seriously in a personal search for God's will, and to recognise it when it manifests itself to us. Whole communities of people also take time together to engage in a process of *communal* discernment.

We are fortunate that over the past generation there has been a great awakening to the importance of discernment. The best-known approach is the one called 'discernment of spirits' as worked out in some detail by St Ignatius Loyola. For those who are deeply involved in Ignatian spirituality, discernment is a very specific process designed to help the individual or group to have a sense of whether or not a proposed action is 'consonant' with the following of Christ.

The presupposition of the Ignatian approach to discernment seems to be that behind the everyday consciousness of the person there is some kind of 'deeper self' which plays a privileged role as an instrument of enlightenment by God. One gets in touch with this deeper self in prayer. It comes to consciousness in the form of spiritual feelings of 'consolation' or 'desolation'. These feelings are the normal way in which one discovers, or 'checks out', whether a proposed course of action is in conformity with the will of God. So the discernment process depends crucially on the ability to recognise the spiritual feeling of 'consolation'. It also involves learning to link such 'consolation' to specific proposed courses of action; and learning to know when a sense of 'consolation' can be interpreted as an indication of divine approval. Ignatius allowed also for a more rational approach but seemed to see it as a 'fall-back' – perhaps even a second-best – style of discernment.

Other Approaches

The Ignatian approach is very valuable but I do not think it is sufficient. In some cases it may be necessary to undertake a certain amount of professional counselling or therapy. In this we can deal with serious psychological wounds or blocks which would prevent one from engaging in realistic discernment.

In addition to the Ignatian model of discernment, it can be very useful to make use of a variety of other ways of accessing the deepest desires of our heart and the more intuitive side of ourselves. I am sure I am not alone in finding that some decisions are best made not in a time of formal prayerful discernment but simply through 'taking space'. For me, this often involves leaving aside my regular occupations and preoccupations and going for a long walk in the hills. When in this way I 'get out from under' the immediate pressure of the decision I want to make, I often find that the pieces fall into place very naturally. It is as though a deeper part of me does the discerning – and does it more effectively when the more rational thinking part of me gets partly 'switched off'. It would seem that, when discursive reason plays a less determining role, there is more space for the Spirit to work in the depths of my spirit, evoking inspirations which well up into my consciousness.

Going out on the hills is one way of 'switching off' my excessive reliance on a purely rational-discursive approach to decision-making. Going to sleep is another way. I often find that inspirations and guidance slip 'ready-made' into my mind just as I drift off to sleep at night or in the instant of waking up in the morning. In what I call these 'twilight' moments, a particular direction or decision on some important issue seems to be presented to me, accompanied by a kind of invitation for me to ratify it. Over time I have come to recognise the particular quality which characterises certain inspirations and guidance and which invites me to trust them as coming from the heart – and, hopefully, from the Spirit – rather than as a wild impulse or a 'far-out' idea.

Quite a lot of people keep track of their dreams or take part in dream workshops in order to get in touch with their unconscious. In this way they seek guidance in their lives. Mark Patrick Hederman recommends the use of the tarot cards for the same reason (Hederman: 2003). Until quite recently most

Christians would have believed that such practices are superstitious; and even today they are rejected by many as pointless or
misguided at best, and perhaps sinful. But the work of Carl Jung
has made it quite respectable to work with the symbolic material
of dreams or with the tarot symbols. And some Christians have
now integrated these approaches into their spirituality and see it
as a way in which they may be touched by the Spirit. They can
justify this by pointing out that, in the Bible, God frequently
spoke to people through dreams and symbols.

I believe that we can be helped to discern better by using
processes or techniques which enable us to get in touch with the
more intuitive side of ourselves. For I think that our intuitive
capacity is a privileged instrument used by the Holy Spirit in
guiding us on life's journey. As part of my work, I facilitate two
such processes. One is called 'The Transformation Retreat'. It
brings together a group of individuals, who may not have known
each other previously, to search together for a way forward for
each, on his or her personal journey. The other, called
'Frameworks for Change', is designed specifically for existing
leadership or management teams who wish to integrate spirituality and management, and to develop their ability to get in
touch with their creative and intuitive powers. The participants
find these processes helpful in uncovering the deep desires of
their hearts and in getting guidance from the Spirit.

It would be a serious mistake to imagine that the Spirit of God
is the immediate source of all 'guidance' or insights which well
up from the depths in this way. There are blocks and wounds in
everybody's heart and these can cause the 'message' to get
distorted. The question we need to ask is not: 'Does this impulse
come from the Spirit?' but *To what extent* is it from the Spirit?' To
answer that question we need to have a sense of how free and
open we are. For the Holy Spirit is effectively at work in us to the
extent that we are fully free and authentic (cf. Rom 8:10, 23).

Conclusion
In this chapter I have been giving an outline of what I consider

to be the distinctive features of a *Christian* spirituality, as distinct from the many other spiritualities in the world today. I hope that it has become clear that what characterises the Christian approach above all is a personal relationship with each of the persons of the Trinity. I also hope that it is now evident that our relationships with God are more about finding sources of spiritual strength and nourishment than about discovering distinctive moral obligations. As Christians we do not have a whole range of special concerns and moral duties which are different from those of people who are not followers of Jesus. In fact the moral and political agenda of Christians overlaps to a very considerable extent – and sometimes entirely – with that of committed people of other religions or of none. In this chapter I have mentioned some of these concerns in passing. In the next chapter I hope to present them in a more comprehensive and systematic form.

CHAPTER 2

'Worldly' Ingredients of Spirituality

I began the previous chapter by noting that, while some people understand spirituality as having to do with their relationship with God, many others focus instead on 'worldly' values such as justice, or human relationships, or being nourished by nature. It is important to note that God is never in competition with any of these 'worldly' values or commitments. As Paulo Coelho says, '... no heart has ever suffered when it goes in search of its dreams, because every second of the search is a second's encounter with God and with eternity' (Coelho 137).

We Christians do not have to choose between God and human values because we know that God is never identified with any particular aspect of the world (cf. Jn 4:23). In fact those who think of spirituality in terms of their relationship with God nearly always believe that God is calling them to work out their spirituality through some 'worldly' commitment such as caring for the poor (e.g. Mother Teresa), or the struggle for justice (e.g. Moses and the liberation theologians). They find that as they strive to live authentically in their everyday lives they grow in understanding and love for God and find in God a sure source of hope and commitment.

Nevertheless, a lot of people – especially in the Western world – now articulate their spirituality with little or no reference to God. So it is important to spell out the values to which they devote themselves and through which they find nourishment for the spirit. These same values also constitute what we might call 'the working agenda' of Christians. For these 'worldly' concerns and values are the terrain on which we walk on our journey towards God and with God. In the present chapter I propose to list them under twelve major headings and to give a short description of each.

Twelve 'Ingredients'
People have a variety of different emphases in their spirituality, ranging from those who seek to develop personal tranquillity to those who engage passionately in the struggle for justice. This variety is good but it would be a pity if somebody were to focus on just one or two aspects while neglecting all the others. I find it helpful at times to think of spirituality as though it were a cake into which we have to put a wide variety of ingredients. There is room for a lot of variety in the mix. Different people may give more or less emphasis to particular values, depending on the inclination and personal call of each individual. But our spirituality is inadequate or unbalanced if it ignores or entirely neglects any one of them. In the following pages I give a short account of each of twelve different 'worldly' values which should go into the 'mix' to provide a balanced spirituality. The twelve are:

1. Ecological Wisdom
2. Option for the Poor
3. The Struggle for Liberation and Structural Justice
4. Reconciliation and Peacemaking
5. Respect for Cultural Differences
6. Leisure, Celebration, and Contemplation
7. Integration of Sexuality
8. Community-building through Collaboration
9. Interpersonal Respect and Love
10. Personal Qualities, Virtues, and Attitudes
11. Vulnerability
12. Openness to Enrichment and Challenge

(It is important to note that I have not listed our relationships with God as a distinct ingredient alongside the other twelve. This is because the God aspect can integrate with each of the other ingredients.)

1. Ecological Wisdom

By ecological wisdom I mean a fundamental *respect* for the patterns of nature and a deep *awareness* of myself as part of the web of life here on earth. This is present in an unreflected way in primal peoples all over the world. But the modern Western pattern of living has replaced it with an exploitative attitude to our environment.

There are two main reasons why ecological wisdom is a crucial part of a genuine spirituality today. The first is that it is a matter of justice. When we use the resources of the earth wastefully we are stealing from future generations. Furthermore, the wasteful use of resources by rich nations and classes takes place at the expense of poor nations and people. For instance, land that is badly needed by the peasants of Kenya and Brazil to grow their food of maize or rice is taken to grow coffee for well-off people; and as Sean McDonagh points out (2003a), water has now become a precious resource which rich people and powerful nations are 'cornering' for their own benefit at the expense of the weak and the poor.

The second reason why ecological wisdom is crucial to spirituality is that we need to be in touch with unpolluted earth and sea to nourish our spirit. We cannot survive and thrive unless we are in touch with the beauty of nature, and experience at times the freedom and space of a wilderness place. These are not luxuries but necessities of the human spirit.

2. Option for the Poor

A big test of whether we are living a fully human life is whether or not we have a real concern for those who are poor, or oppressed, or discriminated against, or sick, or old, or disadvantaged (handicapped) in body or mind, or left on the margins of society. But concern is not enough; we are called to make a choice to be on the side of all such people. This involves two aspects. Firstly, we need to be in solidarity with them in an experiential way. That means sharing their lives in some degree, and in this way nourishing within us the beautiful virtue of compassion – since the word 'compassion' means 'suffering with'. So the experiential aspect of option for the poor has to do partly with our style of life and partly with the fundamental attitude with which we approach people, the world, and even our own lives.

But why should compassion be so central to our spirituality? Peter McVerry (43-4) gives a striking explanation:

> God's preferential option for the poor and the powerless comes, not from loving the poor and the powerless more than the rest of us, but because God is compassion. The God who is compassion must have a special concern and care for those children who are suffering, who are in danger or in pain. … And how better could God reveal that God is compassion than to usher into the kingdom all those who were made to suffer here on earth, whose dignity was taken away from them, who were unwanted and rejected. The kingdom belongs to the poor. So I am left wondering do I get in or not! … If through my compassion, I have made friends with the poor, then they will welcome me into the kingdom …

The second aspect of option for the poor has more to do with political action. It calls us to work to ensure that the structures of society are shaped to protect the rights and dignity of poor or marginalised people. This is the topic which I shall deal with in the following paragraphs, under the heading 'The Struggle for Liberation and Structural Justice'. Indeed it may seem strange that I have chosen to list option for the poor as a separate topic from this struggle. The reason I have done so is that prior to any struggle for justice it is essential that we experience compassion. Our struggle for a just society may be – indeed should be – driven partly by outrage and righteous anger. But behind that anger we need to be motivated by compassion, for otherwise our spirituality will not be fruitful and nourishing for ourselves or others.

3. The Struggle for Liberation and Structural Justice

The third ingredient of spirituality is commitment to structural justice. Our world is marred by three major types of structural injustice. These are: (i) *exploitation* of the poor by the rich;

(ii) *discrimination* on the basis of gender, race, or status; and
(iii) *oppression* of the weak by the powerful, both in the political
sphere and in the sphere of culture – for instance, through
domination of news services, TV, and the film industry.

One might imagine that our first responsibility in the face of
such systematic injustice would be to challenge it. But we are
learning that there is something else that must come before that.
We must first of all allow ourselves to experience solidarity with
the victims of injustice. We learn this from the prophets and
from seeing the effects on ourselves and others of attempts to
correct injustice from outside, from above. This experience of
solidarity comes through some measure of practical sharing in
the plight of those who are the victims of injustice.

The next stage of our response to structural injustice must be
to understand its causes. Without this, our response will be hap-
hazard and ineffectual, a tackling of the symptoms without getting at the roots. So we need to engage in what is called 'social
analysis', which involves serious study of the patterns of poverty
as well as the fundamental causes and the forces that are preventing change. The most effective kind of social analysis is one
which is not just academic but which gives a central role to 'on
the ground' research and sharing by local people (see Freire
1985 and 1996).

Then comes a further stage which is to challenge injustice.
Here we come to the key word 'struggle'. This notion of a spirituality of struggle is something new; it contrasts sharply with the
type of spirituality which most of us were brought up with. We
had heard, of course, how the martyrs suffered for their faith.
But the impression was given that their refusal to bow to persec-
uting authorities was primarily a passive resistance rather than
an active struggle. Furthermore, they were presented mainly as
suffering, not for issues of social justice, but for their unwilling-
ness to abandon Catholic doctrine (taken in a very narrow religious
sense) or their refusal to dishonour Catholic religious symbols
such as the crucifix.

What liberation theology has given us is a whole new light

on Christian spirituality – an active involvement in struggle on behalf of those who are victims of injustice. This requires us to find a place in our spirituality for righteous anger. It also calls for a new kind of fortitude – the ability to continue the struggle in the face of an apparently hopeless situation, and despite the fear that the struggle will cost us our livelihood and perhaps even our lives. If we are to live out a genuine spirituality of struggle we must also develop the virtue of prudence to a high degree – knowing when to resist openly and when to work more quietly, when to stand up strongly and when to bend and make some compromise.

Moreover, we have to learn how to preserve a certain equanimity of soul in the midst of the struggle and despite all the stress which is part of the life of anybody who works for justice. Our efforts will seem puny in the face of the forces of injustice, so we need a spirituality which enables us to hope against all hope. We know that much of our effort will be futile, but we believe that some of the seed we sow may produce a hundredfold; and we cannot know beforehand which seed will bear fruit.

The final stage of the struggle for liberation is the creation of alternatives. It is only from a purely logical point of view that it is the final stage. For in practice it must go hand in hand with the challenge to injustice, and cannot be postponed until the justice struggle is completed. In the creation of alternatives the crucial point is to ensure that the values we are promoting are already embodied in the means we choose to promote them. The new world which we are privileged to work for must already become visible in some degree in the midst of this distorted world. How can it be recognised? I suggest that it will be a world where every action will be worthwhile and rewarding in itself, so that the distinction between means and ends will dissolve. But for such a spirituality to be realistic in our world it must include as part of it a belief that new life can come through suffering and even death.

4. Reconciliation and Peacemaking

The fourth ingredient of spirituality has to do with peace. It is not simply a matter of *being* peaceful but of *making* peace. There can be no true peace without justice. Peace is a flower that can come to bloom only out of a just balance in a family, a community, a nation, and in international society. This means that though there is a tension between struggle and peacemaking, the two are not incompatible. To struggle for justice it is not necessary to abandon one's commitment to peace – indeed at times such a struggle may be the only way to work for true peace.

When powerful nations, groups, or individuals are looking for peace, their sense of insecurity often drives them to intimidate others. They seek to protect themselves by imposing an unjust peace on other individuals or groups. Such a peace is unjust because it does not respect the rights of others. In the name of 'security', vast resources of scarce materials and of human creativity are squandered on the arms race, when they ought to be used instead to overcome poverty and to promote human development. Weaker nations, groups, or individuals may feel compelled to acquiesce sullenly in a situation of injustice. This is a false peace, for as soon as an opportunity arises the old grievance comes to the surface again.

We see this, for example, in such cases as the 'unequal treaties' made between China and the European powers in the nineteenth century. And in our own lives we will recall occasions when old grievances surfaced again to undermine our relationship with others. Insecurity is part of the human condition; so the search for true peace must be built on acceptance of this fact. A spirituality of peacemaking is one which acknowledges our vulnerability and even at times increases it by taking the risk of trusting others.

One of the obstacles to real peace is to keep saying 'peace, peace' where there is no peace (Jer 6:14). To make genuine peace it will often be necessary to break down a false peace, an uneasy truce or brittle accommodation which is built on fear or short-term self-interest. Peacemakers must at times take the risk of uncovering grievances (their own or others') that have been papered over. Only then can people come to grips with the fears and hurts that prevent lasting peace.

To create peace we must go beyond justice to reconciliation. For peace implies that individuals, local communities, and nations can form a real community, with encounter and true dialogue between its members. Such encounter is constantly being threatened by injuries, misunderstandings and hurts – and by the need to challenge injustices whether real or imagined. So there is need for on-going forgiveness and reconciliation. Furthermore, as Segundo Galilea (80-1) points out, the spirit of reconciliation must imbue even our life-and-death struggles for justice. Forgiveness and reconciliation will be almost impossible at the end of the struggle unless, while we are still in the midst of the struggle, we humanise it by respecting the human rights of our enemies or opponents.

5. Respect for Cultural Differences

Until recently, people in the West – including church leaders and theologians – were inclined to assume that Western culture and theology was superior to other cultures. We were particularly inclined to look down on people who lived in tribal societies, practising what we would now call 'primal religion'. We called them 'pagans' and assumed that we were much more 'advanced' than they. Even today a good deal of this attitude lingers on, though the language is not so crude. It is widely assumed that the role of economists, planners, and 'development workers' in non-Western countries is to ensure that the Western model of 'development' is adopted by these peoples.

Nowadays, those of us from 'the West' (or the Westernised sectors of other countries) who work with such peoples are usually given orientation courses to open up for us the richness of the non-Western cultures. This is helpful and it can enable the participants to avoid some bad mistakes. But it must be said that part of the Western mode of thought and feeling seems to be a kind of superiority complex or cultural arrogance in relation to other cultures; and this comes to the fore when people are under pressure. So the development of genuine respect for other cultures is a difficult and long-term project. But it is one which is enormously important if one is to live out a truly life-giving spirituality. It is particularly important in today's world in which there is no longer any country where the population is purely homogeneous; everybody now has to face up to the reality of cultural diversity.

6. Leisure, Celebration, and Contemplation

We are inclined to think of the 'earthly' or 'worldly' aspect of spirituality in a way that puts the emphasis on our moral efforts – what we do, and our struggle to live a fully human life. There is a danger that we will ignore the other side of life and spirituality – the relaxed and contemplative and enjoyable side. We need to remember the proverb, 'All work and no play makes Jack/Jill a dull boy/girl.' And not just dull but also less than fully human. It is important to hold in mind that the whole purpose of our efforts and our struggles is to achieve fulfilment, for ourselves and for the world. So we need at times to anticipate that fulfilment, by relaxing, enjoying, and contemplating.

Joy, serenity, and wonder are three of the greatest gifts of the Spirit. We need to appreciate them – and to make sure that there is room in our lives for them. We all need to celebrate and re-create with others at times – mainly with family and friends, sometimes with the local community, occasionally with the whole nation, and even with like-minded women and men all over the world. We also need 'space' and time for ourselves – to be alone with nature, allowing our spirit to be nourished by the waters, the air, the earth, the stars, and the plants and animals.

7. Integration of Sexuality

Under this heading I want to consider three distinct but related points. They are: (a) the overcoming of dualism, (b) taking account of gender differences, and (c) respect for difference in sexual orientation.

(a) *Overcoming Dualism.* One of the most urgent challenges facing spiritually sensitive people today is the development of a spirituality which values and respects human sexuality. For sexuality is such an important part of the 'make-up' of the human person that it is essential that we integrate it into our spirituality. In fact, however, we in the Western world have great difficulty in achieving this integration. Of course, human sexuality is such a powerful force that people of other cultures also find it difficult to handle it well. But there are particular difficulties in Western culture. We have inherited from the Greeks, and from the Zoroastrian religion, a strong tradition of dualism – a tendency to split off the spirit from the body and to treat the body as in some way evil or at least as inferior to the soul or the spirit. Western Christianity took on a good lot of this dualistic attitude, particularly in relation to all aspects of sexuality.

In English-speaking countries this took the form of a rather puritan approach which caused very many people to have a guilt-laden experience of their sexuality. In more recent times Western people – Christians and non-Christians – have been trying to shake off this legacy of guilt. This, in turn, has caused us further problems. One of the most serious of these is the extraordinary increase in pornography and the way in which it has been moved from the margins and has infiltrated the mainstream of everyday life. The production of pornographic material involves very serious exploitation of women, men, and children; and it can hardly be doubted that the whole pornographic 'industry' leads on to further exploitation and to debasement of people's attitude to sexuality.

We have to find a way of integrating into our spirituality the rich experiences and energy of sexual love. In some respects this challenge is an age-old one. But in recent times it has taken a radically new turn, and has been given new urgency, by the development of various forms of contraception and by the growing sense that the world is over-populated. Sexual activity is no longer so clearly linked to reproduction. So we need to develop a spirituality of sexuality which takes account of this new reality. I shall return to this topic in later chapters.

(b) Gender Differences. There are notable differences between women and men in the style and pattern of their spirituality. It is not easy to know how much of these differences are due to cultural conditioning (e.g. patriarchal traditions and practices) and are therefore changeable and, on the other hand, how much of the differences are genetic and basically unchangeable. There are indications that quite a lot is genetic: from an early age little girls experience life 'in a different key' from young boys. But, whatever their source, it is important to respect the differences – and even to foster them if they help us to flourish.

Respect for the differences between women and men does not in any way imply that people of one gender are superior to those of the other gender. On the contrary, respect in this situation means ensuring that there is real equality in law and in practice between women and men, while allowing for the different gifts and capacities of each. An important part of a genuine spirituality today is a commitment to dismantling the age-old structures and practices of patriarchy, which, in most cultures, have kept women in a subordinate role.

A first step in this direction is the avoidance of all sexist language. There are two stages in this. The first involves refusing to accept the disclaimer which people sometimes make, namely, 'women are included when I use the word "man" or the masculine pronoun'. A second step in resisting sexism is to avoid speaking about God in language which would give the impression that God is male. This second stage poses real difficulties for those who pray the psalms and many of the traditional Christian prayers. But over the past few years a rich resource of new translations has been built up, to ease this difficulty. The trouble is that the Vatican authorities have been very slow to recognise the new translations, and have insisted strongly on retaining – and even at times re-introducing – language which many people nowadays find blatantly sexist and offensive.

I feel sad and angry that a lot of what could be most valuable in the Christian and Islamic traditions has been left on the margins or even dismissed because the religious leaders have mostly been men. My own limited experience convinces me that, if women's spirituality were taken seriously, our religions would be more flexible and less legalistic. They would also be less narrowly intellectual and more experiential – even mystical; I think they would pay more attention to the mysterious religious experiences (visions, voices, etc) which play an important part in the spirituality of some people – and especially of women.

The theologies which have emerged from the women's movement have enriched us all enormously. But I venture to suggest that a lot of this theology is still written in a somewhat intellectual and academic style – perhaps because it has to fit into a Western and rather patriarchal university context. However, alongside this, there is the development of women's spirituality through storytelling and the sharing of spiritual experiences. I look forward to the time when there is a greater welcome for this approach, as it will add depth and warmth to our theological reflection on the spiritual journeys of women and men – and also of children.

(c) Sexual Orientation. It is commonly accepted that there is a stage in the sexual development of many young people where they find themselves attracted to people of their own sex. For the great majority, this is a temporary stage and as they grow older they move on to become definitely heterosexual in their orientation. However, a certain proportion of adult men and women find that their sexual orientation is clearly homosexual, and some adults have a bi-sexual orientation.

It is not clear to what extent a gay or lesbian orientation is due to the genetic make-up of the person and to what extent it is caused or shaped by some of the experiences of the person's early life. Whatever the cause, it is important that we of the majority learn to accept and respect those who have a different sexual orientation. It is perhaps even more important that they themselves accept that their sexual orientation is different from that of the majority, and that they learn to live comfortably with that reality.

I am not concerned here primarily with the issue of the

morality of homosexual activity but with the prior question of a
person's fundamental sexual nature and orientation. Down
through history there has been a lot of overt or tacit persecution
of gay and lesbian people. Even today, homophobia is quite widespread. This makes it extremely difficult for gays and lesbians to
'own' their sexuality and to give it the important place in their
spirituality which it should have. Some of them try to escape
from their sexual feelings entirely while others acknowledge
their different orientation but only within a 'secret world'.
Acceptance and respect by the majority for those who have a
different sexual orientation will make it easier for the minority to
accept themselves as they are. Acceptance, by both the majority
and the minority, of the diversity of sexual orientations will lead
to an enrichment of our overall spirituality of sexuality. All of us
may be helped to move in that direction by James Alison's powerful and moving book, *On Being Liked* (2003: especially 78-99).

8. Community-building through Collaboration

One of the very best ways in which we can nourish our spirituality is through having a good working relationship with others.
On the other hand, if our relationships at work and in our local
community are stressful, this makes it very difficult to retain the
peace of soul which is a requirement of a healthy spirituality.

Good working relationships are built on mutual trust. It
seems to come naturally to some people to be open and trusting
towards others, whereas others find it a constant challenge.
Simple exercises of listening and sharing can be used at first to
develop an atmosphere of trust; and a good facilitator can help
to create an atmosphere where people 'feel safe' to be open with
each other. Those who work with groups or communities know
that trust is something which has to be built up in the group, and
that without that trust the group will soon fall apart.

It is not enough to listen and to share. We need also to plan
together. Here, too, it is important to do exercises together and
to learn some planning techniques. But techniques alone are not
enough, for they can be used to manipulate others. We need to

be morally converted if we are to avoid this temptation. In practice this means finding a delicate balance where we are able to put forward our ideas and suggestions with some confidence and able to stand by what we see as basic principles and values, while at the same time treating the views and proposals of others with genuine respect.

It is very helpful if the members of the team or community can find agreement on their overall aim and the values they stand for. They can then go on to work out their strategy and tactics for achieving their common purpose. At that stage the ideal is that different members of the group throw their ideas and suggestions into the common pool, and then 'let them go'. This means that everybody can evaluate and build on the various pooled ideas, scarcely adverting to who first proposed them.

People often find meetings – and especially planning meetings – burdensome. One of the main reasons for this is that they do not allow sufficient time for the meetings. So they get into a vicious circle: the meetings are stressful because there is too much to be done in too little time; and people are unwilling to give more time because the meetings leave them tired and 'raw'. It is important to break out of this vicious circle by making a special effort to have a different kind of meeting – one in which the participants have a very good experience and come out of the meeting feeling 'nourished in spirit'. This means that our spirituality includes such very practical things as ensuring that our planning meetings are productive, creative, and even enjoyable.

9. Interpersonal Respect and Love

The ninth ingredient of spirituality is respect and love for the people with whom each of us comes into personal contact. I am thinking here not of our relationships with large groups but rather with our friends and the members of our own family or religious community. The topic is vast and well explored, so here I shall just mention two points.

If love is genuine it must always include respect. (So, parents who truly love their children must be careful not to manipulate them to fit in with the parents' ambitions or wishes.) The key to being respectful in interpersonal relationships is to engage in genuine dialogue. This comes easier to some than to others. But all of us can benefit from learning techniques of listening, sharing, giving feedback, confronting, non-verbal communication, and even how to be silent with others. These are the basic 'tools' we need in order to promote dialogue and build real community.

When we communicate with others it is of course essential to be honest. And emotional honesty is just as important as moral and intellectual honesty. If I do not 'come clean' with you about my feelings, I am cutting myself off, leaving you in the dark, so that you cannot easily respond to me. If I refuse to take the risk of acknowledging my fears and perhaps even my suspicions about you, then I am likely to try to manipulate you. But if I regularly share with you both my admiration and my unease, then you will know you are not being attacked when I express dissatisfaction, and you are not being flattered when I praise you.

10. Personal Qualities, Virtues, and Attitudes

There is a range of inter-connected qualities which are associated with the purely personal aspect of spirituality. The first of these is integrity. This word 'integrity' is very useful because it has two shades of meaning. On the one hand, it refers to the kind of intellectual and emotional honesty to which I have just referred. On the other hand, it suggests a kind of wholeness, an integral development of all aspects of the human personality. There is a close relationship between the two shades of meaning. For it is only by dedicating myself to the long haul of personal development that I can hope to attain full honesty in my relationships with others – or indeed (if I am a believer) with God.

In thinking of the attainment of personal integrity it is helpful to make use of two different models of change. One can think in terms of healing the psychological hurts and lacks of the past. But this therapeutic model needs to be supplemented by a model of growth, where the emphasis is not so much on the wounds of the past as on making full use in the present and future of our emerging gifts—or those that are still undiscovered.

We may be helped by using more and more sophisticated systems and techniques to promote our personal growth – Enneagram, Myers-Briggs, psychotherapy, yoga, etc. Yet the ideal to strive for is not sophistication but a kind of simplicity. 'Transparency' is the word which best expresses the personal quality that we should aim for. It suggests a person who is 'without guile' and is truly open to others.

When I think of attitudes which are characteristic of the person whose spirituality is balanced and wholesome at the personal level, three qualities come to mind. They are gratitude, serenity, and hope. *Gratitude* is a very fundamental aspect of genuine spirituality. At times it is focused on a particular event such as success in some project, or escape from some danger, or the kindness of some friend. But occasionally a person experiences a wave of gratitude which is more all-embracing. It comes as a gift which flows into one's heart as one looks back on life as a whole, or as one luxuriates in a present sense of well-being and giftedness.

This global sense of gratitude is very liberating. It brings a kind of transcendence, by lifting the person out of self-absorption and personal concerns. It can easily lead on to an outpouring of praise which may also have the same global quality. Those who believe in a personal God will feel drawn to lift up their arms – literally or metaphorically – to praise and thank God. Those who do not have a sense of being close to a personal God may still find that this praise-reaction wells up within them and seeks expression through dance or some other bodily gesture. They may focus their praise on nature or the cosmos or they may be content to leave it unfocused and nameless.

Very closely related to gratitude is the quality of *serenity*. To be serene does not mean that one is passive. In fact serenity can co-exist with quite a lot of activity, with some suffering, and even with a certain amount of stress. It includes calmness but is a quality which goes deeper than psychological composure. It is a tranquillity of spirit which comes from entrusting oneself into the flow of life or into the hands of God. Those who are serene have a lot of inner freedom – freedom from undue desire to impress others, and freedom from the tendency to be constantly evaluating and judging themselves very harshly. This serenity is one of the greatest graces one can receive when one is ill – and, above all, when one is facing death.

Gratitude is evoked mainly when one looks to the past, and serenity is very much a quality of the present. When one looks to the future the corresponding attitude and virtue is *hope*. This too is experienced as a gift, an ability to trust in God or in the flow of life. We have a sense that it is a gift because it can exist alongside a keen awareness of threats and evils of all kinds. So it is very different from the kind of naïve optimism of those who refuse to face up to present reality and impending problems. Once again it has a certain characteristic of transcendence about it, since it lifts one beyond human calculations and enables one to 'hope beyond all hope'.

I want to add the word 'mindfulness' to the other qualities and virtues associated with the personal aspect of spirituality, even though I know that this word may seem strange to many of those who are interested in spirituality. The notion of 'mindfulness' is very central to Buddhist spirituality and it is one which has a lot to offer to those of us brought up in a different spiritual tradition. It is such a rich concept that it is hard to pin it down in words. It calls one to be fully present to oneself, and this involves being single-minded in doing whatever one is doing (even very 'ordinary' things like eating, or walking), rather than doing it in a distracted way while thinking of something else. So it means that one is living fully in the present moment rather than anticipating the future or pining for the past.

This is a real challenge for many of us who live a Western lifestyle. We find it hard to be present to ourselves. We tend to lose ourselves in fantasies of the past or the future, rather than living fully in the present moment. Yet we sense that a crucial aspect of the call to personal integrity is an invitation to cultivate this kind of presence or mindfulness so that we can live out each moment in peace, at ease with ourselves.

11. *Vulnerability*

As I said in the previous chapter (when writing about Jesus), vulnerability lies at the very heart of spirituality. There is a paradox here. In developing our spirituality we must aim to be strong and learn to overcome our many weaknesses. And yet we realise at some deep level that we have to come before others – and before God – not as people who have 'got it all together' but rather as fragile and inadequate. If we try to hide our vulnerability from God or from others we set up a barrier to genuine communication, and we introduce an element of dishonesty into the relationship. It is not that we should set out to be weak and vulnerable. But we must acknowledge that that is how we are – and we must even learn to make a virtue of it.

The paradox of vulnerability does not become resolved as we develop our spirituality. In fact it may well become more intense. For as we grow in sensitivity we become more open to be wounded by the insensitivity of others and by their deliberate or unconscious cruelty. Furthermore, it is quite likely that we will begin to sense deep within ourselves a restlessness which leaves us dissatisfied and brings a sense of alienation from ourselves and others. Here we are touching in to a very primal level of vulnerability. Is there any remedy for this deep existential discontent and sense of emptiness? Yes, it can be healed – or at least eased – but only by an experience of very profound tenderness (cf. O'Shea 11-2). This can be mediated to us through another person – and the challenge for us then is to 'let it in'. Sometimes too it may come as a deeply personal experience with no immediate relationship to another person. But however it comes, it is always experienced as an unmerited gift or grace.

There is a second and more painful aspect to our vulnerability. For some of that vulnerability comes not from a growth in sensitivity but from a sense of shame and guilt. Most young people go through a stage where they feel intensely self-conscious and inadequate – and even, at times, ashamed of being who they are. If they are accepted and loved they usually grow out of this. However, for some people this remains a major problem even when they have grown into adulthood. It is a legacy of damage done to them in childhood: they did not receive the unconditional love and respect which they needed in order to grow in self-confidence. For these people a central feature of their spirituality throughout their lives will be the challenge of learning to overcome – or even to live fairly comfortably with – this sense of inadequacy and deep-seated shame about their whole being. In chapter 5, I shall return to the question of shame, especially in relation to our sexuality.

Those who have not been unduly damaged in childhood may also suffer at times from a sense of failure, weakness, inadequacy, and shame. This often springs from an awareness of having done something morally wrong, or from bad habits which we have failed to shake off (e.g. excessive drinking or eating, smoking, laziness, or compulsive patterns of work). If we are comfortable about using overtly religious language we can say that we know we are sinners and we are weighed down in some degree by our sense of sinfulness. So we feel guilty and ashamed. That is not something we can rejoice in or even make a virtue of. Yet we have to find some way in which we can come before God and before people without denying that reality but somehow taking it into the relationship.

12. Openness to Enrichment and Challenge
Spirituality is not something which we can attain once-for-all. We have to keep growing, constantly open to new insights and new challenges. Otherwise we stagnate and our spirituality becomes fossilised and shrivelled up. As the poet Patrick Kavanagh says (256), 'God must be allowed to surprise us.'

There is a constant temptation to settle for our present achievements and present challenges – to tell ourselves that 'we have enough on our plate already'. Especially as we grow older we find ourselves inclined to look back rather than forward. And of course it is important to root ourselves more firmly in our own life-story and to nourish our spirituality by getting deeper into the spiritual tradition in which we have grown. But that is only one half of the journey of spiritual development. The other and more exciting part involves listening out for the voice of the Spirit, who is inviting us to 'launch out into the deep' (Lk 5:4).

Occasionally that 'voice' of the Spirit may be clear and explicit. But more commonly it comes in the form of intimations and hints which are all too easy to miss. So we need to cultivate an attitude not merely of openness but even of expectancy. We need to invite the Spirit to show us the new things that are coming to pass in our own lives and in the wider world. The challenge is spelled out for us in the book of Isaiah (43: 19): 'I am about to do a new thing; now it springs forth, do you not perceive it?'

A Tension

It is comparatively easy to outline all these different aspects of spirituality. But what is far more challenging is to try to fit them together in daily life. Frequently one will experience a tension between the different elements. For instance, the desire to share the lifestyle of the poor may not fit easily with the need for 'space' to nourish the spirit. Individuals and communities have to work out a way of prioritising the different values. In doing so they must take account of the particular traditions of different groups, of the special needs of each person, and – above all – of the very personal call experienced by anybody who tries seriously to be in touch with God or with the deepest human values.

We need also to recognise that the particular call of each of us may grow and develop as we grow older – and even that it may change quite significantly. Furthermore, it is important to take account of what Patricia Higgins wisely calls 'cycles of involve-ment', where a person may feel called to withdraw for a time from on-the-ground involvement, for any one of a variety of reasons: 'I may have to sacrifice the sense of being in touch on the ground in order to upskill, do other much needed background work, or simply take time for other recreative things to restore my energy and enthusiasm.' (130).

Having described these twelve components of spirituality I

have to add that this rather analytic approach is in danger of draining spirituality of some of its vitality and excitement. Furthermore, for me personally the most stimulating and life-giving aspect of spirituality is the commitment to any or all of these 'worldly' values with a sense of personal closeness to God. So I would suggest that any Christian who reads this chapter should relate each part of it to the account of Christian spirituality which I outlined in the previous chapter. We need to take seriously the 'worldly' values described in this chapter; but it is best to do so in constant dialogue with God about our efforts and our failures, our occasional despondency or depression – and the hope which springs up in us as gift at the most unlikely times.

CHAPTER 3

Spirituality and Religion

Nowadays many people in the West and the Westernised world look back on their early years with a feeling that they were brought up in a quite repressive version of Christianity. Of these, a small number have converted to some other religion, such as Islam or Buddhism. Others have left aside the repressive 'baggage' and have come to a more authentic understanding of Christianity. But a large number of those who have these bad memories have abandoned their childhood religion and become indifferent or actively hostile to all forms of organised religion. So the word 'religion' has become a rather unpopular word. At the same time the word 'spirituality' has come into vogue and a lot of people – whether or not they see themselves as 'religious' – have become very interested in developing their spirituality.

Religious leaders, and all committed religious believers, must resist the temptation to imagine that if people would 'get back to their religion' then there would be no need for all this interest in spirituality. They should instead see the development of interest in spirituality as a hopeful sign and should encourage people to develop their spirituality. For spirituality lies at the heart of any genuine religion. In Section One of this chapter I shall try to spell out the relationship between the two. I hope this will show how religions at their best can be 'carriers' of spirituality. I hope it will also throw light on what can go wrong and explain why people can become disenchanted with organised religion. In Section Two I shall go on to examine how well the present-day Catholic Church is living up to the challenge of offering people a spirituality that is appropriate for today's world.

Spirituality as a Personal Call

Spirituality in its most basic sense is a very *personal* reality. Of course it is true that most people have been reared in the spirituality of their family and local community. But such an inherited spirituality does not become fully effective until the person begins to 'own' or appropriate it personally. So any account of spirituality will be fully convincing only to the extent that it finds echoes in our own personal experience of trying to be fully human and responsive to God or to a call from 'beyond' us, or from deep within us.

Taking spirituality in a personal sense, it can be seen as that which from within me and beyond me calls me to be more authentically human, more fully all that I am destined to be. All of us, believers and non-believers, experience such an inner call in some degree. Non-believers may see it is a call which comes from deep within the person. Religious believers agree, but hold that God is also at work in it. Christians say that God's Spirit speaks to each person's spirit, inviting each of us to a fulfilment beyond all imagining. We believe that God's Spirit does not just work from outside us but moves and moulds our inmost being, so that the voice of the Spirit becomes our own inner voice as well (cf. Rom 8:16).

The suggestion that each of us experiences an inner call, an invitation to fulfil our own personal destiny, may be dismissed as just a pious fantasy by those who bury their inner life under a welter of activism, and also by those whose life is given over to distractions and triviality. But one indication that the notion of such an inner call 'rings a bell' for multitudes of people in very many different cultures is the astonishing success of the little book *The Alchemist* by Paulo Coelho. This fable tells how a shepherd boy follows his dream, his call, through dangers and desert, resisting the temptation to give up the journey, and constantly looking out for the clues and the guides sent by Providence to enable him to fulfil his destiny. The book has been translated into several languages and millions of people have read it and found in it an encouragement to listen to their own personal call.

The inner call, echoing in the deepest part of each person's spirit, is an invitation to each of us to respond. If we choose to answer authentically, our response will normally have two distinct aspects. There is a contemplative aspect, for instance, allowing ourselves to be moved by the experience of God's providential care, or by the experience of seeing a new-born infant, or by looking at the stars, or being struck dumb by the dignity of somebody who is living in great poverty. There is also an active aspect, for instance, working to overcome oppression and injustice, or to promote reconciliation, or to foster environmental awareness.

Spirituality is not just a call. It also includes the power to respond to that call. So I think of it as an energy which inspires and animates me. It is not just a futile aspiration but one which has a built-in power to lead me beyond my present limitations towards what I feel myself called to be. When I follow this aspiration and allow myself to be led by it, then I find myself growing spiritually and becoming what I am called to be.

The 'Shape' of my Spirit

I also find it helpful to think of my spirituality as 'the shape of my spirit', in the sense that it more or less determines how I feel and think and act. In calling it 'the shape of my spirit' I am not at all suggesting that it has nothing to do with my body. In fact my spirituality eventually becomes embodied in my body – and so it becomes visible to a considerable extent. For instance, some people are visibly gloomy while others are obviously cheerful and bright; some people are frenetically active, while others are serene; some are cold and distant, while others are warm and welcoming; some are so suspicious of others that they even look shifty-eyed, while others are open and trusting in their relationships with others. All these are aspects of a person's temperament but they also have a lot to do with one's spirituality. We can think of one's temperament as the raw material on which one is called to work; and that temperament is moulded and modified through the spirituality one chooses to live by.

At present I experience a gap between my inner call or aspiration or destiny and my present inadequate stance or 'shape'. I often have an inner struggle to live up to my high ideals – and I sometimes fail to do so. But my life's task is to allow the gap between the ideal and the actual to be narrowed, partly by my own response and partly by the help of others – and, as a believer, I add, mainly by God's grace. In this way, I believe, I will eventually grow into my destiny. I will then be able to say that I have answered God's call and become the person God has known and loved from the beginning and has led to perfection 'with leading strings of love' (Hosea 11:4). (Somebody who is not a religious believer may say, 'I have become the person I felt called to be.')

Journey

I have been suggesting that we think of spirituality as a call, and noting that part of that call is an awareness that we have not yet responded adequately or lived up fully to that call. This can help us to realise that when clarifying the nature of spirituality it is not enough just to focus on the present moment of time, as though we were taking a snap-shot. We are historical beings, persons whose lives are spread out in time. So we need to broaden our conception of spirituality to see it as a personal life-journey; and then we must go further to situate that personal journey within a much broader sweep of history.

When I look at spirituality from the perspective of a personal journey, I find it helpful to imagine it (or even to draw it on paper) in relation to 'the river of my life'. This visual image makes it easier to look back and pick out important moments in my life history. Looking back in this way helps me to identify the time when I first had some inklings or intimations of a new call. I can then move on to try to identify when that rather vague and wordless call in my heart came to full consciousness in my mind.

I can also recall moments or periods of new insight, of conversion or breakthrough, of being blocked or depressed, of failure and of new beginnings. Furthermore, I can look forward, trying to sense or have an intuition about where my heart – or the Spirit of God – is calling me to move on the next stage of the journey. In my own experience, and that of others whom I know well, this 'looking forward' is not primarily a matter of rational forecasting and planning but of getting in touch with one's deepest aspirations and hopes which may be only partly conscious.

Spirituality as a Tradition
So far I have been considering spirituality as something very personal to each one of us – a call and a set of attitudes and commitments. But none of us is an isolated individual. Our spirituality is bound to have an impact on those with whom we come into close contact. Some people have such a magnetic personality and such an attractive spirituality that they inspire others to adopt their spirituality. In this way individuals (or small close-knit groups) can become core figures around whom followers or 'disciples' tend to gather. In this way new spiritual traditions come into being, due to the inspiration of founding figures – people who tried to live authentically and to be open to God or spirit. In some cases the founding figures set out consciously to start a new spiritual tradition, while in other cases it happens almost against their will.

This means that, in addition to being deeply personal, a spirituality may also be a religious or ethical *tradition* into which people may be 'formed' or moulded. Indeed many of us were brought up in a particular religious or moral tradition that existed long before we were born, a tradition in which we were 'socialised' so that it moulded our religious or spiritual sensibilities (feelings) and attitudes in a particular way. Examples are:
- the Protestant, Orthodox, Ethiopian, Independent African, and Western Catholic traditions in Christianity;
- the Sunni, Shia, Sufi and Wahabi traditions in Islam;
- the Tibetan and Zen traditions in Buddhism.

In the case of primal religions, such as the various African Traditional Religions, it is not possible to identify any founding figures, since their origins are lost in the mists of time. But these are very powerful spiritual traditions which find expression not in creeds or systems but in mindsets, dances, symbols, rituals, and myths.

In addition to these overtly spiritual traditions we should also take account of the fact that nowadays many people grow up in families which do not believe in God and do not consider themselves religious. These people would be very slow to use the word 'spirituality' about their inheritance; but they might speak of 'an ethical tradition' – for instance, agnostic humanism in the West, or even perhaps one of the different versions of Marxism. In so far as these shape people's ethical values they can be seen as more or less equivalent to spiritualities.

All of the above are traditions into which many people are born. But, as they mature, some people (a relatively small number) freely choose to switch allegiance. They may move over to a different tradition of spirituality from that in which they were reared.

Furthermore, within most of the major spiritual traditions there is room for a great variety of interpretations and variations. So there arise more particular traditions which may differ from each other but which all exist within the older broader tradition. Within the Catholic tradition, for instance, some people find themselves attracted to the ideals and values of a particular religious movement such as the Franciscans, or the various congregations which adopt an Ignatian spirituality, or the groups who have been inspired by Nano Nagle, Catherine Macauley, Charles de Foucauld, Jean Vanier, or Edwina Gately.

People who come as aspirants to join any of these movements make a deliberate choice to insert themselves into the spiritual tradition of that movement. But it is important to remember that when individuals consciously insert themselves into any such tradition they are not abandoning the very personal commitment that lies at the heart of genuine spirituality. Rather they are choosing a particular style in which to live out their personal commitment.

Spirituality and Religion

Nowadays many reflective people are happy to adopt and develop a spirituality but are quite opposed to the idea of religion. So what is the difference? I think the best way to answer this question is to see how a spiritual tradition can evolve into a religion. I would say that a spiritual tradition has developed into being a religion when it becomes fixed, when it develops rules which people are expected to follow, when it spells out its basic beliefs as 'teachings' or 'doctrines' which people are asked to accept, and when a set of authority figures emerge within it to ensure that the tradition is followed.

When we speak about a religion in contrast to a spirituality we are referring mainly to an institutionalised spiritual tradition. The whole point of the religious structures (rules, doctrines, and authorities) is to preserve and foster the spirituality so that it develops as a life-giving spiritual tradition, one which is open to new insights while retaining all that is best of its original inspiration. We might say that the spirituality is like the spirit or the soul which gives the tradition and the religion life, and which ensures that it is life-giving. The religious structures (rules, doctrines, authorities) are like the body (or perhaps a scaffolding) which holds the spiritual tradition in shape. Without the spirituality, the religion is dead. It restricts our spiritual freedom and creativity; and it can easily become spiritually repressive.

A certain amount of organisation or institutionalisation can be very helpful. Without it, a spiritual tradition is likely to remain vague; and it can develop into a number of different competing interpretations of the tradition – some of which may be damaging or dangerous. So, at best, the structures of religion can safeguard a spiritual tradition, can help to purify and develop it, and can ensure that it is handed on faithfully to future generations.

Furthermore, people who share a spiritual tradition frequently become involved in providing social services, such as education, or care for the sick or for the old; and they sometimes become engaged in community development and even in political and economic development. When people in a particular spiritual tradition reach that point they need quite a lot of organisation, to deal with issues which are not 'religious' in the strict sense.

However, trouble arises if the organisational side of the whole project starts to gain so much prominence that the spirituality begins to take second place. The religious system is then likely to become unduly rigid, tending to restrict people's response to spirit or the Spirit, instead of inviting them to ever greater openness of spirit. Quite frequently, when the religious system becomes rigid, those with spiritual authority begin to abuse their power. At that point the religion has become a serious obstacle to true spirituality.

Fundamentalism

In recent times fundamentalism has developed in the major religions – especially in Hinduism, Islam, Judaism, and Christianity. Those who adopt the fundamentalist approach will not, of course, accept that they are fundamentalists. They will say they are simply returning to the original sources and basics of their religion – for instance, to the Bible or the Koran. Fundamentalism emerges in situations where the process of modernisation has disrupted people's lives and caused insecurity in people's beliefs and values. It is a reaction, an attempt by insecure people to defend themselves and others against rapid changes in the social, political, economic, cultural, and religious spheres.

In fact, then, fundamentalism is a modern development rather than a genuine return to the past (cf. Gray 2003: 3, 76-9). It is a desperate attempt to avoid the challenges of the present and the future by picking out some elements from the past, while ignoring other more important elements (cf. Armstrong 164-174). This narrow selection of elements from the past is then given a particular 'slant' or interpretation and turned into a very rigid set of rules and beliefs which are imposed in a fanatical way.

It is significant that fundamentalism in Islam, Hinduisim,

Judaism, and Christianity is used to impose a rigid patriarchal system in which women's behaviour is regulated in a way which can be quite tyrannical; and this oppression can be internalised by many of the women themselves. Islamic and Christian fundamentalists ignore the very important ways in which both Jesus and Mohammed challenged the dominant culture of their time and brought a lot of liberation to women.

In the world today the fundamentalisms of the different religions are 'playing into' each other, in the sense that, while strongly opposed to each other they are actually reinforcing each other. It is easy for Christians to see how this is taking place in Israel/Palestine where Islamic fundamentalism and Jewish fundamentalism come face to face, and in India where Hindu fundamentalism and Islamic fundamentalism confront each other. Christians may be more reluctant to acknowledge that, on the global stage, the rise of Islamic fundamentalism is partly caused by the Christian fundamentalism which has become a major political force in the United States.

Recently in the USA a new type of fundamentalism has come to the fore and has come to dominate the foreign policy of the Bush presidency. It is a mixture of old-fashioned Christian fundamentalism with a right-wing political agenda. The result is a secularised version of fundamentalism in which hard-line expansionist political policies are promoted using the rhetoric of evangelical Christianity. For instance, the overthrow of the government of Iraq, and the imprisonment without trial of people suspected of terrorism, are justified as part of 'the war on evil'. Christianity is not the only religion which can be corrupted and turned into a secularised nationalism, or can allow itself to be 'instrumentalised' in the interests of nation-building. John May describes how this happened to Buddhism in Sri Lanka, China, Korea, and Japan (May 18 and 146).

SECTION TWO: HOW WELL DOES THE CATHOLIC CHURCH MEASURE UP?

In this second section of the present chapter I want to address the question of how well the present-day Catholic Church is carrying out its fundamental task of being a 'carrier' in today's world of the rich and authentic spirituality of Christianity. The first thing to say is that the Catholic Church has an enormously rich spiritual tradition, stretching right back to the time of Jesus and the first Christians. So we can nourish our spirituality by drawing on a whole treasure-house of doctrines, values, symbols, rituals, and institutions. I shall mention first some of the valuable elements and then go on to note some areas where I think there are inadequacies and distortions which need to be corrected.

The Catholic Church has inherited and still uses a set of very powerful religious rituals (e.g. the eucharist and other sacraments) and symbols (e.g. the crucifix) which 'carry' and nourish the faith and devotion of millions in practically every one of the hundreds of different cultures in today's world. The church has also inherited a body of clear doctrines which spell out the essential elements of the Christian faith; and it has a body of moral and socio-political teaching which shapes the behaviour of its members and has a major influence even on those who do not share the Christian faith. It has a multitude of popular devotions – special prayers, novenas, pilgrimages, etc – which can channel the energies of its members; and new forms of devotion are constantly emerging to replace those which fall out of favour. It has a tradition of being a major patron of the arts, and it has a treasury of religious art and architecture which still nourishes the faith of believers.

As a result of Vatican II, additional sources of nourishment for spirituality have become available to Catholics. One is the use of vernacular languages and culturally appropriate music in the liturgy. This has enabled people to play a much more active part in the eucharist and to have a greater sense of being a community in doing so.

The Council also authorised and promoted a much greater

use of the scriptures for private devotion and in public worship. Prior to Vatican II many Catholics had experienced the Bible as the preserve of Protestants. But in the intervening forty years it has gradually come to be used more widely by Catholics as a major source of nourishment for their spirituality – though there is still a long way to go in this regard.

Reflection on scripture is now a central feature of Christian life in those of the 'young churches' where the basic Christian community approach has been adopted. 'Ordinary Christians' there are encouraged to 'read' the Bible in the light of their own situation, following the pattern developed by Ernesto Cardenal in *The Gospel in Solentiname*.

In the West, the situation is quite different. Here the majority of practising Catholics still have little familiarity with the Bible. But the scriptures now play a major role in the life of many priests, most members of religious orders, and a relatively small number of committed lay Christians. For these people, the old devotional 'books of meditation' have been abandoned, replaced by direct recourse to the living words of the Old and New Testament. But there remains a wide gap between these 'post-Vatican II' Christians and a large segment of Catholics who have become devotees of a variety of new devotions. Some of these recent devotions seem to embody and promote a spirituality of 'gloom and doom' which is a long way from the central thrust of the good news of the gospel.

Variety
One of the most valuable elements in the Catholic Church is that the faith has become inculturated and embodied not only in the Western Rite but also in several other 'rites', such as the Uniate Churches of the Eastern Rite and the 'St Thomas Christians' of India. This means that the church authorities accept in principle that there is not just one definitive and normative way of articulating and giving expression to the Catholic faith. It can be embodied in a whole variety of different ways in the different cultures of the world. Indeed, the differences between the four

gospels are a clear indication that such different embodiments and interpretations existed in Christianity from the very beginning.

Another valuable aspect is the pluriformity of spiritualities which exist alongside each other within the one church. There are rich traditions of spirituality to support and nourish those who wish to dedicate their whole lives to contemplation. In both the Eastern and the Western church there have been many great mystics, and several of these stand at the head of different 'schools' of mysticism. Among the outstanding mystics within the Western church were Teresa of Avila, John of the Cross, the unknown author of *The Cloud of Unknowing*, Julian of Norwich, and Meister Eckhart.

It is rather ironic that nowadays, when people in the West become interested in mysticism, they often look to the Hindu or Buddhist religions for inspiration and guidance. They seem to be unaware of the rich resources of mystical meditation and prayer which are much nearer home, and perhaps much closer culturally to them than the cultures of Asia. It is a serious failure of communication on the part of the church in the West that it has failed to make its mystical heritage better known and more available to spiritual 'searchers'. There are, however, some exceptions. Matthew Fox (2000) has done a lot to make the mysticism of Meister Eckhart known, not merely to practising Christians but to a much wider range of spiritual 'searchers'. And the Benedictine, John Main (1980 and 1998) developed a school of meditation which brings together elements from the Eastern religions as well as from the Christian tradition, and which provides spiritual nourishment for a great many people at the present time.

Within the unity of the church there are also hundreds of varieties of more active spiritualities which are embodied in ancient or more recent traditions. These spiritual traditions support and challenge people who feel called to any one of a great variety of options, ranging from sharing life with handicapped people to engaging in inter-faith dialogue with non-Christians.

Many of these more specialised spiritualities find an institutional expression in the hundreds of different religious orders, congregations, societies, and institutes, each of which has its own particular 'charism' or gift for the church and the world. This means that the institutional side of the church is by no means monolithic. Alongside the hierarchical structures (pope, bishops, priests, deacons, lay ministries) there is a whole variety of religious orders which in some ways offer alternative structures within which people's spirituality can be 'carried' and nourished.

Down through history, individuals and whole groups from within the religious orders and congregations have at times provided a very effective challenge to the hierarchical authorities. Francis of Assisi, Catherine of Siena, Mary Ward, and Vincent de Paul are just four of the hundreds of prophetic figures who challenged the church leaders of their time by offering an alternative and more authentic understanding of key aspects of the message of Jesus. And these alternatives became embodied in spiritual traditions which carried them on to later generations. This means that challenge, and even a certain measure of defiance, can be accommodated and encouraged within the unity of the church.

This process of challenge from within the church itself is still operative today and it offers us hope that fairly radical transformation can take place without a total rejection of the present authorities. What it means in practice is that there are individuals and whole groups who promote and model new approaches, while remaining fundamentally loyal to the church and respectful of its authorities. They are keenly aware of many inadequacies, wrong attitudes, and other distortions which make the present-day church less effective as a 'carrier' and nourisher of genuine spirituality than it should be.

In the previous chapter I listed twelve 'ingredients' of spirituality. I propose now to examine briefly how well the present-day Catholic Church measures up in relation to these items. In addition to mentioning areas where the church has done well, I venture now to point out some of the inadequacies which trouble

me. But in doing so I am very aware that I have my own prejud-
ices and blind-spots. So I make these comments and suggestions
in a tentative way and in the hope of being corrected and enriched
by the views of others.

The Church and Ecology
Where does the Catholic Church stand in relation to the first
item on my list, namely, ecological wisdom? Its present leadership is supportive in principle of the ecological agenda. A strong
statement on the environment was issued by Pope John Paul II
for the World Day of Peace of 1990. This argues that failure to
respect the integrity of creation is a rejection of God's plan and
does damage to human life (cf. Dorr 1992: 334, 348 and 369; and
Keenan 69-72).

In his 1991 encyclical *Centesimus Annus* (CA 37), the pope
referred to the 'prior God-given purpose' of the earth, insisting
that humans may develop this purpose but must not betray it.
But he went on immediately (CA 38) to refer to 'the more serious
destruction of the human environment'. It is unfortunate that he
makes this contrast, almost as though one were opposed to the
other; and his words 'more serious' are a clear indication of his
priorities.

In 2002 the pope joined with the Ecumenical Patriarch
Bartholomew I, in signing a Declaration on the Environment (S
McDonagh 2003a: 101). Nevertheless, ecology does not seem to
have a very high priority for the Vatican; and it seems to be
ambivalent at best on one issue which has a very high priority for
most environmental campaigners – that of genetic modification
of crops. Most of the Catholic bishops, with a few notable exceptions (cf. S. McDonagh 2003a and 2003b) have not taken a strong
stand on the ecological issue. There is little indication that
church authorities are giving practical support to those who are
campaigning on such environmental issues as genetic modification of plants.

There is an ample basis in scripture – especially in the psalms
and the gospels – for the development of an ecologically-sensitive

spirituality. But the Vatican is extremely cautious about giving any overt support to Catholic ecological theologians or campaigners. I suspect that this may be at least partly because these church leaders are concerned about the dangers of a new form of paganism – worship of Mother Earth. The result of their caution is that they are doing little to promote an understanding of the Christian faith which emphasises the presence of God in nature and which gives a prominent role to nature mysticism.

Liberation and Option for the Poor

Next we consider the topics of option for the poor and the struggle for liberation and justice. Over the past generation there emerged within the Catholic Church one of the most important developments in Christian spirituality since the time of the Reformation. It was the movement for liberation theology and basic ecclesial communities. This movement made a major contribution towards the development of a spirituality which promoted great lay participation, and which involved solidarity with marginalised people, a radical option for the poor, and a commitment to struggle for structural justice in the world. Beginning in Latin America, it brought new energy and hope to millions of people around the world. It empowered millions of lay Christians; and it was embraced and supported by very many priests and by the members and leadership of many religious orders, as well as by a significant number of local bishops in Latin America and elsewhere. It is hardly going too far to say that it was even adopted officially by the Latin American bishops at the Medellin Conference in 1968.

Sadly, however, the reaction of the official church in Rome was lukewarm at best and decidedly negative at worst. Rome hesitantly adopted some of the new language – for instance by speaking of 'a preferential but not exclusive option for the poor'. And when the pope visited Third World countries he undoubtedly took a very strong stance against a variety of oppressive governments. But against this must be set the constant stream of warnings about the dangers of politicising the Christian faith.

More damaging was the failure of Rome to give support to local bishops who challenged oppressive governments. In general, Rome has acted on the assumption that change must be brought about, not through confrontation 'from below', but mainly through a change of direction by those who are in power (cf. Dorr 1992: 331-2, 376).

The hostility of the Vatican towards liberation theology becomes very evident in its policies in relation to local bishops and religious leaders. There seems to be a sustained commitment to marginalising bishops who favoured the new approach. Whenever the opportunity arose they were replaced with men strongly opposed to anything that smacks of liberation theology. Rome even took the unusual step of replacing elected leaders of religious orders who were seen as too sympathetic to the liberationist approach. The result of these policies has been to dishearten those who felt inspired by the development of a spirituality of liberation within the church.

We may ask why has Rome reacted so negatively in the face of such an important development in Christian spirituality. The obvious answer is that Rome is quite accustomed to dealing with powerful rulers, challenging them and eventually working out some accommodation with them. So the Vatican is not convinced that it would be preferable to switch sides and come down overtly on the side of oppressed and angry people who are struggling for political liberation, sometimes by violent means. Furthermore, some of the suspicion of liberation theology may well be due to the fact that the institutional church is itself a very authoritarian institution at present. So the Vatican, and many local bishops, are fearful of a movement which challenges authorities to become much more democratic and to share power with those who are now largely voiceless.

Many Catholics today find the structures and attitudes of church authorities rigid and dominating. They are shocked when they notice that Rome seems to find it easier to come to an accommodation with right-wing regimes than with those of the left. They are scandalised when to see how much resistance there is in Rome to anything that smacks of liberationist spirituality. All this is a very serious hindrance to the development of a rich and nourishing spirituality for many Catholics today. I shall return in my final chapter to the issue of the need for a more participatory style of authority in the church.

Peace-making

I move on now to consider the record of the Catholic Church in relation to reconciliation and peace-making. In some respects the record is a good one. The most outstanding example in recent times has been the very strong and explicit opposition of the pope to the invasion of Iraq in 2003. Furthermore, the Rome-based Caritas Internationalis (which acts as a co-ordinating agency for Catholic development agencies and charities throughout the world) has become a major promoter of reconciliation in the world.

On the other hand, reconciliation between Catholics and other Christians in troubled areas such as Northern Ireland and the Balkans has been made much more difficult by the stance taken by Rome on some crucial issues. The intransigence of the Vatican, and of some local church authorities, on the issue of eucharistic sharing with Anglicans and Protestants has been a major problem. So too has been Rome's stance in relation to the ordination of women.

At the local level, the resistance of Irish bishops to integrated schooling in Northern Ireland has been a source of frustration for many who wish to bridge the gap between Protestants and Catholics. On such issues, Geraldine Smyth criticises what she calls the churches' 'increasing incapacity to transcend their own institutional weight" (Smith 96). This is undoubtedly a major obstacle to the development of a balanced spirituality by Christians in these areas.

Cultural Diversity

How well does the Catholic Church measure up in relation to respecting cultural differences? As I said above, Vatican II led to a big advance in this field. But, unfortunately, there is a still a long way to go. In many non-Western countries local church leaders would love to develop a liturgy that would draw on the resources of the local culture. But Rome persists in adopting an extremely cautious stance, which effectively blocks progress.

What may well be even more damaging is that Rome insists that the Western code of canon law be applied in the 'young churches' of the non-Western world. This is an indication that Rome interprets the unity of the church as a strict uniformity – and this in turn is understood as adherence to the pattern set down by the Vatican authorities.

Over the past fifty years, the church has succeeded admirably in giving leadership roles, both at home and in Rome itself, to 'people of colour'. But unfortunately the value of this witness against racial prejudice has been greatly undermined by the policy of the Vatican in promoting only those who adopt a very 'Roman' theology and style. This means that at times the strongest resistance to real cultural pluralism in liturgy and in other aspects of church life comes, not directly from Rome, but from local church leaders.

It never seems to occur to the Vatican authorities that some of the young churches might flourish better if they were attached to one of the Eastern Rites rather than to the Roman Rite. So the Eastern Rites are becoming more and more marginalised. Consequently, the spiritual traditions of the East are not being fed into the young churches. In this way the worldwide church and the peoples of the world are being deprived of a very rich resource of spirituality.

Contemplation
The Catholic Church has always valued the contemplative voc-ation and it continues to give support to religious congregations whose particular gift or charism is contemplation. But the number of those who commit themselves to the contemplative life on a full-time basis and for the whole of their lives is bound to remain quite tiny in proportion to the overall membership of the church.

Where the church has not done so well is in fostering a truly contemplative dimension in the everyday lives of 'ordinary' Christians. Many of these would be greatly helped if church leaders were to set up more training programmes for those who would like to learn how to meditate or how to pray, and more centres where they could 'take time out' to pray and meditate.

Gender and Sexuality

I shall treat this topic extensively in chapters 4, 5, and 6. At this stage the main point I wish to note is that the present-day church has inherited a bad legacy on these topics and is doing very little to change it. The Vatican has insisted quite aggressively on the continued use of sexist language in Roman documents and liturgical texts. It has declared that the topic of women's ordination may not even be discussed. These are just two indications of Rome's failure to take account of the anguish and outrage of many committed Christian women and men in the face of a callous insensitivity by church authorities on gender issues. Rome has also been quite intransigent in relation to various issues of sexual morality. For instance, it has adopted a very harsh line in regard to homosexuality. And it has even insisted that the partners of people infected with HIV / AIDS may not use condoms to protect themselves against infection. So the church has a long way to go in the areas of gender and sexuality if it is to provide a spirituality which speaks to Christians today.

Spirituality and Psychological Maturity

A key development over the past generation has been a very close integration of spirituality with psychological maturity. This is now so taken for granted that even we older people have almost forgotten that forty years ago we saw very little connection between psychology and spirituality. Finding a linkage between them has been one of the major breakthroughs in the post Vatican II era. In fact I think that it and the emergence of liberation theology have been the two biggest developments in recent centuries.

As a result of this breakthrough, we now see a close connection between the topics of community-building, interpersonal respect, personal integrity and vulnerability. Catholic authorities have become very aware of how important it is that church ministers and members of religious communities should receive a solid formation leading to psychological maturity. The documents issued by the Vatican on this topic are very insistent on this point – and the sex-abuse scandals have made church authorities more aware of it than ever. As a result, formation programmes nowadays are radically different from what they were a generation ago.

However, this is not universally true. There are still quite a number of more conservative religious congregations of men and of women which take in candidates at a young age and train them in the kind of 'hothouse' spirituality which is bound to inhibit the development of psychological and sexual maturity. Furthermore, there are some seminaries in non-Western countries where the number of students is so large that there is no real possibility of giving them the individual attention which the new formation programmes require.

In the Western world the religious orders and congregations – especially those of women – have, by and large, made a very serious effort to provide renewal programmes designed to remedy the inadequacies in the formation programmes to which their older members were subjected. Sadly, many dioceses have been slow to provide similar corrective renewal programmes for their priests – and many priests have been quite reluctant to take part in the programmes which are available.

What about the situation of lay people? For about twenty years after Vatican II the religious programmes offered to laity were made up mainly of theological lectures. In more recent years a much wider variety of courses has become available. So the present situation is that, alongside the more academically-oriented theological courses, there are quite a lot of programmes which have a strong psychological component and where the focus is more on spirituality or on training for pastoral ministry.

The initiative for these latter courses has generally come from committed people 'on the ground' rather than from Rome or from the bishops. But, whatever its source, this development is to be welcomed as it leads to the fostering and nourishment of people's spirituality – and also to a healthy pluralism in spirituality.

A Wide Gap

The final item on my list of twelve 'ingredients' of spirituality was openness to enrichment and challenge. This is one area where there is a very wide gap among committed lay Catholics between conservatives and liberals. What I find sad is that in recent years the church authorities – especially those in Rome – are generally located on the conservative side. One aspect of this resistance to change is an attitude to Vatican documents which is practically fundamentalist.

Those of us who experienced the excitement and spiritual liberation of the Vatican II years are not merely disappointed but also scandalised at the extent to which the Roman authorities have been attempting to 'roll back' the Council's changes. On a whole spectrum of major spiritual issues very many Catholics now find that their deepest spiritual instincts are in conflict with the Roman view. These issues range from liturgical matters to issues about sexuality, and from the question of sexist language to dialogue with other religious traditions – especially Buddhism and 'New Age' spirituality. Instead of finding support for their spirituality in the documents and statements coming from Rome – and in the leaders appointed by Rome – very many open-minded Catholics find themselves more and more alienated and are looking elsewhere for spiritual nourishment.

CHAPTER 4

The Unfolding of Sexuality

In this chapter I propose to look closely at the experience and meaning of sexuality. In this way I hope to provide a basis for a spirituality of sexuality without making any very explicit reference to God or Jesus. In the next chapter I shall consider the more explicitly Christian dimension of the spirituality of sexuality.

What is Sexuality?
There is a certain confusion about what exactly we are referring to when we talk about sexuality. I think it is helpful to locate its meaning between two extremes. On the one hand, there are those who restrict the meaning unduly by using the word as a euphemism for sex or genitality, that is, explicitly sexual behaviour. We need to take a much broader view than this. On the other hand, I think it is better not to define sexuality quite as broadly as Ronald Rolheiser does – in his otherwise very helpful treatment of the subject – effectively equating it with all forms of creativity (Rolheiser 1998: 184-8).

Sexuality may perhaps be seen as a dimension of life which is located between creativity, sensuality, and intimacy – and which partly overlaps with each of them. Diarmuid O'Murchu catches the experiential core of it when he says:

> Our sexuality consists of all those feelings, moods, and emotions that require a certain quality and quantity of closeness, intimacy, tactility, and love if we are to become, and help each other become, the fully evolved people that God intends us to be. (1999: 49-50)

Elsewhere he describes sexuality as he envisages it to have been in primal societies many centuries ago, long before 'the hang-ups and deviations of contemporary culture' interfered with it:

> There is an undeniable sense of the goodness of the human
> body, the sensuousness of the flesh, the intimacy and close-
> ness of human bonding (and a close affiliation with other
> life-forms), the erotic delight in the pleasures and joys of life.
> (1998: 86)

Looked at from a more analytical point of view, sexuality is seen
to be a very complex reality which permeates all of human life. I
think there are three central aspects to it. Firstly, there is the *fact*
of being a woman or a man. This fact affects practically every
aspect of how life is lived out both in its biological aspects and in
its cultural aspects. For instance, there is the primary biological
fact that women are capable of bearing children, whereas men
are not; and at the cultural level there is the reality that most of
the cultures of the world are patriarchal and therefore give more
privilege and power to men than to women.

The second aspect of sexuality is the *awareness* of being female
or male. This awareness of one's gender adds a whole new
dimension to the factual situation. It means that women experience themselves in a way that is significantly different from the
way men experience themselves. A person's gender has a very
big influence on what one considers to be important, how one
looks at other people, and how one behaves. The differences
spring partly from biological factors and partly from cultural
conditioning – and it is not easy to know at what point the biological
shades into the cultural.

Various studies by psychologists have produced a good deal
of evidence that even at a very early age little girls tend to behave
in a notably different way from boys. They are more interested
in developing harmonious relationships in their group, whereas
little boys tend to be more competitive and to set up a hierarchy
of dominance. It is not clear to what extent this pattern springs
from 'nature' rather than from 'nurture'. However, there is little
doubt that in most cultures this difference in pattern extends
into adulthood. So 'the man's world' feels quite different to 'the
woman's world'. The differences were spelled out in a popular
and practical way by the psychotherapist John Grey in his book,
Men Are from Mars, Women Are from Venus.

The third crucial element in sexuality is the experience of *sexual attraction* for another person – usually a person of the opposite sex. Here we have moved from issues of gender to overtly sexual issues. For very many people the most central and powerful aspect of sexual attraction is the experience that is called 'falling in love'. In my account of the unfolding of sexuality I shall focus on this experience of falling in love, and then go on to explore where it tends to lead one.

But, before doing so, I want to note that the way women and men relate to each other in their everyday interactions is significantly different from the way they relate to those of their own sex. Even if a woman and a man are not sexually attracted to each other, both of them are quite aware of a certain current or frisson of sexual energy in their relationship with each other. In other words, the gender of the person with whom we are relating is never an irrelevant or neutral element in the relationship. Sexuality in this general sense permeates all our human relationships.

It is also important to note that although there is a close link between sexuality and love, each of them extends into spheres of life which have little to do with the other. For instance, the sexual play of the infant with his or her own body has little connection with love; and there are forms of sexual domination and abusive behaviour which are the antithesis of loving behaviour.

Having acknowledged that sexuality is not confined to the experience of a loving relationship with another person, I want here to focus mainly on that aspect of sexuality which involves loving relationships. I begin by looking closely at what for many, if not most, people is the high-point of their experience of sexuality, namely, 'falling in love'. Patrick Kavanagh's 'Raglan Road' (187) is a very powerful song-poem about this kind of sexual love:

> On Raglan Road on an autumn day I saw her first and knew
> That her dark hair would weave a snare that I might one day rue;
> I saw the danger, yet I walked along the enchanted way,
> And I said, let grief be a fallen leaf at the dawning of the day.

Already in these first few lines the poet succeeds in communic-
ating the sense that falling in love has an element of enchantment about it. He is aware of the risks but is so 'ensnared' and
taken out of himself that he chooses to ignore the danger. No
wonder, then, that the ancient Greeks believed that this experience of falling passionately in love was due to enchantment by
some divinity – specifically by the goddess Aphrodite or the god
Eros. Only the power of deities like these could explain how a
woman like Helen would abandon her husband Menelaus to
elope with Paris, a prince of Troy.

Both Kavanagh's poem and the story of Helen indicate that
sexuality is the area of our lives which seems least amenable to
rational control. In some respects it seems to operate at a 'higher'
level than reason, evoking in us great generosity and self-sacrifice
and leading to decision-making based on intuition and an
exceptional level of interpersonal sensitivity. In other respects it
seems to operate at a 'lower' level, closer to the animal pattern of
experience and behaviour. However, it may be better not to
think in terms of either 'higher' or 'lower' but simply to acknowledge that our sexuality works to a considerable extent independently of reason. Sexual attraction and falling in love seem to
be autonomous, in the sense that they are not amenable to our
usual way of deciding our behaviour.

Aspects and Stages

Sexual love or *eros* is a profound and complex reality which
unfolds in several stages. At first one may have little or no sense
of where it will lead one in its later stages. Furthermore, it is not
the only form of love. *Eros* can co-exist with various other kinds
of love; indeed a central aspect of its inner dynamic is that it calls
forth these other types of love and integrates them.

Romance is the first stage of *eros*. It comes to young teenagers
in the form of a growing sexual awareness and sexual interest,
mixed with a sense of lightness and hope (which can be quite
unrealistic), as well as a good deal of anxiety and shame about
their appearance. Before long (indeed sometimes from the very

beginning) *eros* becomes focused on one particular person who becomes the object of romantic attraction. The sexual attraction of one person for another (somebody of the opposite sex, except in cases where the person is gay or lesbian) may begin as admiration of the other and as a desire to impress and be admired by the other.

There is a *playful* form of love which comes to the fore in the early stages of sexual attraction. We see it where two people are flirting with each other, exploring the possibility of getting into a deeper relationship. In a truly successful relationship of love this inter-personal playfulness will endure and may surface at quite unexpected moments.

Romantic attraction to another person gives way to a much more profound experience when one 'falls in love'. At this point the attraction has developed into a kind of 'enchantment'. One becomes almost completely preoccupied with thoughts and fantasies of the person with whom one is in love. It is not inaccurate to describe it as an experience of blind infatuation – except that the word 'infatuation' is rather judgemental and fails to convey the life-giving energy and sense of gift and of miracle or magic which is part of the experience. Being in love gives one a sense of sparkling new life and lifts one out of the mundane reality of everyday living. So the word 'enchantment' may be more appropriate since it conveys the positive aspects as well as the sense of being 'taken over' by the attraction.

There is at first a high degree of unrealism – almost of blindness – in the lover's image of the other. The image is 'unreal' because it is not based on an accurate observation of the other person. Its main source is the preconception of the 'ideal other' which is unconsciously held by the person who has fallen in love. (Jungian psychologists relate this to the power of the unconscious *anima* in every man and the unconscious *animus* in every woman; they maintain that what the person has 'fallen in love' with is mainly the unconscious side of his or her own personality.) It may be quite a long time before the person comes to have a more realistic conception of the other. But part of the wonder of *eros* is that people can continue to be in love with each other even when they have attained a quite accurate sense of each other's inadequacies and faults.

Once *eros* comes into its full flowering it becomes a *passion*, that is, an emotion which is so strong that it is very difficult to control. In the case of sexual passion at its most powerful there is an almost overwhelming desire to be close to the beloved. We tend to associate the word 'passion' with violence. But in the case of sexual passion, while there may be a whiff of violence in the air, there is generally an overwhelming feeling of tenderness. Emily Bronte, in her account of the passionate love between Catherine Earnshaw and Heathcliff in *Wuthering Heights*, conveys very well the violent dimension of sexual passion; one has the sense that there is tenderness there also, but it remains largely unexpressed, perhaps even unacknowledged, by these two extremely strong-willed lovers.

At the heart of sexual passion is the desire to 'possess' the other and to be 'possessed' by the other. When I refer to the desire to 'possess the other', I am using the word to cover a whole spectrum of attitudes. It can be a very literal clinging on to the other, or a desire to control the other as 'mine', or simply a desire to be physically and emotionally close to the other, coupled with an assurance that there is a certain exclusiveness about the relationship. But, wherever one is located on this spectrum, there is always an inner dynamic which draws one towards having sexual intercourse with the other person. That is at the heart of this experience of sexuality or love in the form of *eros*; and this dynamic or 'intentionality' remains even in cases where the people concerned have no intention of acting on it.

The desire to 'possess' and 'be possessed' takes a very bodily form – it comes as a strong urge for mutual nakedness. In everyday life, people have very strong inhibitions against exposing themselves; the sense of shame is quite powerful. *Eros* incites one to overcome this shame and allow oneself to be naked before the other.

Needless to say, to allow oneself to be naked before one's

beloved is a major act of trust. It is a very powerful image of being open. But it is important not to interpret this nakedness in a purely metaphorical way. What is in question is a very real physical 'hunger' for skin-to-skin contact. We may assume that one basis for this craving for skin contact is an unconscious body memory of the time when one was an infant in skin-to-skin contact with the mother's breast. But, whatever its background, it is experienced in the present by people in love as a strong urge to touch and be touched, to explore the body of the beloved, and allow one's own body to be explored in turn.

This mutual exploration normally finds its high point in the act of sexual intercourse, but it also takes place in touches and embraces which do not culminate in intercourse. Ben Kimmerling argues convincingly that, when two people who are in love with each other respond to their *conscious* urge to explore each others' bodies, they are in this way meeting a deep *unconscious* need which each of them has to know and accept his or her own adult body: 'Each partner, by delighting in the other, reveals to him/her the wholesomeness of his/her body' (Kimmerling 1986, 302).

I would add that loving touch is a very powerful cause of healing (cf. Donnelly 48). This is something that both animals and humans know instinctively, as is shown by the way they treat their young who have been hurt. And there is plenty of anecdotal and scientific evidence that children or animals which have been psychologically damaged by abuse can be fully or partly healed when they are held and touched in a loving way. One element in the strong urge of two lovers to hold and be held by each other is this instinct to comfort and heal – and to be comforted and healed by the other. The more sustained and intimate the contact, the more likely it is to bring a profound degree of comfort and healing. Apart from the relationship between a mother and her unborn child, sexual intercourse is the most intimate physical contact that is possible between two people. So it can play a very important role in healing the psychological wounds which people have sustained – provided the context is right and it is a genuine act of love.

Any sexual relationship, no matter how intense, can quite easily degenerate into one of mutual or one-sided exploitation. To ensure that this does not happen, it is essential to allow *eros* to develop into a deep bond of *friendship* between the partners. Aspects of this friendship-love are: ease in one another's company, common interests, sensitivity to each other's feelings and moods, and, above all, mutual respect and care for each other.

Alongside these various aspects and developments of *eros* there is also what we may call the *domestic* aspect of love – the inclination to share a home (and perhaps a garden), to eat together, to sleep together, to plan life together. At this point the 'magic' and rather unrealistic quality of romantic love is brought 'down to earth' by a healthy note of realism.

Kimmerling suggests that there is a further stage in the journey into intimacy. It is a movement into truth and authenticity in the emotional sphere. Here the challenge is for each partner to accept the full range of feelings which are experienced by himself or herself and by the partner. Some of the negative emotions which well up are so powerful that the person is temporarily overwhelmed and is in danger of becoming physically violent. Kimmerling maintains that, when one partner goes 'over the edge' in this way, the other can provide a 'safety net of love' which prevents a fall into chaos. In this way the moment of weakness becomes the occasion in which a new and deeper bond of trust is forged. The partners can agree to grow, stretch, and take risks within the wider space provided by the joint 'safety net' of both partners (Kimmerling 1986, 306-7).

At this stage *eros* has already developed to a point where generosity and self-sacrifice have become far more prominent in the relationship. What has taken place is a radically new advance of an inclination which was a characteristic of *eros* even at a very early stage. For the person who is sexually attracted to another and falls in love very soon finds a strong inclination to be generous to the other, to give gifts, support, and time unstintingly – generally without thinking of recompense, or in terms of a bargain. In the later stages of a sexual partnership this dimension comes more and more to the fore.

'The Lonely Self'

In a stable relationship of sexual love the partners reach a stage at which there is a change in the dynamic. Up to now they have been moving ever closer together, growing more deeply in intimacy. But the next stage is the process which Kimmerling calls 'discovering of the lonely self' – and respecting one's partner when he or she makes this discovery. When a person's more immediate needs (to have one's body and one's whole range of emotions accepted and loved) are met, other needs begin to surface. These include the need for privacy and independence, and also 'the right to experience moral confusion, religious doubt, crisis of faith, … uncertainty – even uncertainty about the relationship itself – and the need for time (sometimes a great deal of time) to sort out … inner conflicts …' (Kimmerling 1986: 365). At this point, genuine love means 'offering the gift of freedom within which this search for autonomy can take place'.

> It is a 'letting be' sort of loving … a stillness rather than an activity, a holding back rather than a jumping in to help – a waiting! It is a type of loving which requires patience, endurance and strength. Above all it is a love which requires faith and hope. It is a type of love which is costly and difficult because it does not have immediate results. … It is the beginning of non-possessive love. (366)

The relationship of the partners has now moved into a different stage. The partners are in a phase of differentiation, where it may seem that they are growing apart, and where they may fear that they really are moving apart. But what is happening is that each of them is discovering that at the core of human existence there is a profound loneliness. Before they met each other they had experienced loneliness, but it was a 'hopeful loneliness' because it 'seemed possible that the pangs could be assuaged if only the right person came along'. Now, however, 'the right person has come along and yet the love which now exists between these two people succeeds only in heightening each partner's awareness of his/her own isolation.' (366-7)

Move to Community

In addition to these different aspects of love which are present in *eros*, or become linked to it from a fairly early stage, there are practical developments of love which are latent at first but which are called forth over time as part of the inner dynamic of *eros*. The most obvious of these is the desire for one or more children. Having children opens up the parents in a radical way. They move from being focused to a very high degree on each other to finding themselves extremely preoccupied with the child or children. At its best this turning outward to the child is experienced as a wonderful completion and enrichment of the parents' love for each other. But almost invariably in practice it stretches their love – and their whole being – almost to breaking-point. It calls forth in them a degree of generosity and self-sacrifice which would have seemed almost unthinkable at an earlier stage of the relationship. And yet all this is an intrinsic part of the unfolding of the dynamic of *eros* or sexual attraction.

The next stage to which the inner dynamic of *eros* leads those who engage with it is the turning outward to the local community. This happens quite naturally as the children grow older and become involved in activities such as schooling and sports in the locality (cf. Rolheiser 1998: 190). A further stage is when parents reach out beyond the family connections to become involved in welfare projects (e.g. care for the elderly) or to pursue other interests (e.g. the arts) or other concerns (e.g. environment or peace-making or world justice issues). These wider involvements may become more significant in parents' lives once their children are reared. *Eros* unfolds further as the couple engage in such activities together and bring new life and richer meaning into their lives.

Kimmerling holds that the move towards community and universality is part of the inner dynamic of love from an early stage. She goes on to give a very interesting account of how it may come to the fore in a rather dramatic way. A new upsurge of *eros* energy may burst unexpectedly into a person's life, in an event which she calls 'enter the stranger'. She suggests that a couple, who over many years have developed a mature relationship with each other and a healthy spirituality of sexuality, may be presented with a very new kind of challenge. This is to find a way in which one of these partners can relate in a loving and healing way with some radically new reality – a person or perhaps a group – which comes into that person's life and may be quite undeveloped and needy in the whole sphere of human relationships (Kimmerling 1986: 454-461).

According to Kimmerling (464) 'the stranger' may be anybody – 'a young child or an old man, a beautiful woman or a handicapped baby'. Or it could be 'a spouse or family member who becomes a stranger through behaviour which seems unacceptable'. It could also be a group. But the crucial point is that the 'stranger's love becomes so palpable that the needs of the self are deliberately put aside'. This, she maintains, is a crucially important development, because now, for the first time, the person is loving another in a way which is utterly devoid of self-interest. It is an act of 'utmost tenderness', given 'as pure gift' (460).

But what form does this response of selfless love take? It may come 'in a thousand ways ... by a single gesture or a lifetime of service, by a smile or a kiss ... by a word or by silence' (464). In whatever form it comes, what matters is that the response be a totally free and generous act of self-giving. It is in this abandonment of self-interest that the person uncovers 'the deepest human need of all, deeper even than the need to be loved'. 'It is the need to love', and by loving in this utterly generous way to become 'an instrument of divine outreaching' (461).

What I understand Kimmerling to be saying is that love, of its very nature, seeks to be both totally *personal* and utterly *universal*: personal, in the sense of being focused on the other person in a way which makes the other be absolutely unique; and at the same time universal in the sense of reaching out in an unlimited way to all (462). The love which God has for us has both of these elements in full degree. But in the case of our human love, it takes some time before both aspects can be fully present.

In early adulthood, as each of us discovers our personal call or vocation, we find ourselves drawn in one of two directions. On the one hand, we may move towards a personal one-to-one relationship which is at first somewhat exclusive. On the other hand, we may be drawn towards a celibate way of life; in this case we are giving first priority to the universal dimension of love – embodied, for instance, in care for refugees, or the victims of racism. She spells out elsewhere the development of the celibate call (Kimmerling 1993). Focusing here on the unfolding of the personal one-to-one love of sexual partners, she holds that a major breakthrough occurs when one of them takes the enormous risk of accepting and loving 'the stranger'. For in this first act of fully selfless love the universal and personal dimensions of love come together, and so the person is privileged to love as God loves, and in this way becomes an instrument of God's love.

If this situation of 'meeting the stranger' occurs as Kimmerling describes, it will be the culmination of the expansion of love from being a one-to-one affair to reaching out to the wider human community. For 'the stranger' here represents the part of humanity which had previously been unknown, or not taken into account, or not deemed deserving of our love.

It is, however, obvious that this whole situation will stretch the love of the partners in a way they have never experienced before. They will now have to cope with new and very difficult but understandable emotions and inclinations. There will be a temptation of the 'left out' partner to become suspicious and jealous. Responding to this (or anticipating it) the other partner may feel disloyal or guilty and be tempted to become secretive or manipulative. If the partners succeed in working through this testing time, their relationship will have developed into a much deeper, more trusting, and more open one. No wonder, then, that Kimmerling sees this stage of love as one in which the person (or partners) may be conscious of sharing in the creative and life-giving love of God – and even of being themselves agents of this divine love.

Ben Kimmerling has here identified a very important dimension of sexual love. By using the dramatic phase 'enter the stranger' she deliberately highlighted the newness and the element of breakthrough to selfless love. However, she had previously noted that, once a child has come into the relationship between two people, selfless love is already present, in a way that is more familiar and therefore more socially acceptable (455). The point is that, from the beginning, love is tending towards openness and universality. So the breakthrough is in one sense an organic development, a making overt and explicit of a dynamism that is latent in any genuine love.

I would want to take this a stage further by saying that the breakthrough to selfless love is not necessarily an all-or-nothing affair. Like most human processes, it can be present to a greater or lesser extent. It may take a very long time before one is able to leave aside all personal self-interest. And even if that stage is achieved one may slip back again. So the pattern of breakthrough may not be very obviously dramatic. Furthermore, people who are truly religious are aware that God is calling them to a selfless love which is modelled on, and shares in, divine love. So there is a two-way process: the entry of 'the stranger' enables people to come to a love that has the quality of divine love. But at the same time their experience of God's love and their awareness of God's call give them a strong incentive to allow their love to become ever more generous and more open to 'the stranger'.

Letting Go

The final stage of the *eros* dynamic is that of letting go. This, of course, is the very antithesis of the initial stage of *eros* which is the desire to possess and to be possessed. Not surprisingly, then, it can be very difficult. But death is part of the reality of life and it is only very rarely that both partners die at the same time; so the bereaved person has to 'let go'. The total breakdown of a loving relationship is also an experience which some people have to endure.

It is clear, then, that when two people enter into a sexual relationship, an implicit aspect of that relationship is the likelihood that one or other of them will at some stage have to cope with the loss of the sexual partner; and in the case of marriage breakdown both partners will have that experience of loss. Only people who are unusually reflective or philosophical or pessimistic are likely to pay much attention to this reality while they are still experiencing the wonder of first love. But, at some deep and perhaps unacknowledged level, this consideration does have an influence on people's decisions about whether or not to take the risk of following the dynamic of *eros* by committing themselves wholeheartedly to each other.

When the dreadful moment of loss comes – usually after many years, but in some cases after a short time – then *eros* unfolds into or calls forth a particularly poignant aspect of love. Love, in its mourning mode, is a peculiarly complex emotion. A grief which is almost unbearable, bitter-sweet memories, regrets, guilt, sadness, anger, hopelessness, loneliness – all these are mixed up together, along with other less predictable feelings.

But the very first form of mourning-love is likely to be emotional numbness, an inability to feel anything – except a vague feeling of guilt for being so 'unfeeling'. For those who have to endure this numbness it may be some small comfort to be reassured that this is a perfectly natural reaction. They may need to be reminded that it is a defence of the psyche in the face of the shock of death and loss, and that at the right time the tears will come. And in the case of those who are coping with the death of the partner, as distinct from the breakdown of the relationship, there may be, beyond the tears or mixed in with them, an experience of love which endures beyond the grave.

In many non-Western societies there is a kind of 'postscript' to the unfolding of the *eros* drive. This is the entry of the dead person into the company of the ancestors. The ancestors are seen as an important part of the extended family, able to exercise a benign influence – but also able to cause trouble for the family if they are neglected or insulted. This suggests that, in these non-

Western cultures, as soon as two young people begin to court each other they already have some vague or implicit awareness that their relationship may extend even beyond death, since a dead partner will join the company of the family ancestors.

Variations
The way in which *eros* unfolds depends very largely, as I have been suggesting, on the age of the person and the stage which the relationship has reached. However, there is room for a great lot of variation in the way in which *eros* is experienced and unfolds. The culture in which one has been reared has an enormous influence on how one experiences sexuality. For instance, the desire for children is very high on the agenda of most Africans from a very early stage.

It is fairly well-known that in Africa there is a tendency to think that a marriage is not really stable (perhaps not even fully consummated) until a child is born. What is perhaps less well-known is that, among some tribal peoples, before marriage a woman is expected to have already proved that she can conceive a child. The priority given to the ability to have children also explains behaviour which Westerners would see as incest: older family members may feel they have a duty to ensure that the younger members are sexually experienced before entering into marriage.

The gender of the person also has a considerable influence on how sexuality is experienced. It can be quite dangerous to make generalisations about gender, since there are great differences between individuals. But it seems that generally – at least in Western cultures – the desire for sexual intercourse is very prominent in the early stages of a man's experience of *eros*. For women generally it seems that the more immediate desire at first is to be admired, wanted, touched, held, and to 'possess' the other in the sense described above. My experience of working in Africa inclines me to believe that for many Africans the desire to procreate is to the fore from a very early stage in both men and women. It is arguable that among some teenager women in areas of high unemployment in the Western world the desire to have a child has recently come to have a more prominent role; apparently these young women see this as a way of putting meaning into their personal lives and of finding a significant role in society.

Another factor which is very relevant is the sexual orient-ation of the person. There was a widespread tendency in the past (and it is still present among many today) to assume that heterosexuality is the only acceptable form of sexuality, and that there is therefore something wrong about being of a gay or lesbian orientation. It will be a great service to the world if we can develop a spirituality of sexuality which helps people to be comfortable with homosexuality in themselves or others.

Having come to terms with the fact that a certain proportion of women are lesbian and of men are gay, we now have to con-sider a factor which is closely related to this but may not be quite the same. It is the fact that people can find themselves at any point on a wide spectrum, ranging from very male at one end of the spectrum to very female at the other end. We are dealing here with something more than the widely-accepted fact that, from a psychological point of view, all women have some masculine elements in their make-up, and all men have feminine elements. We have to go further and recognise that, in a small number of people, the boundary between the male and the female is very blurred; nature may not conform to the very sharp boundaries which logic prefers. Some men are endowed with a lot of typically female features; some women have char-acteristics which are typically male; and a small proportion of people who look like men are genetically female and vice versa.

The consequence of all this is that the biological make-up of some women and men at times sends them 'mixed messages' about their sexuality; and in the case of a small minority of people these 'mixed messages' are very confusing indeed. This helps to explain why some people experience themselves as bisexual. It also helps to explain the lengths to which some people may go to try resolve their confusion about their sexual identity – including behaviour which others would consider to be weird (e.g. cross-dressing) or actions which seem brutal and bizarre (e.g. sex change operations).

There is one further source of variation in the way different individuals experience their sexuality. It is the degree to which a particular person is highly sexed or is less intensely so. (This is not the same thing as where the person is located on the male-female spectrum.) Why should one person be hyper-sexual while another person seems to have relatively little preoccupation with sex? It is probably a combination of the biochemistry of the individual with his or her psychological history. But, whatever the causes may be, it is important that we take account of the notable differences between people in this regard.

A Promise Unfulfilled

Sexuality of its very nature promises more than it can deliver. The very word 'sex' comes from the Latin *secare* and suggests being 'cut off'. Our sexuality is felt as a longing for completion, for union. And as soon as this longing becomes focused on another person it includes a belief – indeed a kind of certainty – that through union with this person one will no longer be 'cut off' but will feel fulfilled and made whole. This belief or certainty is not at all based on any kind of rational calculation. It is a quite irrational feeling which goes against a lot of evidence. Nevertheless, its power can be almost overwhelming.

In this regard sex is quite similar to other human activities. As little children we tend to set our hearts on some object of desire, assuming that it will give us perfect enjoyment or fulfilment. But the reality seldom lives up to our expectation – and even if it does, the satisfaction pales after some time. Even when we move into adulthood the same pattern repeats itself time after time. The main difference in the case of sexual attraction is that the pull is generally more demanding, the hope of complete fulfilment much stronger, and both are less amenable to rational control.

A successful sexual relationship goes a long way towards living up to its promise. There is pleasure, joy, comfort, fulfilment, and a real sense of union in the act of sexual intercourse at its best. Indeed it can bring about a sense of the blurring of the boundaries between 'you' and 'me' so that, as the Bible says, the two become 'one flesh'. Furthermore, a successful on-going sexual partnership brings shared pleasure, ease, support, companionship, and deep friendship. These very positive experiences of sexual love teach us that whether love comes as a response to our initiative or comes 'out of the blue', it always comes as gift, not something which we have earned.

But neither the intimacy of the sexual act nor the warmth and security of an on-going sexual relationship can fully satisfy the human person's deep hunger for self-transcendence and unity. We find within ourselves a primordial aloneness which is part of being human. And, as I pointed out above, following Kimmerling's analysis, the deepening love between two people heightens rather than diminishes their awareness of this loneliness. So those who expect sexual activity or an on-going sexual relationship to rid them of that sense of being 'cut off' are doomed to disappointment. They have expected more from the experience of sex than it can give them.

If even a successful sexual relationship cannot satisfy one completely, how much more is this the case in brief sexual liaisons, or in long-term relationships where the partners are not getting on well together. In such situations people may be tempted to 'shop around', or to become promiscuous, or to get involved in pornography, in the hope that a lot of sexual activity may make up for a lack of quality. This proves to be an illusion – but it is difficult for people to learn that lesson, since by then they may have become addicted to sex to a greater or lesser degree. The reality is that the sexual activities and relationships of very many people, while they may bring some pleasure and release of tension, are not very fulfilling and are often a source of further tension and of many problems. For them, the promise of sexual attraction to bring fulfilment and union has given rise to disappointment and perhaps disillusionment.

Those who have a firm belief in an afterlife can find a rather easy solution to the problem of the unfulfilled promise of *eros*. They can claim that the very purpose of this incompleteness of union and joy in our present sexual experiences is to point us beyond the present life. For them, the gap between the promise and its realisation will be bridged in the life to come, when our hearts will be filled with a joy which no one shall take away from us. Our task in this life is simply to make our peace with our present inadequacy or incompletion, mainly through living in the hope which comes from a promise of fulfilment in the next life. In the meantime we must give up 'false messianic expectations' (Rohlheiser 1998: 197).

Those of us who are less certain about the future, or whose ideas about the next life are more tentative, may find ourselves unable to invoke the certainty of perfect fulfilment and joy in a future life as an easy solution to the problem of present incompleteness. Nevertheless we may find *eros* in its different manifestations to be a source of hope. For *eros* is already an experience of partial transcendence. It carries us beyond ourselves, puts us in touch with that part of ourselves which longs for intimacy with the other and for a union in which we can feel no longer 'cut off' but fully whole. However inadequate our present experience of self-transcendence may be, *eros* at least points us in the right direction.

Eros intimates to us that fulfilment and happiness are to be found, not through a single-minded pursuit of our own pleasure, or through the acquisition of more and more possessions, or through exercising power over others. It is found instead through giving our love to another (or others) warmly, generously, spontaneously, and even at times a little madly. So *eros* hints that the way to grow and flourish is through entering into and holding on to relationships which challenge us to entrust ourselves to others; relationships which will unfold into new possibilities and new risks, constantly stretching us to go further; relationships which require that we grow both in our aspirations and our achievements. The experience of loving also invites us to become more aware of our fragility and so to ask for help; to be more conscious also of our inadequacies and failures and so of our need to seek forgiveness. Furthermore, it invites us to undertake the surprisingly difficult enterprise of allowing ourselves to be loved, accepted, and forgiven unconditionally.

Even the aspect of *eros* which puts us in touch with our primordial dis-ease does not have to be seen as a burden – or not only as a burden. That restlessness deep within us which is experienced as an unfulfilled promise can be interpreted not as a source of disillusionment but as an invitation to hope. The hope which we scarcely dare to name is that, if we recognise and receive with open hands the many gifts of love which are showered on us on our present journey, then God (or whatever power is at work in giving us these gifts of love) will give us the ultimate gift: rest for our restless hearts through a union and completion 'which no eye has seen, nor ear heard, and which the human heart cannot imagine' (1 Cor 2:9).

Spirituality

It may seem that I have spent a very long time in describing the different dimensions of sexuality without saying anything about the spirituality of sexuality. In response I can only say that perhaps sixty percent of the work of developing a spirituality of sexuality is coming to understand the rich complexity of sexual experience and ridding ourselves of misconceptions about it.

The remaining forty percent is a matter of accepting gratefully what is on offer without trying to grab more. This means, firstly, that a key aspect of a wholesome spirituality is being at ease with, and grateful for, our sexuality and with the different aspects of it which unfold over time. It also means exercising moderation – even when we are in the midst of the wonder and 'enchantment' of falling in love. But this must not be a puritan type of restraint which would kill the joy of sexuality, or a very calculating restraint which would empty it of its lightness and spontaneity.

The lesson which Christianity at its best has to teach our present-day world is that we are likely to 'kill the goose that lays the golden egg' if we make it our primary aim to get as much sexual pleasure as possible. Pleasure is part of the experience, but we miss the full joy if we are unwilling to accept that sexual pleasure comes as part of a 'package'. The primary components of the 'package' are generous love of the other, entrusting ourselves to the other, and allowing ourselves to be loved; the pleasure comes best when it is not pursued directly (cf. Cozzens 28).

CHAPTER 5

Shame, Intimacy, and Spirituality

There are two main positive emotions associated with sexuality. The first is 'interest-excitement' which arises once the possibility of a sexual encounter comes on the horizon. The second is 'enjoyment-joy' which comes during the encounter and after it, if the experience has been one of genuine intimacy. 'Interest-excitement' creates a tension, and 'enjoyment-joy' is a relaxation of this tension, a coming to rest in a kind of fulfilment which completes the sexual emotional cycle. Nathanson puts this very well:

> The part of love that is exciting and makes the heart pound owes its power to interest-excitement; the part of love that makes us feel calm, safe, relaxed, and untroubled owes its power to enjoyment-joy (240-1).

Shame

Unfortunately, however, these positive emotions never come in a pure form; in practice, they are always inextricably linked to some negative emotions. Of all the negative, painful emotions associated with sex, by far the most common, the most powerful, and the most damaging is shame. Shame comes in varying degrees, ranging from shyness, to embarrassment, to feeling ashamed, to being utterly humiliated.

I propose to devote some pages to exploring the nature of shame, and its damaging effects. Then I shall go on to consider how best to handle it and lessen its harmful effects. My reason for devoting so much space to this topic is that many people – perhaps Christians even more than others – carry a heavy load of shame. This makes it almost impossible for them to handle their sexuality in a healthy way. It undermines and corrupts the spirituality of sexuality. Shame generates a false spirituality which damages people severely and which is also passed on from one generation to the next.

The emotion of shame, in its technical sense, is not just a feeling. It is a feeling linked to a set of memories of previous feelings of the same kind (Nathanson 50). When a feeling of shame arises, it immediately triggers these shame-filled memories which amplify the feeling enormously and cause it to go on and on, as long as these memories keep triggering further shame.

Shame is not just something that occurs in our awareness – our feelings and emotions. It is first of all something that happens to our bodies; and it also interferes with our ability to think. When we are ashamed there is

> … a sudden drooping, a loss of posture, a slump, a turning away of gaze (and therefore a reduction in our ability to interact with another person), a cognitive shock that renders us momentarily unable to think clearly, then an avalanche of shame-related cognitions that force us to think about our worst and most damaged self (Nathanson 291).

Linked to Sex

Why is it that shame is so inextricably linked to what should be such a positive and enjoyable experience as sexual activity? It is mainly because from our very earliest years we have accumulated a whole reservoir of memories of being shamed and humiliated – and very many of these memories are about events which have to do with sex.

It begins at a very early age. A baby boy may be made to feel he has done something wrong when he has a sexual erection – and particularly if he seems to be interested in it or proud of it. A baby girl may be made to feel she has done something wrong if she exposes herself. The shame associated with toilet training easily gets associated with the sexual organs. Furthermore, it is quite common for young children to pick up and take on the embarrassment or shame of the adults around them when some-thing sexual is said or done. When children come to puberty there are endless occasions for shame, associated with normal bodily functions – menstruation for girls and nocturnal emissions or visible erections at inopportune times for boys.

However, shame is not just something that comes as a result of a prudish upbringing. It goes far deeper than that. 'The core of shame', says Nathanson (235), 'is the feeling that we are unlovable.' So shame is triggered by anything which suggests to us that we are not beautiful, or kind, or generous, or brave, or strong, or worthwhile in any one of an endless number of ways. Furthermore, it is also triggered by any word, or gesture, or hint, or memory that reminds us of previous suggestions or indications that we are inadequate or have failed in any of these ways. And because sex is such a powerful and all-pervasive force in human life it is inevitable that many if not most of these triggers will be associated with sex.

What makes the linkage between sex and shame even more likely is what happens during adolescence. This is a time when sexuality is a most pervasive force. And it is during this period that young people develop an image of themselves as lovable or not lovable from a sexual point of view. In this scenario there are endless opportunities for embarrassment, shame, and humiliation, as any of us will realise when we recall that period of our own lives. So the teenager fills up the reservoir of shame to the brim. During those years, or much later in life, the walls of the reservoir can be breached by a chance word or glance. Then a deluge of shame pours out and engulfs the person for anything from a few moments to the rest of the person's life.

Shame is a very painful and unpleasant emotion; at its worst it makes a person feel totally wiped out, wanting to have the ground open up to swallow the person. But the major problems arise not from shame itself but from the stratagems which people use to defend themselves from feeling humiliated in this way. There are four different defence strategies and, by and large, each of us is inclined to opt mainly for one of them. They are named by Nathanson as 'avoidance', 'attack self', 'attack other', and 'withdrawal'. He describes them at considerable

length (305-377). I shall examine each of them briefly, drawing
on his treatment, but relating each of them particularly to current
issues about spirituality. I shall concentrate especially on how
these shame-reducing stratagems give rise to distortions in
spirituality which have been – and may still be – characteristic of
many Christians, perhaps especially Catholics in the English-
speaking world.

Avoidance

'Avoidance' is a well-known psychological stratagem. What is
perhaps less well known is the many ways in which it is used by
people to defend themselves against the shame attached to sex.
The people who adopt an avoidance strategy to escape shame
are suffering from a very poor self-image, taken on in childhood
in the environment of an unloving home (Nathanson 340-1).
They carry into adulthood a great deal of shame, stemming from
the belief that there is something very seriously wrong with
them. They live with the constant fear that others will notice this
defect and so they will be shamed further. So they use a variety
of avoidance strategies to distract people's attention away from
this major defect.

They may seek to impress people by displaying trophies or
other evidence of their achievements. Or they may go to enormous
trouble and expense to make themselves look beautiful (if they
are women), or to make their body look powerful (if they are
men). Another strategy is to go into a secret world where they
identify totally with some powerful hero or beautiful heroine.
Yet another is to become very competitive and become so
powerful that people would be afraid to do anything which
would trigger their sense of shame. Surprisingly, perhaps, one
of the strategies used by men for avoiding shame is 'macho'
behaviour, including a flaunting of their sexual prowess. In
women the corresponding strategy is a flaunting of their sexuality in what would be seen as a 'shameless' manner.

The crucial point behind all these strategies is that they are
attempts by extremely insecure people to deceive those around

them. They are showing the world an image that is the exact opposite of their image of themselves. They present themselves as competent, tough, attractive, and sexy. This is done in order to ensure that others will not see them as they think and feel they really are – incompetent, weak, unattractive, and (above all) sexually defective and unlovable. Their highest priority, then, is to avoid any kind of intimacy where their secret defect might be discovered.

There are two rather obvious ways in which this defence against shame can give rise to a distorted spirituality. The first way is by becoming a 'workaholic', and developing a spirituality which puts all the emphasis on work. Those who adopt this pattern want to prove to others, and to themselves, that they are worthwhile. They think they can do so by working excessively, and by their great achievements. (Those familiar with the Enneagram will recognise this as a 'Three' pattern.)

Perfectionism is another way in which an attempt to defend oneself against shame can give rise to a damaging spirituality and way of life. A perfectionist spirituality may effectively glorify compulsive cleanliness and tidiness ('cleanliness is next to godliness'). Or it may put excessive emphasis on being right or 'getting things right'. This leads to a lot of harsh judgements on oneself and on others. Needless to say, this is a quite destructive type of spirituality. Furthermore, it generates further shame, which provides more 'fuel' for self-condemnation in a downward spiral. (In Enneagram terms this is a 'One' pattern.)

Both of these distorted forms of spirituality can be characteristic not only of an individual but also of a whole group of people. It can happen, for instance, that a religious community – or a whole religious Congregation – can adopt (or inherit) a spirituality that is unduly perfectionist or puts far too much emphasis on work and on achievements. This can allow individuals within the group to feel quite humble, while at the same time having an excessive corporate pride in the wonderful cleanliness and order of 'our hospital', or the great success of 'our school' or 'our project'. In this way the individual's sense of shame is doubly distanced.

Attacking Oneself

Some people adopt a quite different approach. They set out to avoid or minimise shame by pre-empting the shaming words or actions of others. So they do to themselves what they fear others may do to them (Nathanson 329). The milder forms of this are shyness, deference, and conformity. All of these send out the message, 'I recognise that I am less important than you.' And the sub-text is, 'so there is no need for you to shame me, to put me down, to humiliate me.'

A more sophisticated version of this approach is used by those who make jokes at their own expense. Fearing that they will be shamed by the jokes of others about them, they forestall that humiliation by 'getting in first' with a less virulent version of the joke. They see this as a good bargain. By paying the price of a small amount of self-inflicted shame, they disarm those who might have shamed them much more severely, and win these dangerous people over to their side.

A much more severe form of this approach is masochism. According to Nathanson (333-4), it is not that those who engage in masochistic sex really enjoy being hurt and humiliated. But for them there is something that would be even worse, namely, being abandoned and isolated. They are suffering from such an intolerable weight of inner shame that they submit to bondage, sending out the message: 'I need you so much that I'm even prepared to let you cause me pain, rather than have you abandon me.' Of course this kind of distorted thinking sounds bizarre to those who are not trapped in the quagmire of shame and distorted sexuality. But we can see the same pattern at work, in a slightly more credible form, in the case of the battered wife who defends her abuser.

Even in its less pathological forms, this type of defence against shame damages and distorts one's spirituality. It generates an unhealthy form of humility which sees shame as a virtue, or at least as something which should be fostered to some extent. In the past, this emphasis on humility was a fundamental feature of the formation programmes in novitiates and seminaries.

Those in charge of these training programmes set out deliberately to train the candidates in humility – quite often by humiliating them. So, in some cases at least, the 'attack self' pattern had actually been replaced by the 'attack other' pattern which I shall look at next.

Attacking Others
Social constraints and personal experience combine to teach us that it is risky to get openly angry with others. These others may punish us for our anger, either physically or by withdrawing their friendship. But people who feel their whole identity threatened by the thought of being seen as weak, incompetent, or stupid may become so enraged that they attack those whom they see as posing the threat. If that seems too risky, they may attack somebody else, in order to prove to themselves and the world that they are not weak and incompetent. In either case, the basic motivation is the avoidance of shame.

There is a vast spectrum of ways in which we can attack others, ranging from unkind words or contemptuous looks to murder or declaring war on them. In the sexual sphere there are endless scenarios where a person reacts to a personal experience of shame by shaming somebody else. If this stratagem for escaping shame is to be effective, the transfer of shame from self to other must take place so instantly that it is done automatically and generally without conscious awareness. So the rapist may almost believe his excuse that 'she was asking for it'. Again, the person who is sexually attracted to an unavailable person may immediately alleviate the shame by making a disparaging sexual comment about the other – or by fantasising a situation where the other is sexually submissive or humiliated.

In a sado-masochistic relationship, one partner's pattern of 'attack other' is matched to the other partner's pattern of 'attack self' (Nathanson 372). The same linked patterns are present in marriages where one partner continues to accept physical or emotional battering by the other. In cases of sexual abuse of children or adolescents, the abuser often succeeds in establishing the same kind of dominance over the victim. Furthermore, the abuser cleverly uses the victim's shame to generate or amplify a feeling in the victim that he or she was responsible for the abuse, and to blackmail the victim into acquiescence in the abuse.

One might imagine that no credible spirituality could include any incentive to attack others. Sadly however, this is not the case. As I mentioned already, novices and candidates for the priesthood were quite frequently shamed and humiliated deliberately by people in charge of their training-programmes. Instead of discouraging such behaviour, the spirituality of the time actually encouraged it. And this spirituality was also taught to lay Catholics. Many conscientious parents and teachers adopted a certain degree of this damaging spirituality – and imagined themselves to be virtuous in doing so.

The same kind of distorted spirituality was used in the past to justify clerical domination. A priest whose sexuality is undeveloped, or whose sexual development has gone awry, is almost certain to carry a heavy burden of shame in relation to all things sexual. A rather common way of lessening this shame is to dominate and even humiliate others. This type of spiritual domination is still practised by some priests, especially in areas where the clergy are still respected and even feared.

Clerical control and domination can occur in various spheres of life. But it is particularly damaging when it occurs in matters related to sex – for instance, in the way the priest advises or passes harsh judgement on people who come to him with sexual problems. In judging others and exercising strict control over them, the priest is trying to give the impression to them and to himself that he is an expert in these matters. In this way he is seeking to lessen the shame arising from his ignorance and confusion in relation to sex. A much more extreme form of this domination takes place in cases of sexual abuse of children or of other vulnerable people by priests or others with spiritual authority. I shall return to this a little later. But before doing so, I want to examine the stratagem of *withdrawal*, because it, too, is relevant to the issue of sexual abuse.

Withdrawal

Withdrawal is the fourth of the stratagems used by shame-filled people to avoid or lessen their burden of shame. In some respects it is the most radical of all, because it is more or less an attempt to de-sexualise oneself. It is important to understand the difference between avoidance and withdrawal. In avoidance, the person seeks to block out the shame associated with sex but does not give up the sexual activity itself. On the other hand, withdrawal involves distancing oneself to a greater or lesser degree from the whole area of sexuality.

Minimal forms of withdrawal are the politeness which causes us not to meet the eyes of the other, together with such unconscious gestures as putting our hands to our mouth or biting our lip. In a more severe form, withdrawal manifests itself in frigidity and impotence, or an almost complete lack of interest in sex. The most serious forms can be very severe depression or almost complete inability to leave home or to meet strangers.

There are many ways in which the withdrawal pattern has damaged the spirituality in which people of my generation were brought up. Perhaps the most obvious is a major deficiency in the training-formation given to those preparing for priesthood, and for life in religious congregations. It is no exaggeration to say that these young men and women were encouraged to ignore their sexuality as far as possible. 'Occasions of sin' were to be avoided. Therefore these young people must distract themselves at once from any sexual fantasies which came into their minds; and prayer was seen as the best way to get rid of 'bad thoughts'. Sexual desires had to be avoided as far as possible; and if they came into consciousness they were to be ignored, or actively resisted and banished.

Looking back, we can now see that the whole area of sexuality was dealt with by a policy of withdrawal. What is particularly disturbing about this approach is that it was not just an official policy which was ignored in practice. It actually 'succeeded' to a very considerable extent, in the sense that it was internalised by those on whom it was imposed. When these young women and men entered the novitiate or seminary their normal sexual development came to an abrupt end. From then on, all the irruptions of sexuality in their life were consigned to a purely private world, seldom shared even with a confessor or spiritual director. This was a secret world surrounded by guilt and permeated with shame.

Guilt and shame were the two emotions associated with sex. From a psychological point of view, guilt is a combination of shame and fear. The distorted spirituality of the time gave a rather prominent place to guilt and fear. Guilt was closely linked to fear of punishment by God, who was presented as a judge who could see into one's heart. Guilt and fear were never far from the mind, for the church teaching was that any deliberate 'giving in' to sexual thoughts, desires, or looks (not to mention touches) was a mortal sin. Provided the person had 'full knowledge and full consent', every sexual sin was punishable by hell for all eternity. The dominant spirituality also encouraged people to feel ashamed of their sins. However, shame was left curiously undefined – probably because it is so obvious that it is a feeling and the importance of feelings was greatly played down in the spirituality of the time.

The fact that feelings of shame were evoked but left undefined meant that people could not 'get a handle' on shame, to work out whether or to what extent it was appropriate in any given situation. This increased its power enormously. Everything to do with sex was contaminated with shame. The resultant pathological 'spirituality' of sexuality was passed on to each succeeding generation by people who themselves had been moulded in the same hothouse atmosphere. Furthermore, the priests, sisters, and brothers, trained and moulded in this distorted attitude to sex, passed it on in their preaching, teaching, and pastoral ministry to generations of lay Catholics. So the reaction of withdrawal was not just a *personal* pathological response to sex; it was also a *corporate* dis-ease affecting the church as a whole.

It is not so long ago that a very prudish kind of modesty was imposed on young people – especially on girls. While dressing and undressing, even in private, they were expected to keep their bodies covered. And it is probably quite true that at least some convent girls were advised not to be naked even in the bath – 'for the sake of the holy angels'. We look back now with some amusement at these prudish attitudes. But they were not at all funny at the time. They reflected a serious determination to teach people to withdraw as far as possible from anything that would remind them of their sexuality. These practices were inculcated with the intention of ensuring that people would not act shamefully and so would avoid feeling ashamed. Of course they actually generated a lot more shame – and some of that shame still troubles people fifty or sixty years later.

Celibacy

When we think about the different ways in which withdrawal can take place, we have to face up to questions about celibacy. These questions arise at two levels, the institutional and the personal. At the institutional level, it must be recognised that the Catholic Church's emphasis on celibacy has been influenced by a dualistic philosophy which undervalued and distrusted the body and especially the sexual. But it is also important to ask to what extent the psychological process of withdrawal was at work. Looking back at the spirituality of celibacy which was current before Vatican II, we must ask, was it not inviting priests and vowed religious to 'withdraw' from their sexuality as far as possible?

At the personal level, those of us who chose a celibate way of life at a fairly early age have to ask ourselves to what extent our choice was influenced by a largely unconscious desire to withdraw from the shame we associated with sex. And we then have to ask ourselves a further question: to what extent have we moved on from where we were at that early age? Have we now developed a more wholesome attitude to our own sexuality? I shall return to these issues towards the end of the next chapter, when I explore the spirituality of celibacy.

Distorted Theology and Child Sexual Abuse
The phenomenon of withdrawal helps to explain the extremely
inadequate and distorted theology of sex found in the manuals
of moral theology used for centuries up to the time of Vatican II.
What was presented in them as theology consisted mainly of a
description of different kinds of sexual sins, all of them described
in biological terms. There was little of no reference to a context
of interpersonal relationships, still less to issues about respect
and intimacy.

This can be understood when we advert to the fact that theologians and Church leaders were using the stratagem of withdrawal to lessen their feelings of shame in relation to sex. In
doing so they were filtering out all the feelings attached to sexuality. They were marginalising a whole range of emotions – not
just shame but also love, loyalty, fidelity, excitement, jealousy,
anger, grief, betrayal, dependency, and domination. What was
left was a description of sex such as might be given by an
anatomist. Consequently, the moral rules which they presented
as 'natural law', were actually based on anatomy and biology,
rather than on human relationships.

Against that background we can begin to understand the
otherwise extraordinary fact that child sexual abuse was not
mentioned in the manuals, or in the courses of moral theology. It
was 'the sin that was absent', and was therefore unknown to
many who should have known about it. (In so far as the moral
theologians of the time took account of the sexual abuse of children, they included it under the heading of incest; this meant that
what they saw as the evil of the action was not precisely the
abuse of a child but rather the sexual relationship with a close
relative.)

I have to admit that for most of my life I was quite unaware
of the reality of such abuse. I didn't know anything about
paedophilia – despite the fact that I had taken a doctorate in theology and had taught theology for several years in a seminary.
How could I have been so uninformed? I suppose I was sheltered
by the tacit conspiracy in the media and in society in general to

cover up a reality which must have been well known to social
workers, police, and medical people. Nevertheless, I am shocked
that during all my studies of moral theology I never heard of this
sin. It is not as though our teachers and those who wrote the
manuals of theology were too prudish to refer to various sexual
perversions. When we studied moral theology we worked
through what purported to be a comprehensive list of sexual
aberrations. But I have no memory of hearing or reading anything about child sexual abuse at that time or for many years
afterwards.

A Blind Spot
I think it is very likely that at least some of those who wrote the
manuals of moral theology knew that child sexual abuse occurred.
And they must have had at least some awareness of the harm
that it did to the victim, even though they would not have been
at all as aware of the damage as we are today. What then prevented them from dealing with paedophilia alongside the other
sexual sins? One would have expected that not only would it be
mentioned but that it would have been included on the list of
'sins which cry out to heaven for vengeance'. It seems there was
a collective blind-spot which caused those who knew of this sin
to fail to mention it in their books and lectures.

I suggest that the theological blind-spot about paedophilia is
to be explained in terms of the psychological process of withdrawal. The theologians who used the stratagem of withdrawal
were effectively eliminating from their awareness all the interpersonal and relational aspects of the sexual abuse. In trying to
filter out their own shame about sex, they also filtered out empathy
with the victim. So they had little or no awareness of what was
really being done to the child or vulnerable adult who was being
abused. If asked, 'what is happening to this person?', they
would have responded in clinical anatomical terms, completely
ignoring the nightmare of feelings being generated in the victim.

Furthermore, whole generations of moral theologians supported each other in generating and continually fostering this

blindness. The manualists of each succeeding generation practised
the same withdrawal from feelings associated with sex, and they
carried on the same way of thinking. Over three or four centuries
they built up a very solid tradition and an almost incontrovert-
ible body of 'accepted wisdom' which was, in reality, a quite
distorted theology and a damaging spirituality.

How could hundreds of theologians have more or less ignored
the difference between sexual intercourse with an adult and
with a child? Well, they were thinking more of bodies than of
people. So the fact that the 'other body' was that of a child was
not seen as relevant to the act 'in itself'. Furthermore, all sexual
acts outside of marriage were considered to be intrinsically evil,
that is, evil in themselves independently of their consequences.
So, child sexual abuse was seen as just one particular instance of
such an evil act. Therefore these theologians saw no need to
advert to the horrific consequences of this specific act, that is, the
damage done to the child.

The Consequences
The failure of theologians to name child sexual abuse as a sin has
obviously played a part in the cover-up of this shocking evil in
society. It meant that there was no mention of the sin of paedophilia in the programmes of moral instruction in schools, col-
leges, and seminaries – or in Sunday sermons or parish missions.
So this was one element in the great conspiracy of silence which
allowed sexual abuse to be ignored or played down for so long
in our society. Furthermore, the fact that child sexual abuse was
not listed as a specific type of sin meant that there were no warnings about the wrongness of the kind of actions that are now
termed the 'grooming' of potential victims – for instance, curry-
ing the favour of children by giving them sweets or other gifts.

The spirituality which was fostered in the church for several
centuries made it extremely difficult for victims of sexual abuse
to tell what was happening to them, because of the extremely
heavy charge of shame and guilt which surrounded sexual activity. In fact, victims of sexual abuse ended up feeling responsible

and guilty for the evil that was being done to them. This applied above all to abuse by 'church-people'. These abusers employed a particularly damaging mixture of different stratagems for defending themselves against shame.

The 'attack other' pattern is the most obvious of these strategies. In fact the victim was attacked at two levels, firstly by the actual sexual abuse, and secondly by having the shame and guilt of the perpetrator loaded on to the victim. But the 'withdrawal' stratagem was also at work – probably in the abusers and certainly in the environment in which the abuser operated. The result was that the abuser felt no real empathy with the victim of the abuse, no sensitivity to the enormous emotional damage that was being done.

However, we must not make the mistake of focusing almost exclusively on sexual abuse by 'church-people'. The statistics show clearly that the great majority of sex abusers of children are relatives of the victim. In these cases, too, the prevailing spirituality made it very difficult indeed for the abused child to seek redress. For one thing there was an excessive and unnuanced emphasis on the rights of parents over their children. Furthermore, the burden of shame was greatly increased by the heavy emphasis in Christian spirituality on the serious guilt attached to almost every sexual action. This made it even harder for the victim to break the secrecy and tell anybody about the abuse.

The distorted moral theology of the time also had a very serious effect on the *perpetrators* of sexual abuse. Shame and guilt made it extremely difficult for people to ask for advice or guidance about their sexual behaviour – and perhaps particularly about aberrant inclinations or actions. Furthermore, the false conscience which was imposed on people by a misguided theology made it hard for them to distinguish between healthy and unhealthy sexual desires and activities.

No wonder, then, that some people failed to develop a delicacy of conscience in relation to activities which were abusive and seriously sinful. Abusers may even have told themselves that they 'might as well be hung for a sheep as for a lamb'. In other

words, those who were tempted to abuse a child sexually may
have argued that, even if this was sinful, it was no worse (or not
much worse) than more conventional sexual activity. They
could see it as just one more of the many kinds of sexual activity
which were all labelled as mortal sins.

I am not saying that the defective theology of the time was
the primary cause of paedophilia. But I think it helped to sustain
a polluted spiritual atmosphere and a seriously unhealthy silence
in which sexual abuse of children was not named openly and
was covered up when it occurred. This was an atmosphere in
which the innocent were not warned against abuse and in which
the guilty had plenty of opportunity to practise abuse and a very
good chance of getting away with it.

Spiritual Abuse: Legalism and False Conscience

I think there is a link between clerical *sexual* abuse and a much
more widespread *spiritual* abuse which was inflicted on the people
of my generation. When I refer to spiritual abuse in this context I
am thinking of two closely related things: the reduction of spirituality and morality to legalism, and the imposition of a damaged
and distorted conscience on very many people.

There was so much emphasis on guilt and punishment in
relation to sexual sins that the fundamental Christian belief in a
loving God was undermined to a considerable extent. The idea
that God is love was, of course, acknowledged in theory. But, in
practice, God was seen much more as a law-maker, a harsh
judge, and a kind of spiritual policeman. In this way our spirituality became seriously distorted and oppressive. It was largely
reduced to a legalistic notion of obeying God's commands. I feel
sure that people of my generation will agree that what I am
describing here is not a caricature but is a fairly accurate picture
of the spirituality that was presented to us in the years before the
Vatican Council.

This kind of theology also led to a serious undermining of the
very notion of morality. There was little or no emphasis on the
notion of moral values, or on the concept of morality as a call to

do good for its own sake, without reference to reward or punishment. In popular preaching and teaching at that time, moral activity was reduced to obeying God's laws and commands. Christians were taught that a major reason for avoiding evil actions was to escape being sent by God to suffer in hell for all eternity. The horrific punishment of hell was not intrinsically related to the evil action in any obvious way. The result was that genuine morality was replaced by a fear-ful legalism. And the imposition of this distorted theology on Christian believers amounted to spiritual abuse.

Closely related to this is the second aspect of spiritual abuse. The misguided moral theology of the past immersed normal sexual desires and responses in a quagmire of shame, guilt, and confusion. It generated a distorted conscience in very many people by leading them to think that they were falling quite frequently into mortal sin – for instance, when they 'went courting', or even when they thought about 'going courting'! Furthermore, very many young Catholics were put through agonies of shame and guilt about masturbation, which was harshly described as 'self-abuse'.

This rigorist moral teaching blocked people in the development of moral sensitivity in sexual matters. That damage to moral conscience in the sphere of sexuality came on top of the more general damage done by the wholesale reduction of morality and spirituality to a fearful legalism. Together they lie at the heart of the spiritual abuse which was inflicted on so many of the people of my time. And this spiritual abuse itself contributed significantly to the development of the distorted theology and spirituality which was a major component in the environment in which sexual abuse took place.

Urgent Need for Change

I hope it is now clear why I have devoted several pages to the exploration of shame and various damaging reactions to it. It is because this throws a lot of light on the distorted and dysfunctional theology and spirituality of sexuality which was dominant in the church in recent centuries – at least up to Vatican II, and to some extent even up to the present. If we are to develop a healthy spirituality of sexuality we must face the challenge of correcting the inadequate and at times distorted theology and spirituality which we have inherited. We cannot any longer assume that what is presented to us as the 'traditional Catholic teaching' on sex and sexuality is an accurate and adequate reflection of what Jesus stands for.

All of this 'traditional' teaching is culturally conditioned, and some aspects of it stem not from the Bible but from neo-Platonist philosophy and Gnostic sources. Furthermore, it fails to take adequate account of major social and technological changes which have taken place in relatively recent times – for instance, the major problem of over-population in the poorest parts of the world, the HIV/AIDS pandemic, the development of effective means of contraception, the women's movement and the growing acceptance of the equality of women with men, the increase in the number of women going out to work, and the move from the extended family to the nuclear family.

The spirituality of sexuality which was pervasive in the church up to Vatican II was quite inadequate and has done a lot of damage. Unfortunately, some senior Vatican authorities are still defending major elements of it. I hope the earlier part of this chapter has made it clear that this distorted spirituality does not stem only from a dualistic heritage in philosophy and theology, or from a failure to take account of modern technological and social developments. In addition to all that – and perhaps more profoundly damaging – is a seriously pathological element which can only be understood in psychological terms. This is why the analysis of shame is relevant. And it means that a major part of the development of a wholesome spirituality of sexuality must be some more effective way of handling shame, especially shame associated with sex.

Dealing with Shame
Feelings of shame will control our behaviour and our attitudes

so long as they remain under the surface. So, if we wish to develop a healthy spirituality, it is important that we acknowledge the reality and power of shame, and that we recognise ways in which we have unconsciously allowed it to affect us. It is quite important to identify which of the various stratagems we commonly resort to, in our efforts to minimise our feelings of shame. Do we habitually withdraw, or do we practise avoidance? If so, how has this behaviour prevented us living a wholesome life? In what situations are we attacking ourselves, 'putting ourselves down' in a damaging way? When do we try to minimise our shame by attacking others – and in what ways?

It may take a long time before we can answer these questions honestly and accurately. It is quite likely that it will require difficult and painful soul-searching. But the reward is great. For the more we succeed in bringing to light the ways in which shame has determined our attitudes and lifestyle, the more we will be able to live our lives in freedom, with less stress, and with greater respect and openness towards others.

Nathanson (378-396) gives a very interesting account of how the load of shame can be lifted by humour. First, the tension is raised by the mention of something secret, shameful, and 'unmentionable'; then the tension is suddenly lowered by making a joke about it. But it is not every kind of humour which dissipates shame. Some jokes are barbs at somebody's expense; they are instances of the 'attack other' pattern, intended to humiliate the other person. The humour which lessens shame is of the type which is compassionate and creates a bond of empathy between people.

Loving Intimacy

The best way in which shame can be dissolved, and the damage done by shame can be healed, is by being lovingly accepted by another person. The most natural place in which this happens is in loving intimacy between sexual partners. At this point I need only recall the account I gave, in the previous chapter, of this kind of love. There is the entrusting of one's naked body to the beloved, fully open and exposed, totally vulnerable. And this act of trust is not betrayed. The person is accepted, touched, embraced, held in love. At the same time this act of trust is reciprocated: one is privileged to touch, embrace, and hold the other in loving acceptance.

It is well also to recall Ben Kimmerling's insistence on two stages in this loving acceptance, as outlined in the previous chapter. First there is the unconditional acceptance by the other of one's body. In the light of the analysis of shame given above, we can now see how important this is. In our damaged world the body is a primary source and locus of shame. To have it accepted with tender love dissolves the shame at least for that precious time – and it can go a long way to enabling the person to accept his or her own body without shame. It can even heal some or all of the shame-filled wounds of the past.

The second stage goes deeper still. In the presence of the beloved, the lover is permitted to have the whole range of his or her emotions come to the surface and be lovingly accepted. Even the most negative feelings – the hateful jealousy and suspicions, the desire to possess in a controlling way, the greedy desire for more pleasure or for some novel, or weird, or cruel experience, the fears that one's sexuality is perverted, the burst of violent hatred or of disgust and nausea, the feeling of boredom – all those emotions which are so shameful that they are buried in a deep almost inaccessible place, all can be brought into the light and accepted in love.

It is important to point out that what melts and heals shame is not sex but loving intimacy. But what do we mean by intimacy? Kimmerling gives a helpful description.

Intimacy … is an attitude of truth and authenticity: an open space which is free of physical distaste, emotional blocks and intellectual prejudice. It is about availability. It is about appropriate, relevant and truthful disclosure in every relation-ship. It is about revealing vulnerability as well as strength. It is about transparency. It can exist not only in private relation-ships – though that is usually where one first learns about it –

it can exist in public relationships too. In its presence people feel deeply moved: they feel invited to change and grow. In this kind of intimacy a person is fully present to others and so God is present too. (Kimmerling 1993: 88)

It often happens that sex is used as a substitute for intimacy and love. This is obviously the case where somebody has sex with a prostitute. But it is by no means limited to such situations. In fact Nathanson, in referring to the fact that very young people have sex nowadays, says 'I suspect that this represents a move away from intimacy toward the use of sex for its druglike properties.' (293). So there may be the most intimate skin-to-skin contact without any real intimacy.

Indeed, eye-to-eye contact may often be a better 'carrier' and sign of genuine intimacy than skin contact. The inability to look somebody in the eye is one of the most significant and primordial features of shame. I use the word 'primordial' in the sense that the downcast gaze goes back millions of years and can be seen even in animals – for instance, in the pet dog who knows it has done something forbidden. The person who is in the process of overcoming shame manages bit by bit to look the other in the eye; and when that look is reciprocated with love a wonderful healing takes place. (In the case of visually-impaired people the 'carrier' may be the voice.)

Other Locations of Intimacy

I have said that the intimate loving relationship between two sexual partners is the most 'natural' place where shame can be dissolved and its wounds can be healed. But there are other locations, too, where a fair degree of intimacy can be found; and the greater and more enduring the intimacy, the more shame can be melted away. A warm loving family or extended family; a truly caring and accepting community; and, more especially, a close and enduring friendship – all these can provide an ambience in which a good deal of shame can be faced and dealt with in a healthy way.

Theatrical performances, or certain kinds of public lectures, are more unusual – and perhaps surprising – ways in which people can allow shame to surface and to be relieved and perhaps dissolved. A high degree of intimacy can be achieved even in a relationship between one person on stage and an audience of hundreds. It might seem like a one-way relationship and certainly it lacks the mutuality of one-to-one intimacy. But the gift of the great actor is to establish a very close empathetic bond with the audience, so that those who are present feel that their own secret lives have been touched or revealed, and handled with reverence. Likewise, the person whose lecture is deeply experiential – the speaker who takes the risk of exposing intimate personal secrets – may generate a similar type of rapport with the audience; but only if he or she finds the right balance between cool objectivity and self-indulgent exhibitionism. The secret here, as in everything to do with the healing of shame, is delicate, respectful, courageous love.

I venture to suggest that some degree of intimacy can be achieved even through the written word. If I, as an author, am willing to expose some part of my soul – especially the inner doubts, fears, and agonising that goes on within me – then I am reaching out to my readers, hoping to make a connection that transcends time and space. Some bond of intimacy may be established if I succeed in revealing myself while avoiding sentimentality, mawkishness, excessive self-exposure, and anything that sounds false or contrived. It is a limited kind of intimacy, because it is largely a one-way relationship. (From the writer's point of view it is like dropping a stone from a cliff which is so high that one never hears the splash when it lands!) But even this one-way intimacy may, at its best, be an incentive to the reader to reach out with sensitivity to others and in this way to widen the network of authentically human relationships.

What about the formal therapeutic relationship established between a spiritual guide or a counsellor / therapist and a client? Is intimacy involved here? In therapy the client goes through the difficult and at times shameful process of exposing his or her deepest fears, anxieties, and hopes; one of the hoped-for outcomes is that the client's burden of shame in everyday life will be lessened. The therapist has to be very skilful to help the client reach the point of trust where shameful secrets can be revealed and explored. And the client has to pay money for the benefit of the therapist's skills and time. Nevertheless, it would be a great mistake to assume that the relationship is a purely professional one. The healing, if it occurs, will be accomplished above all through the attention and loving acceptance which the therapist gives the client. So this relationship, too, despite the careful boundaries that are set around it (and partly because of them), is ultimately one of loving intimacy. The wounds of shame are healed only by loving acceptance.

Intimacy with God

Finally, there is the question of God. Can we overcome and heal shame through an intimate relationship with God? The answer, obviously, is 'yes'. If loving acceptance is the answer to shame, then there can be no doubt that God's superabundant love and acceptance of each of us is a supreme source of healing of the wounds of shame. And this is not just an abstract theological theory; there is abundant evidence in the writings of the mystics that their awareness of God's infinite love and care sets them free to stand erect, no longer crippled by shame.

It is true that people who feel overwhelmed by a vivid sense of God's presence, sometimes convey their feelings in words which might suggest a sense of shame. One thinks, for instance, of Isaiah's exclamation: 'Woe is me! I am lost, for I am a man of unclean lips' (Is 6:5). But it is well to remember that this was immediately followed by the touch of a live coal from God's altar, a touch which purified him. In any case, a closer reading of the words of such mystics indicates that their primary feeling is not so much shame in the strict sense, as a sense of creaturely awe before the wonder and majesty of God.

Having insisted that the experience of God's love can heal us of shame, I must add at once that this may not be the easy shortcut which it might seem at first sight. Practically all of us in the older generation were brought up in a spirituality where God is the judge, the one who sees our most secret and shameful thoughts, and who is prepared to condemn us to hell for harbouring sexual thoughts or fantasies. It is not at all easy for somebody with such a conception of God to establish a relationship of loving intimacy with that God.

The fact of the matter is that it is very difficult for anybody to experience themselves as fully loved and accepted by God, unless that person has had some similar experience of love and some degree of intimacy with one or more humans. We were not created as isolated individuals, called to find our lonely way to God. The normal pattern of our lives is to be born into a family where we are loved and where we learn to love. So we cannot expect to have an alternative route – one which enables us to by-pass the experience of human love and human intimacy in order to go directly to God. It is not even clear what the word 'directly' would mean in this context, since God is transcendent, beyond our world. In one sense all contact with God is direct, but in another sense it is always mediated through some aspect of our created world.

Of course, I am not entitled to put any limit on the power of God to touch the human heart. I cannot rule out the possibility that even the most isolated and wounded person may receive the grace of such a powerful experience of intimacy with God that all shame is removed. But if that occurs it is a rare exception. Few people, if any, have been able to by-pass all experience of human love in their journey to God. To say this, is not to put a limit on the power of God. It is simply to take seriously the reality that we humans are both embodied and are part of the human community.

In fact if we really believe the claim of Jesus to be 'The Human One' we must say that he, like us, was called to be loving and intimate with other human beings. We may even go so far as to say that, before he could have an experience of loving intimacy with the One he called 'Abba', he had to experience intimacy and love as an infant in his family; and that as he grew up he had to learn to love and to be intimate in his family and community. This is indicated by the gospel text which says that he 'grew in wisdom and age and grace' (Lk 2:52). Furthermore, it seems that he taught his closest friends that there is no intimacy with God without loving relationships with those around us. St John, 'the disciple whom Jesus loved' is quite blunt about it:

> No one has ever seen God: if we love one another, God is in us and God's love is perfected in us. ... Those who say, 'I love God,' and hate their brothers or sisters, are liars; for those who do not love a brother or sister whom they have seen, cannot love God whom they have not seen. (1 Jn 4:12, 20)

A Christian Spirituality of Sexuality

A Christian spirituality of sexuality is made up for the most part of the kind of general human spirituality which I have been outlining in the previous chapter and this one. Furthermore, it is just one aspect of the overall Christian spirituality which I outlined in Chapter 1 above. So I need only recall and spell out a little more explicitly some of the aspects which have a particular relevance to sexuality. The first of these is that we share in God's creative and providential power in a most striking way through the creative power of loving and being loved. Two people who are deeply in love with each other can enable each other to come alive and flourish to a remarkable extent. Their reaching out in giving and receiving love also helps each of them to heal and be healed at a deep level.

We can rejoice that the Song of Songs is one of the books of the Bible and therefore part of God's sacred word to us. Its richly sensuous and erotic language encourages us to see intimate human sexual love as one of God's greatest gifts to us. This is one fundamental element in a spirituality of sexuality.

A second crucial element springs directly from the title 'the Human One' which Jesus gives himself in the gospels. In taking this title, Jesus provides us with the link between spirituality as a personal relationship with God and spirituality as living fully authentic human lives. The fact that Jesus called himself the

Human One encourages us not to interpret the Song of Songs in a pseudo-spiritual way by seeing it as just an elaborate metaphor of the love affair between God and humanity. Of course, it does give a hint of the intimacy of God's love. But it is first of all one of the most beautiful love poems in human literature, a celebration of sexual love.

The way Jesus related to women is very obviously relevant for the Christian who wishes to develop a spirituality of sexuality. As I pointed out earlier, he posed a radical challenge to the patriarchy of his time. The fact that he treated women as equal to men was shown strikingly – even scandalously – when he called one of the women he healed 'daughter of Abraham'. This indicates that those who wish to follow Jesus must resist sexism and patriarchy.

The lifestyle of Jesus gives us a beautiful example of how to be intimate in a fully human and respectful way. We see a great tenderness in the way he spoke with his friends – with women as well as with men. But at the same time he was quite willing to challenge and rebuke them at times. It is interesting to note that he took the risk of acting in a way that aroused jealousy among his friends and followers. The gospels indicate that he had a closer level of intimacy with Peter, James, and John than with his other disciples. And St John called himself 'the disciple whom Jesus loved'.

The trusting and unconditional love of Jesus for his friends left him very vulnerable, open to be betrayed by Judas and to be denied by Peter. Furthermore, the fact that Jesus was willing to expose his vulnerability by calling on his friends for support in his agony teaches us an important lesson. It indicates that a Christian spirituality of sexuality is one where vulnerability is a crucial virtue and where one must trust others, ask for their support, and take the risk of being 'let down' or rejected.

The attitude of Jesus to the use of power is very relevant in relation to sexuality. Inspired by him, we must avoid two extremes: abuse of power in the sexual sphere, and, on the other hand, failure to accept fully our sexual nature. The sexual sphere is one area where some people misuse their power shamefully. The most blatant examples are cases such as paedophilia and rape, but there are also much more common – sometimes quite subtle – ways in which people abuse or dominate others sexually. All these are instances of the 'attack other' mode of escaping from the shame associated with sexuality.

Other people go in quite the opposite direction, failing to recognise and use their sexual power in a healthy way. They run away from a positive engagement with their own sexuality by adopting one of the other three dysfunctional responses to shame, namely, 'avoidance', 'withdrawal', or 'attack self'. It is important to note that in all three of these responses, as well as in the 'attack other' response, the basic problem is that the person is afraid of taking the risk of intimacy.

I noted in chapter 1 how uncompromising Jesus was in challenging religious forms of domination and authoritarianism. Looking at our own church, it has to be admitted that in recent centuries church leaders and theologians frequently exercised a quite oppressive power in the sexual sphere. One aspect of our spirituality of sexuality must be to avoid and repudiate such abuses of spiritual power, perhaps especially in areas associated with sexuality.

An important aspect of the spirituality of sexuality is knowing when to 'hang on' and when to 'let go'. In the sexual sphere, 'letting go' may mean giving up the attempt to manipulate or control one's partner. It could also mean walking away from a sexual relationship which is abusive. Here again we can learn from Jesus. While still a young man he knew when 'his hour' had come – the time when the only authentic way to go forward was to 'let go' and abandon himself into the hands of God.

Following the example of Jesus, we need to bring the power of healing back from the margins of Christian spirituality and into the mainstream. And one of the most urgent areas of life in which this needs to take place is the sphere of sexuality.

CHAPTER 6

A Christian Spirituality of Celibacy

One of the most striking things about the gospel accounts of Jesus is that they give no suggestion that he had an intimate sexual-genital relationship with anybody. This raises the major issue of a spirituality of celibacy. I will argue a little later that the example of Jesus is a crucial element in a Christian approach to celibacy. But, before coming to that, I want to make some more general observations about the vocation to celibacy and the celibate life-style.

In trying to work out a spirituality of celibacy, it is necessary to take two different situations into account. The first is where a person chooses celibacy as a value in itself; I propose to treat this topic at some length. Then I shall comment briefly on the other situation, which is where a person accepts celibacy not for its own sake but simply as part of 'a package' such as priesthood, or life as a member of a religious community.

In relation to the choice of celibacy as a value in itself, Sipe makes an important preliminary point. 'Celibacy', he says, 'is one way of being human' (Sipe 32). He stresses the fact that it should not be defined in purely negative terms but rather in terms of a commitment 'to live for the good of others' (42). He puts a lot of emphasis on the word 'altruism' (61) and argues that there is even a biological basis for this: in the animal kingdom there are many species which have members that 'are sexually nonreproductive and/or not sexually active, but they serve the group by fostering the well-being and survival of others' (22). Furthermore, the notion of celibacy as a religious value is not confined to Christianity. It is accepted also by Hindus and Buddhists (35).

Solidarity versus Individualism

All this raises a very significant point. In our Western world today it is almost taken for granted that, when we look for meaning and purpose in life, we think first of all in terms of the person in isolation. However, this is a very individualistic way of thinking which only emerged in Western cultures over the past few centuries. In earlier times, people experienced them-selves first of all as part of a community. This sense of being in solidarity with others (including those who have gone before us and those who will come after us) is characteristic of most non-Western cultures even today; and it is quite taken for granted in the biblical world. A crucial part of the development of spirituality is a recovery of this sense of community solidarity. It does not mean the abandonment of our Western sense of the uniqueness of each person; but it does involve moving away from a purely individualistic conception of human fulfilment.

The difference between these two approaches becomes very evident in regard to sexuality. The modern Western approach leads one to assume that each individual has a right – and almost a duty – to have personally fulfilling active sexual relationships. The 'solidarity' approach takes it for granted that different individuals can have very different roles in the community – and that this applies in the sexual sphere as well as in other aspects of life. Within this way of thinking and feeling, it is much easier to accept that some individuals, who are not sexually active in the genital sense, can make an important contribution to the com-munity – and that they can find personal fulfilment in doing so. I think we need to make this shift away from individualism in order to accept Sipe's claim that celibacy is one way of being human and that it is not unnatural (22 and 59).

Taking this a step further, we need to recognise that meaning in life and personal fulfilment can be found in devoted service of others (cf. Sipe 100). Oddly enough, we tend to take this for granted in regard to working for justice or caring for the poor. But we find it more difficult to accept that this is also true in the sphere of sexuality – for here individualism comes to the fore.

This is such a strong cultural prejudice in our present-day Western world that theoretical arguments are not very effective in challenging it. What carries much more weight is the living witness of people like Dorothy Day or Mother Teresa of Calcutta. And of course the outstanding model is Jesus. The gospels present him as one who obviously had intimate friend-ships with various people, but who lived a fully human life without having a genital relationship with anybody.

Psychological and Theological Basis
Even though the witness of celibate people is more convincing than any theological argument, nevertheless we do need some intellectually satisfying account of how celibacy can bring human fulfilment. I think it is best to build such an account on a careful reflection on the very nature of sexual love. In my account of the unfolding of sexuality I tried to bring out the fact that *eros* is not a static reality. It leads one on naturally from the stage where it is focused on personal fulfilment (through possessing the other and being possessed) to later stages where it involves very high degrees of self-sacrifice. So it is a serious mistake to set personal sexual fulfilment over against generosity and altruism as though they pulled us in opposite directions.

Of its very nature, love has two dimensions – the personal and the universal (Kimmerling 1986: 461-3). We humans cannot at first hold both together in full degree. So most people start with a deeply personal relationship to another person. If their love develops properly, they progress after some time to the more universal dimension, starting with the birth of children and eventually moving on to a point where 'the stranger' can be welcomed. (I described this pattern in chapter 4.) However, while this is the usual pattern, it is not the only one. Celibates start at the other end. In their journey of exploration into love, the first dimension to emerge is the universal aspect of love (Kimmerling 1986: 463; 1993: 88).

Loving concern for refugees, or the poor, or abused people – all these are obvious examples of the universal dimension of love. But the primary object of celibate love can also come in other forms. A passion for justice in the world, or a burning concern about preserving the tropical forests, or some other aspect of ecology – these too can be instances of universal love. If we take seriously the fact that all aspects of human life and endeavour have a genuine value, then we can see how the total dedication of a person to art or mathematics or science can also be manifestations of the universal aspect of love.

What I am saying is that, for some people, the primary focus of love is commitment to a sexual partner, while for others it is care for the poor, or a commitment to justice or art. Does this imply that married people cannot be as devoted to the poor, or to justice, or to art, as a celibate person? Not at all. In referring to the *primary* focus of the love of different people, I am not making a direct comparison of the love of the married person with that of the celibate. It would be an impossible and pointless task to try to weigh up how much love each of them can give. I am simply noting an observable fact – that some people, at a particular point in their lives, or even for their whole lifetime, are so single-mindedly devoted to, say, caring for the poor, or working for justice that they do not in fact take the time and energy to nurture a loving sexual-genital relationship with another person.

Superiority?
We need to get away, once for all, from the false idea that the celibate vocation is intrinsically superior to that of the person who opts for a sexual partner. We are dealing here with two different vocations, each of them uniquely personal. Because each person is unique, we cannot compare two different people and decide that one person or one call is superior to the other. Each individual, however, does have to look at his or her own personal options and decide which way of life is right for him or her. Those who are advising or facilitating a person in making this personal choice should not suggest that one way of life is objectively 'higher', or superior in principle to the other.

It would even be wrong to suggest that, in responding to the more universal aspect of love, the celibate is manifesting a greater degree of generosity or nobility than the person who chooses a sexual partner. As I pointed out above, there is a natural progression by which sexual love, which is at first narrowly focused on one person, tends subsequently to broaden out to the wider community. So married people, having already exercised enormous generosity in caring for their children, are normally drawn to broaden the scope of their generosity by reaching out to serve the poor or to work for justice.

Of course, there are some married people who refuse to broaden their horizons; they do not let their love blossom outwards to the wider community. They cling on to the personal dimension of love at the expense of its universal dimension. The temptation for those who choose the celibate path is the very opposite. Starting with the universal dimension, they may fail to realise that love can never be fully itself until it becomes deeply personal. So they remain rather distant in their care for orphans, or the poor, or refugees. In the case of those whose devotion is to justice or care for the earth, their commitment may degenerate into angry fanaticism. In this way, their love fails to blossom; it becomes dried up.

In recent times, unfortunately, we hear of various situations where celibate people fell into this trap. Appointed to run institutions for the care of deprived young people, they gave priority to organisational values. So they were perceived as heartless and cruel, rather than kind and loving. It is evident that this sad failure arises mainly from the unconscious adoption by these celibates of one or other of the various stratagems described in the previous chapter for escaping the shame attached to sex. In the more extreme cases of abuse or cruelty, the 'attack other' pattern is very evident. But the other escape patterns (avoidance, withdrawal, and 'attack self') have also been operative and have done a lot of damage – not only to the celibates themselves but also to the children in their care. If celibates are to develop into warm and caring people, they need to 'own' their sexuality, and devote time and energy into developing the more personal dimension of love.

Because the celibate style of life is not the normal or spontaneous way sexuality develops, it is very likely that, at some point in their lives, those who have opted for celibacy will have to face up to difficult questions about how they are handling their sexuality. Are they trying to escape from acknowledging their sexuality through a pattern of 'withdrawal' or 'avoidance' in the technical psychological sense I outlined in the previous chapter? Are they dealing with their internal tensions by attacking those around them physically, verbally, or psychologically? Have they turned in on themselves, allowed their love to remain coldly impersonal, or to become desiccated through burnout? Or have they, on the other hand, developed an attitude of loving openness to other people – and of genuine interpersonal intimacy with one or more close friends? If all their relationships with others remain distant and impersonal, then there is a serious lack in their human development, no matter how much good work they are doing in other spheres.

Contemplatives

What about those celibates who devote themselves to the contemplative life? Should we say that the distinctive feature of their choice is that they give priority to their love of God rather than to any human love? That may well be how they experience and articulate it. But I think that, from a theological point of view, it is not fully accurate. God the Creator (as distinct from Jesus) is transcendent, beyond our world. So whenever we direct our love to God, it always has to be 'carried' through some agency within this world. For some people the primary 'carrier' of love is commitment to a sexual partner; for others it is care for the poor or the sick; for still others it is devotion to art or science; and, finally, for other people it is living a contemplative life of prayer and meditation. We cannot say that any one of these is, in principle, superior to the others. Any one of them may be the best and highest way for a particular person, depending on that person's individual call.

Sexual energy is not excluded or ignored in any of these

different ways of life, since sexuality is a fundamental aspect of our human existence. But that energy can be channelled or focused in one direction or another. The usual way of doing so is through love of a partner and family. But some people find themselves so passionately drawn to meditation and prayer, or so concerned about the poor or the environment, or so deeply immersed in art or science, that they channel all their energy – including their sexual energy – into that passion. For them, the way forward is the celibate life, freely chosen.

Christian celibates who opt for a life of meditation and contemplation are choosing to sublimate their sexual energy in a very specific way. To outsiders it may seem that they are opting out of the world, becoming indifferent to all the concerns of those who have to face the daily round of family difficulties, tensions at work, and political upheavals. But the reality is generally different. Quite commonly, those who successfully choose the contemplative vocation have a deep and burning concern for the world and its peoples. In them the universal dimension of love burns bright – but not at all at the expense of its personal dimension. They may restrict their contacts with the outside world; but they make up in quality what they have given up in quantity. Their hours of prayer enable them to bring a depth of compassion and understanding to those they meet. And even those who seldom communicate with other people are relating to God and to Jesus in a deeply personal way which is nourishing their humanity and bringing an energy of personal love into the environment.

Supports

I have already referred to Sipe's insistence that celibacy is not 'unnatural'. However, it must also be said that those who opt for celibacy are not following the usual or 'normal' pattern. They are going against a natural biological dynamic that is built in to each of us, and has been inherited from our animal ancestors over millions of years. This means that the initial choice of celibacy is not easy. Furthermore, it means that celibacy involves an on-going series of choices. For the dynamic of *eros* remains; and those who have opted for celibacy may find in themselves, on various occasions during their lives, a strong sexual attraction for some person; so their option for celibacy has to made over and over again.

For this reason it is necessary for celibates to build a support structure which will enable them to remain true to their commitment – and to experience their celibacy as a source of personal growth rather than a burden. Perhaps the most important support for celibacy is a regular practice of meditation and prayer. Sipe puts this very strongly:

> In studying religious celibacy for thirty-five years, I have never found one exception to this fundamental rule: Prayer is necessary to maintain the celibate process. A neglectful prayer life ensures the failure of celibate integration. ... Prayer means facing ourselves as we really are in the safety and privacy of our hearts. (54-5)

A second major support is to talk about one's sexuality with at least one other person in a completely open and honest manner. Once again Sipe makes the point strongly and clearly:

> Honesty is a necessity, not a luxury or an option ... Social isolation can encourage us to overidealize sex and maintain fantasies that sexual activity alone can heal our loneliness. It cannot. Fearless self-knowledge and reality sharing are invaluable correctives to ignorance, naiveté, and natural vulnerabilities. (97)

The person with whom the celibate talks openly may be a friend, or it may be a counsellor or spiritual director. It may be that what is best is to talk quite honestly with both a friend and a counsellor or spiritual support-person.

The third major help that is needed to live a fruitful celibate life is to have a culture or sub-culture which provides an atmosphere of understanding and support. Such support can come from a group of colleagues who are at ease with the living out of their commitment to celibacy. By giving a living witness that this life can be fulfilling and fruitful, they help each of their members to persevere in the commitment through the dark times or difficult patches which are likely to arise.

But the sub-culture created by a group of celibate colleagues can be a hindrance as well as a help. It will be a hindrance if the members of the group generally adopt a selfish and easy-going lifestyle. For the choice of celibacy is a renunciation which does not make sense unless it is part of a wider commitment to frugal living. The whole point of the sexual renunciation is under-mined, and the witness value of celibacy is cancelled out, if the celibate tries to make up for the loss of a sexual relationship by indulging in luxuries of various kinds (the best motor-car, ex-pensive holidays, etc.).

Solidarity with Jesus

For very many Christians who choose to live celibately, by far the most powerful motivation and support is the example of Jesus. They feel strongly called to discipleship and they want to live as Jesus lived. For many of them, the desire to come ever closer to Jesus is so clear and strong, that it becomes the primary driving force of their lives. Everything else seems of secondary importance to them – and that applies even to the very natural urge of *eros*, which in other circumstances would impel them to look for a sexual partner.

There is a danger that apologists for celibacy would read too much into the fact that Jesus did not get married or engage in a genital sexual relationship. I do not think that the fact that Jesus did not get married proves that celibacy is a higher calling or a more privileged or effective way to come close to God. But it certainly suggests that it is not necessary to be sexually active in the full sense, in order to live a fully human life. As I pointed out in a previous chapter, this challenges the assumption in most Western cultures that sexual intercourse is an indispensable part of living a fully human life; and it also challenges the assumption in primal cultures that anybody who has not generated a child is not yet fully human.

Suppose somebody tells me that the reason why he or she

has chosen celibacy is in order to follow Jesus, or to live like Jesus. This answer leaves me somewhat dissatisfied. I need to hear more. When Jesus chose to live celibately what was the positive value to which he was giving witness? The best answer I have found to this question is given by Rolheiser (199):

> ... when Christ went to bed alone at night he was in real solidarity with the many persons who, not by choice but by circumstance, sleep alone.

I think about two friends of mine in this situation. One is a widow, a young woman who recently lost a very loving husband. The other is an even younger woman, a gifted and loving person who for some reason has never yet managed to find a boy-friend. Both of these people – and millions of others – are truly deprived. Each of them is tempted at times to think that life has played a cruel trick on her, preventing her from having her heart's desire – the joy and fulfilment of a loving intimate sexual relationship.

I do not know whether it is any consolation to these women to know that Jesus chose freely to live as they are forced to live. But I can see how some followers of Jesus might wish to join him in such a renunciation as an act of solidarity with people who are sexually deprived, as these two women are deprived. I think people who choose celibacy would be very unwise if they were to claim that their way of life is a proof that those who do not have an active sexual relationship have nothing to complain about or are not really deprived! But, whatever about their *words*, their *witness* in living a fulfilled and loving life could perhaps bring some consolation and be a sign of hope to people who are unwillingly deprived of a loving sexual relationship. But, quite obviously, this could only happen if these celibates succeed in living a full and love-filled life. If they can meet this challenge successfully then the witness of their lives can be a very valuable ministry to others.

Celibate Love and Intimacy
Celibacy is not an alternative to intimacy but a different – often a

more difficult – way of achieving intimacy. Anybody who is celibate must make a commitment to developing a love that is deeply personal as well as universal in its scope. This applies, not just to those who choose celibacy as a value in itself, but also to those who accept celibacy as part of the 'package' of priest-hood. It applies also to those who find themselves celibate because they have failed to find a suitable sexual partner or because their partner has died or left them.

In a previous chapter we saw that intimacy involves holding an open space, in which there is relevant and truthful disclosure, and a presence to the other with transparency and trust. It is very difficult for one to grow in intimacy while holding oneself physically at a distance from everybody. That is because the primary language in which intimacy is learned is the language of touch. (The reason for this presumably goes back to infancy or even to the pre-birth situation when the link between mother and child was primordially a bodily bond.) How, then, can a celibate person grow into intimacy?

Certainly not in the manner laid down in old-style programmes of formation, where physical contact (except in sport) was actively discouraged. And certainly not by the kind of 'withdrawal' I referred to earlier, where the person effectively closes off the whole sexual area of experience. We cannot grow to full maturity and full humanity unless we acknowledge the sexual longing and sexual attractions, and even the falling in love, which are part of the human condition. But that does not mean that we have to act on all our sexual impulses, or seek to become the sexual partner of the person with whom we fall in love.

We can develop a close friendship, and learn to express that friendship in ways which involve some degree of physical intimacy, but which do not go 'all the way' into sexual intercourse. It is not an easy road to choose, and there is no general roadmap which is suitable for everybody. It may feel at times that it is wrong to practise restraint, to hold back from allowing the nat-ural dynamic of intimate touch to find its culmination in sexual intercourse. But Kimmerling points out that sexual intercourse is 'just one means of expressing love' and that 'the celibate person discovers that while the need for love has to be met, the desire for sex does not.' (1993: 93) She goes on to say:

> Though sexual intercourse may be the most intense form of touch it is not the only form of touch which can transform, liberate, and redeem us. Any caring touch can heal us and open us up more fully to God and to others. (1993: 95)

A rather obvious question arises: how far can one go? It is not possible to give any general answer to such a question. Indeed the question itself is not helpful because it suggests that one is thinking in terms of rules – and of stretching the rules as far as possible. The question each person needs to ask is: 'What is the most appropriate way in which I can express my intimate relationship with this person, while at the same time enabling both of us to keep in mind that I am committed to celibacy?' The answer to this question is very personal; it will differ from one person to another; it may be different on different occasions; and it will depend not merely on one's own situation but also upon the other person's response.

An Alternative Approach

In all of what I have written here about celibacy I have presumed that it involves abstinence from full genital sex (sexual intercourse). However, O'Murchu, in his account of the vows taken by members of religious orders (as distinct from the commitment to celibacy taken by priests), defines celibacy quite differently. To put it more accurately, he maintains that 'we ... need to abandon the traditional language "[vow] of celibacy" and adopt the phrase "[vow] for relatedness"' (1999: 49).

In order to do justice to O'Murchu's approach it is important to take account of his overall position. He believes that about 10,000 years ago 'the many sexual hangups that prevail today seem to have been largely unknown'. At that time, there was worship of the Great Mother Goddess which brought a 'wild and often uncontrolled exuberance [which] was quite overtly sexual' and was marked by playfulness (1999: 46). But with the

coming of patriarchy, at the time of the agricultural revolution
around 8,000 years before the Christian era, there came various
distortions and 'hang-ups' in relation to sexuality. O'Murchu
believes that one of the more important tasks of those who take
religious vows is to rescue us from the guilt and 'hang-ups'
associated with sexuality. The aim would be to help people of
our time to recover a sense of playfulness in sexual relationships
and an awareness that 'sexual ecstasy is at the core of divine
creativity' (45).

It is against this background that O'Murchu says: 'The vow
for relatedness is a call to engage with the emerging issues of
psychosexual relating in the contemporary world ...' (49). He
maintains that the person who takes this vow needs to remain
unmarried in order to make this engagement in a countercultural
way. Then he goes on to make this very controversial statement:

> Whether or not the celibate should totally refrain from sexual
> genital intimacy, in a world where such intimacy is no longer
> tied exclusively to marriage, it has at least to remain an open
> question. (1999: 51; cf. 1998:112)

There can be no doubt that O'Murchu is right to emphasise the
importance of relatedness, and the need to explore different
forms of intimacy and appropriate ways to express it. But I am
not convinced that it is wise to suggest that the possibility of
genital intimacy remains an open question for celibates. It is of
course true that life is larger and more complex than any set of
rules we devise to cover all the options. But to suggest that there
may be special circumstances in which one can transcend the
normal rules seems to me to be establishing a further 'rule' – a
category of unusual or exceptional cases where the usual rule
does not apply. In effect, then, to say that this issue is 'an open
question' may well be taken by some as approval for sexual
experimentation, on the grounds that the situation is exceptional.

In seeking to answer the question whether celibates might be
entitled to engage in genital intimacy, it is particularly important to take account of the experience of women. By and large,
women tend to feel more 'bound into' a sexual relationship once

it is established, more inclined to see it as involving commitment on both sides. A woman is therefore more likely to feel betrayed and abandoned if her partner moves on to somebody else – and to feel cheated and let down if the partner refuses to make a binding commitment to her. Furthermore, there is the most obvious argument against O'Murchu's position, namely, that contraception is not 100% effective, so the possibility of pregnancy cannot be totally excluded if the woman is of child-bearing age (unless the woman is prepared to bear a child or to use abortion as a back-up in case of the failure of contraception). In the present culture, which still retains notable elements of patriarchy, intercourse by somebody committed to celibacy could easily lead to further exploitation of women.

It is true that many people today engage in sexual intercourse as a sign of intimacy, or warm friendship, or strong sexual attraction – but with no intention of making an exclusive, life-long commitment to the other person. But it has not at all been proved that this more 'liberal' approach marks a real break-through to a more human way of relating. It may well involve a de-valuing of sexual intimacy. Moreover, O'Murchu's account of sexuality in the pre-patriarchal era seems unduly idyllic. Should we really see the attitudes and sexual practices of that era as a model for the future? And is it wise or realistic to call on vowed celibates to lead the way to such a future?

Finally, there is the issue of whether it is legitimate to replace 'celibacy' with 'relatedness'. To do so seems such a radical re-definition of celibacy that there is little, if any, continuity with the past, or with celibacy as practised in other religions. It leaves us with an understanding of celibacy as a renunciation of marriage and family but not necessarily a renunciation of genital sexual activity. I think we need to face the question of whether or not there can be a real value in the total renunciation of genital activity 'for the sake of the kingdom'.

Renunciation and Transformation of Energy

Celibacy is a form of asceticism, namely, a renunciation of genital activity. If it is to be fruitful, this 'letting go' has to be trans-formed into positive energy. The first and more obvious way of doing this is one familiar to football coaches. They advise their players to 'hold back' from genital activity before a big match, in order to build up a reservoir of energy which can then be 'harnessed' during the match. In somewhat the same way, the celibate can re-focus the sexual energy which is not channeled into genital activity. That energy can be re-directed to any one of a variety of activities – for instance, campaigning for a just and sustainable society, or caring for refugees, or dedication to science or the arts, or commitment to a life of meditation and prayer.

There is a certain risk in this re-focusing of sexual energy. If it is done in a way that lessens one's commitment to intimacy, the celibate becomes 'dried up', no longer open, trusting, sensitive, and vulnerable. This kind of celibacy makes one less than fully human. So it is important that the person committed to celibacy takes practical steps to avoid this danger, by developing and nourishing deep interpersonal relationships with at least a couple of close friends.

Hindus, Buddhists, and Christians have all had a tradition of linking celibacy with meditation and contemplation. What seems to be involved is a refocusing of sexual energy. Mark Patrick Hederman maintains that various meditation techniques are used to train the body, so that the need for sexual gratification is lessened. The energy is redirected 'to the base of the spine and allowed to travel upwards towards the area of the brain' (Hederman 1999: 46). I do not doubt that such a refocusing of sexual energy can take place, but I think it is important that those who use these techniques to help them meditate should not try to de-sexualise themselves.

There is a further way in which the abstinence from genital activity can be re-directed into a positive energy. This renunci-ation is a kind of fasting. It has something in common with fasting from food, or giving up coffee, or chocolate. Suppose I decide to give up coffee for the sake of my health. Each time I refuse a cup of coffee I am likely to feel a little stab of loss. I may develop a habit of allowing that 'stab' to remind me of why I am doing without coffee. And on each occasion I may then 'harness' the energy I expend on the renunciation, to strengthen my commitment to becoming a more healthy person.

The situation of those who commit themselves to celibacy is somewhat similar. They are likely to experience a certain feeling of loss whenever they refuse an opportunity to engage in genital activity, or perhaps when they see the children of their friends. They can develop a habit of using this sense of loss as a reminder of their *purpose* in giving up genital activity. For the Christian celibate this purpose is to be more like Jesus whose renunciation of genital activity was linked to his single-minded commitment to his ministry, to his utter devotion to prayer to God, to the way he allowed himself to be constantly led by the Spirit, to his compassionate and sensitive reaching out to those with whom he came in contact, to his warm and intimate relationship with his friends, and to his solidarity with the poor and deprived – including those who are sexually deprived in one way or another.

Because the celibate remains a fully sexual person, and because sexual energy is not given its 'normal' expression in genital activity, there is likely to be a certain build-up of sexual tension. This will manifest itself in sexual attraction or sexual imagery and fantasy. So the celibate will have no shortage of 'reminders' of the cost of renouncing genital activity. Each of these 'reminders' can then be made an occasion for renewing the commitment to follow Jesus in his celibacy – and for deepening one's faith that this is an authentic way to live a fully human life.

Part of a 'Package'
Celibacy is such a specialised and personal call that it is not wise – and in my opinion not just – for the Catholic Church authorities to insist that everybody who wishes to become a priest in the Western church must take on celibacy (apart, of course, from

previously married Anglican priests). But that is the present discipline in the Catholic Church. It has given rise to serious questioning and grave reservations among very many priests who bought 'the package' when they were young, but who now feel that they did not choose celibacy in full freedom and with full knowledge of the demands it would make on them.

This issue is made more serious by the fact that, until quite recently, church authorities and theologians maintained that celibacy was a higher state than marriage. This incorrect theology was applied not only to the priesthood but also to the vowed religious life. Consequently, present-day questioning of the value of celibacy is not confined to priests. Quite a number of members of religious congregations – women and men – now wonder whether, in taking their vows, they were misled by a false theology which presented celibacy as a vocation superior to marriage.

That false theology of sexuality has now been quietly dropped. But, unfortunately, the church authorities do not seem to have replaced it with a more satisfactory justification of celibacy. The result is that there are many in the Catholic Church who think of themselves as 'stuck with' a celibacy which they chose many years ago and about which they now have serious reservations. They feel now that they were 'cheated' when they were told long ago that the more perfect way to follow Jesus was to take a vow of celibacy.

There is no easy answer for those who find themselves in this situation. Some of them have chosen to give up the priesthood or the religious life. But they have felt it a choice they should not have been asked to make. Some of the most 'priestly' people I know have reluctantly relinquished a fruitful priestly ministry because they became convinced that they were not called to celibacy. When they applied for laicisation, many of them were angered and alienated by the attitude of the church authorities, as reflected in the documents they were asked to sign. These documents give the impression that the authorities see a close analogy between an application for laicisation and an application for a declaration of nullity of a marriage: in each case the key thing to look for is a defect in the original intention of the person. But many of these priests hold that there was nothing seriously wrong about their original intention in choosing to be a priest. They look back on their time in priestly ministry as a fruitful period of their lives. Now that they have chosen to get married, they do not want to repudiate their original choice of priesthood.

Church authorities need to change the present practice. At a very minimum they need to couch the application form for laicisation in more acceptable terms, and to adopt a more sympathetic approach to those who now wish to leave the active ministry. This is a matter of justice and respect, especially in view of the fact that the theology of celibacy which was taken for granted up to quite recently is now seen to have been mistaken.

In the light of the seriousness of this mistake there is a very strong case for a much more radical change – for a process which would offer an opportunity for those who left the priesthood and got married, to explore again the possibility of returning to active ministry. Not all of them would wish to do so; and the character or circumstances of some of them would preclude their return, at least on an immediate basis. But the church authorities are being unduly rigid, and are depriving the Christian community of a rich resource, if they continue to refuse to open the possibility of welcoming back to active ministry priests who left to get married.

Some of those who chose celibacy as 'part of a package', and who now feel trapped by that choice of many years ago, have opted reluctantly to stay in the priesthood or vowed religious life. They have rejected the old theology which told them that celibacy was 'a more perfect' way of following Jesus. But they have not found a satisfactory theology of celibacy to replace the old one. So they may drift along, living celibately but not making any serious effort to 'harness' its energy in a positive direction.

For them, it may perhaps be helpful to reflect on the celibacy of Jesus as an act of solidarity with the many people who, for one reason or another, do not have a satisfactory sexual relationship. Such a reflection may lead these 'reluctant celibates' to believe that they can have a helpful and fruitful ministry to those who, against their will, are sexually deprived. In order to do so they would have to decide that the best practical choice they can make is to continue to accept 'the package', including celibacy; and they would have to choose wholeheartedly, however reluctantly, to live celibately with generosity and love. By doing so they would give a witness to others that it is possible to live a fully human life even if circumstances do not allow one to have a fulfilling sexual relationship. They could in this way give a positive value to their reluctant celibacy by linking it to their ministry.

Education for Celibacy

In a rather striking phrase, Sipe maintains that the Catholic Church operates 'a system that demands celibacy but does not educate for it' (78). One might wish to qualify that statement by noting that, in recent years, a lot more attention is paid to the development of personal maturity in candidates for the priesthood and the vowed religious life; moreover, applicants to seminaries and novitiates are generally screened much more carefully than in the past – and this usually includes professional psychological tests. Furthermore, Vatican guidelines for formation now put a heavy emphasis on the importance of personal growth and maturity.

Nevertheless, it remains true, by and large, that positive education for celibacy is quite inadequate. I think there are two main reasons for this serious lack. Firstly, church authorities, and many of the staff in houses of formation, do not themselves have any very convincing theology of celibacy. They are still rather ambivalent about whether celibacy is 'a more perfect state'. They probably do not proclaim openly that celibacy is a higher value, but they are part of a system which was built around this assumption. This causes a general uneasiness in those who staff the system; and the most convenient way to deal with this uneasiness is to say as little as possible about the subject. Teachers of theology tend to leave the topic of celibacy to spiritual directors or to those who give spiritual conferences or retreats. Consequently, celibacy is dealt with in a rather 'pious' way, rather than as a theological subject which can be probed and debated with some intellectual rigour.

Closely related to this is the second reason for an inadequate education for celibacy. It is that church authorities, by insisting on the inseparability of celibacy and priestly ministry, are demanding too much of a theology of celibacy. As I indicated above, the fact that Jesus chose to be celibate provides a sound basis for linking celibacy with some aspects of ministry. But it is simply not possible to 'prove' that any minister should opt for celibacy. In the present quite repressive church climate it is not easy for theologians to say this openly. And if those who teach theology in formation programmes did say it, they would be opening up a debate about 'compulsory celibacy' – a debate which church authorities have forbidden. All this gives rise to a great reluctance to deal openly with the topic.

There seems to be a general hope that those in formation will somehow 'grow into' celibacy by living a celibate life. The trouble is that there is no longer the kind of widespread unquestioning atmosphere which would allow this process of 'osmosis' to take place. Those in formation are exposed to a great deal of critical comment in the media and elsewhere about celibacy; and the church does not seem to be providing any clear theology and spirituality of celibacy which would counteract this.

What is probably much more serious is what happens when people in formation look to those who have gone before them. They find very few who are willing to share openly about their positive experiences of living a celibate life. For the most part there is a silent 'getting on with the job', with an occasional critical or cynical comment. Every now and then, the word goes round that 'so-and-so' is leaving to get married. What is worse, it occasionally emerges that somebody is not leaving, but is quietly ignoring the rule of celibacy, either through a one-to-one sexual relationship which is incompatible with celibacy, or through more promiscuous sexual activity.

There is no easy solution to this issue. One element of a way forward should be an honest acceptance by church authorities that it is unjust to make such a rigid link between celibacy and priestly ministry. If that link were loosened, it would open the way for a more free choice of celibacy by those who are really willing to take it on.

A second, and much more immediate, step that is required is that those who live a celibate life share openly with each other their experiences of celibacy (cf. Sipe 117). In fact, this is by far the most effective education for celibacy that can be undertaken. This alone can break down the wall of silence, of reserve, and of embarrassment which surrounds the topic. Furthermore, it will provide the raw material for a new and more grounded theology and spirituality of celibacy (and indeed of sexuality) to replace the old theology which we now see to have been both dualistic and unrealistic.

I conclude this chapter by expressing the hope that open sharing of experiences of celibacy – difficulties as well as consolations – will help to take this important spiritual value out of the shadows and back into the mainstream of Christian life. If this is done, it will be major service to those who have already taken on a commitment to celibacy, and to those who may wish to do so in the future. But – just as importantly – it will also provide a great enrichment to the overall theology of sexuality, and will be of immense benefit to all who wish to make their sexuality an integral aspect of their spirituality.

CHAPTER 7

Globalisation and Liberation

Our world is grossly distorted and becoming more distorted day by day; it is badly in need of change. The major cause of the growing imbalance in the world today is the process of globalisation. In other circumstances globalisation could have been a powerful force for good, drawing peoples together and helping to forge all the inhabitants of the world into a truly human community. But the way in which the process is taking place at present is widening the gap between the rich and the poor, the powerful and the powerless; and it is giving rise to very serious ecological damage. In this chapter I propose to give a brief account of the different elements that go to make up the complex process of globalisation. Towards the end of this chapter and in the following chapter I shall go on to suggest how an integral spirituality can inspire us to counteract damaging effects of globalisation and instead draw the benefits which it should make possible.

Economic Globalisation

The central element of globalisation is that the world has become one single marketplace rather than a collection of local and regional economies. This is a process which was gradually coming about over many years – in fact over the past four centuries. But it has speeded up enormously over the past decade as a result of the development of technology, above all in the field of electronic communication (the internet etc). Until 1989 the technologically developed world was split into two – the East and the West. But the Cold War came to an end in that year with the triumph of capitalism. This gave a major boost to the process of globalisation

– particularly since a very crude form of capitalism was embraced not only by the Eastern European countries but also by China (cf. Stiglitz 181-6 who, however, praises China's policies).

It is helpful to distinguish between globalisation and internationalisation. The latter refers mainly to relationships between States or nations. But globalisation is mainly a process which by-passes national boundaries and undercuts the political sovereignty of countries. It comes about through the linkages between multinational corporations or financial institutions (banks etc.) and their subsidiaries in many different countries. So it links people and groups 'without passing through the mediation of States' (Serrano 17).

The major effect of globalisation at the economic level is to increase greatly the penetration of large multinational corporations and international banks into the local markets all over the world. They take over small local industries and financial institutions or put them out of business. Operating through GATS (General Agreement on Trade in Services) they seek to get control of vital goods and services, such as, the water supply, the energy sources, tourism, and the health, culture, and education services (cf. George 16 and Coates 28-35). In this way effective control of the economy of countries largely passes out of the hands of national governments – especially the governments of small countries and of those countries which do not deliberately protect their national industries and banks.

It may be a surprise to most readers to learn that at present the most globalised country in the world is Ireland. As measured by the Washington-based Foreign Policy 'globalisation index', it ranks ahead of Switzerland and Singapore – and far ahead of the USA (O'Toole 2003: 4-5). This is seen by the Irish government as an achievement rather than a problem. The official policy is one of creating an economic, political, and cultural climate which is attractive to foreign investors – especially in the sectors of pharmaceutics and information technology. This has provided a lot of high-quality employment in the country.

But a high price has been paid for this benefit. Firstly, because of the low-tax regime, the gap between the rich and the poor has widened very considerably, and social services are stretched to breaking point. Secondly, every down-turn in the world economy creates a serious crisis in employment in Ireland. Thirdly, other countries – especially the new East European entrants to the European Community – have adopted the same low-tax policies as the Irish government, and their wage-levels are much lower; so future foreign investment is likely to go to these more favourable locations. Finally, the Irish government has felt compelled to 'tone down' its foreign policy – for instance, in regard to opposition to the war on Iraq – for fear of alienating the government of the USA, where most of the foreign investment comes from.

Globalisation is not an intrinsically evil process. There is nothing wrong with the use of technology to promote efficiency and the development of world markets. In fact the world in general and poorer nations in particular could benefit enormously from these modern advances – if they were used to overcome imbalances and injustices and to promote really human development. The problem is that a relatively small number of individuals and corporations use these 'tools' to further their own interests – and the governments of the rich and powerful nations support them in doing so.

The harmful effects of the way in which globalisation is taking place at present in the economic and social spheres were well summed up by Erkki Tuomioja, the Foreign Minister of Finland:

> … today … a growing number of people face complete marginalisation and risk ending up in abject poverty. … globalisation based on neo-liberal free-market values can intensify environmental damage. It can also be socially damaging, destroying sustainable communities and threatening established welfare systems, which can never be replaced by purely market-based solutions. It can threaten core labour standards and weaken trade unions, as well as national and minority cultures. (Tuomioja 2001)

Cultural and Political Globalisation

In addition to this primary form of globalisation which is economic, globalisation is also taking place in the sphere of culture.
Here the principal instruments are the media (television, radio,
newspapers, and news agencies), films, the internet, and international publishing companies. These play a dominant role in
shaping the information people receive, the way they think, the
beliefs they hold, the values they adopt, the fashions they follow,
and the way they live out their lives. What is sad is that all these
means of communication could be used in a way that would be
enormously enriching for people all over the world. They could
open up the treasures of other cultures, and help people to
understand each other better and work together for a peaceful
world. But the problem once again is that a small group of rich
and powerful individuals and corporations control the way the
means of communication are used.

Obviously there is a very close link between the economic
and the cultural aspects of globalisation, since in both cases the
market is controlled by multinational companies and agencies
based almost always in the rich countries of 'the North'. This in
turn gives rise to a political aspect of globalisation. For these
companies are so powerful that they have huge influence with
the governments of the countries of 'the North'. So they pressure
these governments to use their political power at the international level in ways which benefit the multinational companies,
at the expense of weaker countries. For instance, many respectable
authorities believe that the US invasion of Iraq in 2003 was
motivated less by fear of weapons of mass destruction than by
the desire to ensure control of the oil market and to benefit a
variety of American-based companies. No wonder, then, that
Professor John Gray (2003: 97) can say: 'Far from ushering in a
new era of global governance, globalisation is producing a rebirth
of empire.'

Furthermore, the rich countries are the ones which have the
power to determine the policies of the International Monetary
Fund and the World Bank. They have also been dominant in the

World Trade Organisation until very recently; but the new 'G21' grouping of China, India, Brazil, South Africa and other countries of 'the South' has now emerged as an alternative power block – or at least a voice that must be listened to.

Religious Globalisation?
I think there is a good case for saying that even in the sphere of organised religion the process of globalisation is at work. This is very evident in the way Islamic fundamentalism has spread in the world in recent times. It by-passes State boundaries, using instead a mixture of very ancient and very modern means of communication. The zeal of Muslims is aroused by impassioned preaching in the mosques; committed young zealots volunteer to spread the message in other countries; and networks are held together by the use of phones, e-mail and the internet.

Equally striking is the extent to which the process of globalisation has been taking place in the Catholic Church. Church officials in the Vatican have drawn more and more power into their own hands, failing to respect the autonomy of local churches. They have undermined the authority of national conferences of bishops on delicate issues such as inter-church and inter-faith marriages, inter-communion, and abortion counselling. Even in matters like the translation of liturgical texts and the use of the rite of general absolution, Vatican officials have usurped the authority of bishops at the local and regional levels.

In some respects, top Vatican officials are acting like the top management of multinational corporations, using a style of governance which is not participatory or collaborative, and making decisions with very little effective consultation of those whom these decisions affect. In the final chapter of this book I shall return to the question of excessive centralisation of the church; but in this chapter and the following one I shall focus mainly on globalisation in its economic aspects.

Strategies for Change
The process of economic globalisation and the problems associated

with it can only be curbed by firm and decisive political action at national and international level. There is an urgent need for governments and international organisations to enact and enforce laws, regulations, and restrictions which will put effective limits on the power of the giant multinational corporations which are the major agents of the globalisation process. Furthermore, it is essential that governments agree to a major reform of the structures and policies of powerful international financial institutions such as the International Monetary Fund, the World Bank, and the World Trade Organisation. For the present destructive model of globalisation, which is based on the neo-liberal economic system, is supported and implemented by these international agencies (cf. World Faiths Development Dialogue, 7, section 3 b). What is required are very fundamental reforms in the operation of international business.

This leaves us with the fundamental question: how can these reforms be brought about? Noreena Hertz points out that action for change through conventional political channels has now become very ineffective. The reason is that politicians have largely 'sold out' to those who wield economic power. Big business now provides most of the money which pays for the electoral campaigns of the politicians. This means that the politicians are highly unlikely to put effective controls on the process of globalisation (cf. Hertz 80-8).

In the present-day world, four more effective ways of opposing the destructive effects of globalisation have been invented; but, unfortunately, all of them have serious limitations:

– Firstly, people can put pressure on companies by exercising their power not so much as citizens but as customers. For instance, they can organise a boycott of goods which are known to be produced through exploitation of workers or of the environment (Hertz 109-132). This is the basis of various campaigns organised quite successfully by Greenpeace and Amnesty International. But, as Hertz points out, this approach is not really an alternative to action at the governmental level. If it is to succeed, people must have access to reliable information about what companies are actually doing. Some of this information is now available through websites run by committed campaigners (cf. Swinson 2003: 114). But, as Hertz notes (154-5), there is need for governmental action to ensure that business enterprises operate in an accountable and transparent manner.

– Secondly, very large numbers of people can come together in the kind of massive 'direct action' protests mounted in recent years in Seattle, Prague, Gothenburg, and Genoa. Such protests can certainly be a stimulus for change. But it is becoming clear that governments, in conjunction with most of the media, have succeeded in minimising the effect of these protests – partly by forcing them into marginal locations and partly by labelling them as the action of fanatics or 'crackpots'.

– Thirdly, a few successful business people, like Anita Ruddick of 'The Body Shop', have used their enormous economic power to promote moral values such as social justice, respect for the environment, or avoidance of cruelty to animals (Hertz 156-169). This is good, but not enough. Hertz insists (195) that, '… the business community will never place good customer service, ethical trading and social investment above moneymaking whenever the two come into conflict.'

– Fourthly, small-scale investors with a social conscience can put pressure on the companies whose shares they have bought. They can do so by organising protests at AGMs and on other occasions where the directors have to get approval of the shareholders. Furthermore, this kind of pressure can be applied even by people who do not have direct ownership of shares in any company. For they can apply the pressure through the companies who manage their pension funds, since large amounts of stock are held by these pension funds. In this way, companies can be forced to adopt what are now called 'socially responsible investment' policies, whereby they undertake not to engage in business practices which involve exploitation of people or of the earth. (For a comprehensive account of this approach see Sparkes 2002; cf. Hertz 123-6.) Of the various ways of working against exploitation this one has the potential to be the most effective. The difficulty is that so far only a small proportion of investors have adopted it.

We must conclude, then, that neither conventional political activity, nor any of the four alternative strategies I have referred to above, is as yet sufficient to bring about a transformation of the present destructive form of globalisation. But we must not give up. By using a judicious combination of all of these pressures we can hope realistically for genuine progress. However, the fundamental difficulty is that only a fairly small number of people are sufficiently motivated and committed to work for the radical changes which are required. There is need for some new inspiring energy to move people to action – whether that action be at the political level, or through using their power as customers, or in the field of public protest and 'direct action'.

Spirituality as a Motivator for Change

I think that the new energy which is required can come through the development of a rich and balanced spirituality in the workplace. At first sight this seems a rather odd claim to make. We tend spontaneously to think of spirituality as a soothing nourishment for the human spirit rather than a source of fiery energy driving people to change the structures of society. But, as I pointed out in Chapter 2, one of the many ingredients which go to make up an integral spirituality is the struggle for justice in the world. The issue then is not whether spirituality can be an incentive for change but whether in fact a sufficient number of people come to adopt that particular kind of spirituality – and with a sufficient degree of commitment.

How realistic is it to think that an end can be put to the present destructive style of globalisation which is doing so much damage to people and to our world? The answer is that this is a realistic hope only if four conditions are fulfilled: (a) a sufficient number of people must be keenly aware of, and disturbed about, the damage globalisation is doing to themselves, or to people they feel close to, or to issues they are deeply concerned about; (b) they must believe that action by them can really help to bring about the changes that are required; (c) they must be prepared to take such action, even at the cost of a lot of effort and sacrifice on their part; and (d) they must be willing to work together with other committed people to bring about the changes, since the task is far beyond the capacity of any individual or small group.

This means that, in thinking about how change can come, we must look, not just at the big picture of the damage done to the environment or to workers in general, but at the everyday experience of ordinary people at the local level. Looking at particular individuals and groups, we must ask whether they are disturbed about what globalisation is doing to them and those dear to them; and, if so, to what extent they are prepared to devote themselves to working for change.

We need to keep in mind the fundamental insight of the great Brazilian educationalist, Paulo Freire. He saw that people will commit themselves wholeheartedly to the struggle for social change only when their attention is focused on something that, for them, is a 'generative theme' (Freire 1985 and 1996). A 'generative theme' is one which touches a well of deep feelings in them – feelings such as anger or pain or enthusiasm – which can stir them to action in a way which ideas alone can never do.

In 'The Third World'
There are two major groups of people in the world – those of us living fairly comfortable lives mainly in the West or what has come to be called 'the North'; and the vast majority of the world's population who are living near or below the poverty line mainly in 'the South' or the so-called 'Third World'. Because of their different situations, the concerns of these two groups are very different from each other. Consequently, it is very likely that when looking for what will motivate each of these groups to work for change we will find that it is quite different for the two different groups. I propose to look at each in turn. In the remainder of this chapter I shall consider the situation of poor workers in what is rather optimistically called 'the developing world'. In the following chapter I shall go on to look at a spirituality which can motivate people in the Western world to work for change.

Workers are grossly exploited in most of the poorer countries of the world. An ever-increasing number work in the huge factories owned either by multi-national companies, or by local entrepreneurs making goods under contract for 'big name' international corporations. These poor people work very long hours in dangerous conditions, without the protection of trade unions. Others work in small local enterprises under rather similar conditions.

It is no surprise to find that individual workers (and their families) in such situations have strong feelings of anger about their working conditions, and a strong desire to find more con-genial and rewarding work. But that is not sufficient to bring about change. These strong feelings need to be broadened: anger about the person's own situation has to extend into an outraged sense of justice about what is happening also to others in the community, in the country, and in the wider world. This in turn has to be linked with a willingness to co-operate with others in working for change.

Furthermore, if there is to be any serious hope of change, many of those who feel angry must be willing to make great sacrifices, putting their jobs – and even their lives – 'on the line' in the struggle for justice. Finally, these people must have hope and a vision of a better future, in the face of an apparently hopeless situation. Taken together, these feelings, attitudes, and commitments add up to a very powerful spirituality. It is a spirituality which can not only stimulate people to work for change but can also provide them with on-going spiritual nour-ishment in the course of the long struggle for justice.

We can by no means assume that most poor workers in poor countries have developed such a rich spirituality. Quite the contrary in fact. The reality is that, down through history, most poor people found themselves stuck in a kind of fatalism about their situation. They looked for minor improvements but it scarcely occurred to them that the whole structure of society could be changed – or particularly that *they themselves* could play a key role in bringing such changes about.

On very rare occasions a great leader emerged and succeeded in inspiring oppressed people to believe that change is possible and that they should work together to bring it about. But for the most part social and political change did not come from the bottom of society. Even today, the kind of spirituality which appeals to most poor workers in the countries of 'the South', is a rather 'escapist' form of Pentecostalism which calls for personal conversion and gives them warm religious feelings, but does not encourage them to struggle for justice in society.

The emergence of liberation theology was a major breakthrough in this regard. It meant that, for perhaps the first time in history, hope and energy could come not just from an inspiring leader but from a spirituality – and one based firmly on the Bible. No wonder, then, that this re-discovered biblical spirituality of struggle for justice, having emerged in Latin America, spread quite rapidly across the world. What makes it particularly effective is that it is not just a theory, but a whole new approach.

It starts from people's experience on the ground and interprets that experience in the light of the gospel. These poor people come to see how similar their situation is to that of the poor and oppressed people in the Bible. Seeing how the God of the Bible was on the side of those who were poor and exploited, they come to believe that this is still true today. So they learn to have hope and are inspired to work together for justice.

A practical methodology, called 'the psycho-social method', for nourishing and applying this new spirituality and approach among poor people, was worked out by Anne Hope and Sally Timmel (see Hope and Timmel 1995 and 1999). It links the emphasis of Paulo Freire on generative issues and social analysis with practical techniques of group-work and planning. It has played a major role in the spread of a spirituality of liberation in Africa and Asia as well as among disadvantaged communities in Ireland and the UK.

I have written extensively in other books about the use of this method (Dorr 1984: 150-8; Dorr 1990: 138-185; Dorr 2000: 233-8), so I shall not describe it here. However, I must make one important point which is very relevant to the theme of this book. It is that liberation theology – even of a very moderate or 'toned-down' type – is frequently experienced by church leaders and ministers as a threat to their authority. As I noted in an earlier chapter, the Vatican has engaged in a sustained campaign to undermine it, by appointing bishops who are quite hostile to that whole understanding of the Christian faith.

The result is that many of the dioceses in Latin America and the Philippines, where liberation theology had flourished in the past, now have bishops who have dismantled the structures of lay participation and the training programmes for animators. A number of the most active and committed local church ministers have become disheartened by the lack of support for their work. So the Vatican hostility has been quite effective. The lesson is obvious: without active support from church leaders it is very difficult for a spirituality of liberation to flourish and bear full fruit – especially in tackling such a major issue as globalisation.

Most of my own direct experience of the difficulty clergy have with a liberationist spirituality has been at a local level in East and West Africa. When I was working there in training community activists, we found that many bishops and priests were supportive of the programme so long as they saw it as concerned with various forms of self-help and similar kinds of economic development. The main trouble we had in this area was that the bishops generally wanted to control the financial side of the project – and we learned from experience that it was important to maintain a certain financial independence.

However, the programme also involved the empowerment of people in the religious sphere. Once this became evident, quite a lot of the priests began to feel threatened, since they saw it as a threat to their own power. So the programme became 'a sign of contradiction', which sometimes split the clergy three ways. The majority remained rather indifferent and not very supportive; some opposed it actively; and a fairly small number became fully committed to it, seeing it as an effective way of overcoming clericalism and of sharing power with the laity.

CHAPTER 8

Globalisation and Spirituality in the West

In the previous chapter I noted that a spirituality of liberation is a powerful means of opposing the more damaging forms of globalisation in poor countries in 'the South'. We cannot, however, assume that a spirituality which animates poor 'Third World' workers, will be equally appropriate for, and congenial to, the majority of people in the West, in attempting to resist the present model of globalisation. So the question arises, what motivation do we in the West have for committing ourselves to change the way globalisation is taking place?

It has to be acknowledged that, at first sight at least, the people of the West have been beneficiaries rather than victims of the process of globalisation. Over the past generation – and allowing for some 'ups and downs' – there has been a notable improvement in the standard of living of most people in the Western world. One of the main reasons for this is that a lot of everyday food items such as tropical fruit, tea, coffee, and sugar, as well as articles such as clothing and footwear are now available in the West at relatively low prices. And the reason why the prices are low is that these foods and other goods are produced by exploited under-paid workers on huge farms or in 'sweatshop' factories in 'Third World' countries.

The more affluent lifestyle of people in the West comes at a high cost. This cost is paid first of all by the exploited workers in foreign countries whose lives are shortened by excessive work and very unhealthy working conditions (pesticides sprayed on the fruit and toxic chemicals inhaled in factories). Western affluence also comes at the cost of serious damage to the environment: scarce resources are used wastefully and the earth, the air, and the waters are severely polluted.

Many people in the West are beginning to realise that their affluence comes at a considerable cost *to themselves* as well. The more obvious side of this is rising unemployment – especially for less skilled workers, since their work is now done in low-cost countries. But there is also a cost which cannot easily be measured: it is the damaging effect which globalisation has had on people and on human relationships in the workplaces of the West. Globalisation is bringing about a major change in the whole ethos of business and work in the developed world. In recent years, managers and workers have found themselves subjected to ever-increasing psychological pressure at work; and they find that a severely competitive ethos is undermining harmony and trust in the workplace.

Pressures on all
The conventional way of looking at this situation is to see managers and workers as opposed to each other. Managers are seen as the ones whose aim is to make the enterprise more efficient and productive. So they seek to squeeze more and more from their workers, setting ever higher targets, offering incentives to those who exceed the targets, and squeezing out any workers who cannot 'make the grade'.

All this is true, but it conveys only half of the picture. It misses out on the fact that managers themselves are also workers. Those in lower or middle management positions are subject to the same kind of pressures as they are imposing on the workers 'below' them – indeed the pressures at this level are often much greater. And the top management and members of the board of directors find themselves subject to similar severe pressures from the shareholders. The irony is that many of these shareholders – especially in the USA – are themselves 'ordinary workers' in other companies. So it is far too facile to think in terms of labels like 'the villains' (the managers and capitalists) and 'the victims' (ordinary workers). What has happened is that everybody has got trapped in a system which is damaging them all.

An increasing number of workers and managers in the

Western world have come to realise that the damaging ethos of
the modern workplace is an aspect of the whole process of
globalisation. Many of them are concerned above all about the
destructive effects on themselves. They see that their work is
making increasing demands on their energy, and often on their
time. They are often forced to work under great pressure, and
this causes many to become quite 'stressed out'. Furthermore,
those who have a role in management at any level have learned
that to be successful in business they have to become tough, and
somewhat unscrupulous. Many of these people are troubled
about this; their conscience tells them that 'success' comes at too
high a price.

A lot of managers and workers are also concerned not only
about what this new business ethos is doing to themselves, but
also about the effect it has on the general atmosphere and
relationships within the workplace. They feel uneasy about the
style of management and the exercise of authority which now
seems to be expected in big business. They see that the 'successful'
management team is one which exercises control through a
judicious blend of incentives, smooth diplomacy, clever
manipulation, and, when necessary, quite ruthless action. They
see, furthermore, that managers have to be competitive, manipulative, and sycophantic if they want to hold on to their jobs.
And they see the damaging effects this has both on those who are
subject to this kind of ruthless management and on those who
exercise it.

Finally, a growing number of people in the Western world
have serious problems of conscience about the effects of industry
or business (their own and others') in the wider world. For
instance, many are waking up to the fact that the goods, which
they are advertising or stocking or using, are produced in sweatshop conditions by poorly paid and unprotected Third World
workers. Others have begun to advert to the fact that their industry
is selling dangerous products like cigarettes or alcoholic drinks
to vulnerable people. Still others are troubled about the serious
effects their industry has on the environment. Finally, some of

those who work in the international banking sector have become acutely aware of the very restrictive and destructive conditions which are being imposed on poor countries when they look for loans or for a remission of debts.

Spirituality
Faced with so many serious reservations about the effects of globalisation, it is hardly surprising that a growing number of people in the Western world look for a remedy and seek to find it in the world of spirituality. In fact spirituality has become a truly 'generative theme' for quite a number of those who play important roles in the world of work in the Western world. For instance, Bolman and Deal (2001) wrote an influential book which was a call for business leaders to embark on a spiritual journey. And two writers in a well-known management journal wrote: 'We need to integrate spirituality into management. No organisation can survive for long without spirituality and soul' (Mitroff and Denton).

Of course this is not a totally new idea. Seventy years ago Canon Joseph Cardijn was keenly aware of the need for a spirituality of work and he founded the Young Christian Workers to enable people to develop such a spirituality. Again, the 'Movement for a Better World' offered its members a highly developed spirituality of work. 'Opus Dei' also proposed a spirituality which touched every aspect of life, with a particular emphasis on work.

Recently the Abbot of Ampleforth has been working with business leaders, offering the 'Rule of St Benedict' as a guideline for ethics in business; the book which has emerged from this work (Dollard 2002) is interesting; but it does not really address the issue of exploitation of Third World workers caused by globalisation. More recently still, Antonia Swinson (2003) has written a best-selling book which emphasises the importance of spiritual values in the business world. She deals with a variety of ethical issues related to business today; one of these is the issue of challenging companies which are involved in exploitative or unethical activities in remote parts of the world (141-3).

She also puts forward a strong case for recognising the importance of 'social capital' (153-172). Voluntary activity, good neighbourliness, creativity, care for the environment: all these are a kind of wealth which cannot be measured in terms of money. Many of them are being eroded quite rapidly by the lifestyle fostered by globalisation.

Swinson draws on the Christian tradition for the ethical and spiritual values which she advocates; and this explicit reference to the Christian religion obviously appeals to a certain proportion of people in the Western world. However, a different approach is adopted by most of those who now insist on the importance of spiritual values in business: they distinguish sharply between spirituality and religion (cf. McGeachy 2001: 59), and are advocating a spirituality which is more or less independent of any particular religion:

> Most of the people leading the spirit-at-work paradigm shift, or at least those nudging it along, say spirituality at work isn't about believing in a particular religion, although many expressions of spirituality at work stem from various religious traditions – from the Jewish faith to Hinduism to Christianity. It's about taking a broader, more global view of the spiritual dimension which may, for some, encompass their religious beliefs. For example, the spiritual concepts of balance, trust, harmony, communication, values, mission, honesty and co-operation come from religious traditions, but aren't the sole by-product of any one of them (Laabs; cf. Porpora 2001).

Creativity, Ethics, and Spirituality
This movement to bring spiritual values into business has itself by now become a big business. As McGeachy (39) pointed out three years ago, there were over 300 books published on the topic in the previous decade. The movement takes a variety of different forms and covers a wide spectrum of approaches. At one end of that spectrum are those like Peter Senge (1994), Joseph Jaworski (1996), and Danah Zohar (2001), who think of spirituality mainly in terms of bringing greater creativity into work.

Further along the spectrum are those whose main emphasis is on ethical and ecological values. Here we can locate the work of E. F. Schumacher and his many followers. In his best-selling book, *Small is Beautiful*, and his later book *Good Work* (1980), Schumacher put up a compelling case for a scaling down of the whole process of globalisation, partly on ecological grounds and partly in the interests of ensuring that workers would not be treated as commodities. He was perhaps the main inspiration of the movement to promote the use of what is called 'appropriate technology', which means making a judicious choice in each case between simple technologies and quite sophisticated ones, depending on the situation.

In his inspiring book, *The Reinvention of Work*, first published in 1994 and issued in paperback in 1995, Matthew Fox carries on in the tradition of Schumacher but takes it much further and deeper. He emphasises the importance of doing work which one enjoys (96-7) and of allowing creativity to manifest itself in work (114-7). He goes on to describe various rituals which can be used to bring spirituality back into people's everyday working lives (278-295).

Much less radical in approach, but still concerned with the ethical aspects of business today, is the approach of the Caux Round Table. This was a gathering of key business leaders who came together in 1986. They proposed a code of 'Principles for Business', based on the key values of *kyosei* and human dignity. The Japanese concept of *kyosei* means living and working together for the common good, enabling co-operation and mutual prosperity to coexist with healthy and fair competition. The code to which they committed themselves is a praiseworthy statement of ideals and aspirations; but it does not question the basic rules and practices which underpin the process of globalisation. The approach of Catherine McGeachy (2001) is somewhat similar; she emphasises the importance of values in the workplace, but does not explicitly question the fundamental principles of globalisation.

At the other end of the spectrum, the focus is not so much on creativity, or on social, political, or ecological issues but on much more personal concerns of the individual. There are many stressed-out managers and workers whose generative issue is the need for inner peace, and a sense of purpose in their lives. To meet this need, a growing number of religious 'gurus' have emerged to offer these people a spirituality of personal transformation. They teach people to engage in meditation and / or prayer, as a means of becoming more peaceful, more loving, and more disciplined in their way of living.

This is good as far as it goes. It can help people to cope better with stress, but it does not address the other problems created by the modern business ethos. In this sense it is, to some extent, an 'escapist' spirituality – and in this respect it is similar to the Pentecostalism which appeals to many of the poor in the so-called 'Third World'. The difference, however, is that those who become Pentecostalists are seeking a *communal* experience of escape from the drabness and misery of everyday life, whereas the meditation spirituality adopted by some in the Western world is a very *personal and private* experience.

A Spirituality of Management

Many right-minded business people realise that a spirituality of personal calmness is not sufficient. They see that the ethos of the workplace is demanding that they be manipulative and ruthless, and they sense they are losing a part of their soul as a result. So they hunger for, and seek to develop, a type of spirituality which, though still deeply personal, is not so self-centred and inward-looking. It is one which fosters the values of gentleness and vulnerability. This spirituality gives a central place to respect for others, encouraging people to 'let down their guard' and be open, trusting, and vulnerable in front of co-workers (cf. McGeachy 17). This can generate an atmosphere where people are willing to drop the mask which has forced them to 'put a good face on things' and to pretend that 'everything is under control'. These are qualities which find very little place in the modern business world.

At this point personal spirituality has moved beyond the private sphere and has begun to shade into a spirituality of respectful interpersonal relationships. When developed a little further, this evolves into a spirituality of good management. At its best, this meets the need of those for whom the generative issue is that workers should have a sense of participation and 'ownership' of their work. It is a communal spirituality which evokes team spirit and a sense of solidarity with managers and co-workers.

Feeling that they are respected and that their contribution to the enterprise is valued, the workers develop a sense of co-responsibility. They find their work fulfilling, and the work itself and the whole atmosphere of the workplace evokes in them a spirit not only of dedication but also of creativity. But this spirituality will not survive if it remains only at the level of personal attitudes. Like any genuine spirituality it becomes fully incarnated only when it becomes embodied in the managerial structures, practices, and legal or quasi-legal traditions of the business.

Many economists would dismiss such a spirituality as quite unrealistic. They would argue that such 'soft' values as respect and participation will always take second place to the 'hard' economic values of efficiency and profitability. However, a small but significant number of mainstream economists recognise that the 'soft' values can make a great difference even in purely economic terms. For instance, Benedetto Gui, of the Department of Economics in Padua, emphasises the importance of what he calls 'relational goods' (such as good relationships in the workplace). He maintains that high-quality relationships in the workplace 'have an economic dimension' (Gui 2000). This suggests that there is at least some hope that economists may eventually come to accept that spirituality is not irrelevant to economic science but may have a very positive role to play within it.

A Global Spirituality

However, even a truly respectful and participative spirituality of management is not enough. It does not yet take account of the serious problems of conscience which, as I mentioned earlier, trouble many people in relation to the effects of modern business. The reality of globalisation and the competitiveness of the global market create real dilemmas for the owners, managers, and workers of even the most humanely managed business.

Those among them who are more aware of what is happening often feel that they are expected to turn a blind eye to ways in which the survival and success of their company is linked to exploitation. For competition may be 'forcing' them to buy goods made by poor and exploited workers in poor countries. Furthermore, they may be playing down the damage their business is doing to the environment. Any spirituality remains inadequate if it fails to take account of these realities, and of the twinges of conscience to which they give rise.

There is a real continuity between this concern for global issues of exploitation and the personal and managerial spirituality I described earlier. The core values in each case are sensitivity, vulnerability, and respect. When these values are lived out at the personal level they expand quite naturally into interpersonal relationships and into the whole sphere of teamwork, co-responsibility and management. Then those who practice them together find themselves drawn to look outward to the wider world.

Managers and workers who acknowledge their own vulnerability and who are respectful of their co-workers, are drawn to recognise the evil that is taking place in the wider world. At that stage the *personal* spirituality of vulnerability and integrity, together with the *managerial* spirituality of participation and co-responsibility, unfold and extend into a much broader socially-oriented *global* spirituality which includes moral concern for exploited workers and the ravaged environment. Those who take this final step are willing to look closely at how their organisation affects – and is affected by – global issues such as ecology, patriarchy, social justice, and human development at the international level. And they now feel more free to give voice to their qualms of conscience and their questions about the overall ethos of the business, and the effect it is having in the wider world.

It is important – even for very practical management reasons – to take seriously the troubling questions of conscience which affect managers and workers when they advert to ways in which the business in which they work may be exploiting Third World workers, or customers, or the environment. For people will work more comfortably and creatively if they believe that these ethical issues are taken seriously in the company for which they work.

This argument is supported by Bruno Frey (1998), professor of economics in the University of Zurich. He makes use of a wealth of empirical psychological studies to show that, whatever about abstract economic theory, in actual practice people are influenced, not merely by narrowly 'economic' considerations such as price and wages. They also act on the basis of what he calls 'intrinsic motivation' (such as friendship, or interest, or environmental concern). Frey goes on to give an interesting account of the delicate interaction between this 'intrinsic motiv-ation' and the more traditional economic incentives.

I hope the past few pages have made it clear that the only spirituality which is an adequate response to the damaging effects of globalisation is one which is truly integral. This means that it must respond to the spiritual and moral aspirations of people at three distinct levels. These are: (1) the need for personal peace, integrity, and meaning in life; (2) the desire for respect, harmony, co-operation, and participation in management and decision-making in the workplace; and (3) the need to ensure that the business as a whole is making a positive contribution to the wider world – or at least that it is not involved in exploitation of people or of the environment.

Managers and Shared Management
It is particularly important that those who hold managerial posi-tions in business or the financial institutions (banks etc.) should be motivated by such a rich and integral spirituality. As managers they are familiar with the practical ways in which globalisation affects workers, customers, the suppliers of raw materials, and

the environment. They are also familiar with the financial and legal structures within which their business operates. So they, more than anybody else, are in a position to know what kind of changes are needed if the more damaging effects of globalisation are to be avoided.

These managers are in a position to make personal choices which can bring about major changes at the structural level. Within the companies in which they work at present they can argue convincingly in favour of a variety of key changes, putting forward a combination of pragmatic and ethical arguments for the adoption of an approach which avoids the damaging effects of globalisation. If their voices are not heard in their present places of work they can seek out alternative employment, making it clear that their reason for switching jobs is that they choose to work in a company which embodies more ethical values.

In the business world which considers managerial expertise to be of the highest importance, the threat by a key manager to move to a competing company can be a powerful incentive for a board of directors to authorise major changes of policy (cf. Hertz 180). Furthermore, if a number of key people in managerial roles were to commit themselves to support each other in working out and implementing common policies which are morally and socially enlightened, they would become very effective agents of change.

I must add at once that if management and workers adopt the spirituality of management proposed here, namely one of collaboration and teamwork, then *every* worker will have an effective share in management. So all of them will be entitled to be heard when they air their problems of conscience about ways in which they feel the enterprise as a whole may be exploiting suppliers, or customers, or the earth. We must assume that all of the workers can make a valuable contribution to a dialogue about the changes which should be made, in order that the enterprise becomes a truly ethical one.

Furthermore, what I am saying here about 'workers' applies not just to those who work in factories, but also to those who work in the service industries, and to workers in the public services, since all of these have been drawn into the process of globalisation. All who have a share in management can play an important role, individually or collectively, within a wider movement for change. This applies not only to those formally appointed to management roles but also to the general body of workers insofar as they share in management in some degree.

One of the most difficult aspects of working to overcome the evils of globalisation is that at present many of those who call for change do not have enough familiarity with the ways in which the various business enterprises and government departments actually work. The issues are so complex that the vast majority of people feel helpless, not really knowing what changes are required to bring about a truly just, sustainable, and respectful world order.

This sense of paralysis is fostered by economists and other 'experts' who use technical jargon which mystifies non-specialists who are unable to understand it. It is all too easy for these 'insiders' of the world of business and high finance to pick holes in the arguments of those who pass judgements on them from outside that 'world'. So they tend to dismiss the arguments for change and the proposed courses of action as high-minded idealism lacking a realistic understanding of the world of economics. The result is that campaigners for change who come from outside the world of business are unlikely to succeed unless they find allies from within the 'world' they wish to change.

That is why a vital role may be played by even a relatively small number of committed people who are 'insiders'. These are people who have some familiarity either with the workings of a particular business or with the interlocking web of relationships which constitutes the present economic world 'order'. They have a sense of where the power really lies. They know which key changes are required if the system is to be reformed effectively.

This knowledge gives them real power – power which they can use very successfully in the struggle to restructure the world of international economics in the interests of human dignity, justice, and sustainability. Their spirituality calls them to make common cause with those who are disadvantaged and exploited by the present system, and to put both their 'insider' knowledge and their analytical and organisational skills at the service of the movement for transformation of society.

An Emergent Spirituality

The spirituality and ethics I have been outlining is one which finds its roots in the real experiences and felt needs of people engaged in any kind of business – or indeed almost any kind of work in the modern globalised world. It is one which articulates and gives a systematic formulation to those elements of spirituality which many middle-class people in the Western world already find deep in their own hearts as they try to cope with the reality of globalisation.

My belief – and my own experience – is that this emergent spirituality is more credible and attractive to them than an ethics of business life proposed by church leaders, or preachers, or theologians. For the church-people are often seen as outsiders with little or no practical experience of the realities of the business world of today. Transformation can never be imposed from outside. Calls for radical change can be heard only when they strike a chord that the Spirit has already touched within.

My assumption in sketching out this spirituality is that the Spirit is working in the heart of each person – even in the hearts of those business people who are deeply immersed in the process of globalisation. It is all too easy to 'write off' the whole business class and scapegoat them as the villains of the modern world. There are many among them who are troubled by what they see happening around them and even by the operations in which they themselves are engaged. A smaller but still significant number are looking seriously for ways to humanise the process of globalisation. Some even feel their heart calling them to make 'an option for the poor'.

Our aim should be to evoke and foster the spirituality which is already there in germ in their hearts. If they listen to the voice of the Spirit in their hearts, they can make a big contribution to the struggle for justice in the world. In dialogue with the victims of the system, and working alongside other committed activists, they can work out realistic policies and strategies which would be adopted and campaigned for by millions of people on five continents in a mass movement of solidarity to bring about a just and sustainable world order.

CHAPTER 9

Human Experience and Christian Faith

In the opening lines of the Vatican II document on 'The Church in the Modern World' *(Gaudium et Spes)*, the leaders of the church referred to 'the joys and hopes, the griefs and anxieties of the people of our time'. Speaking on our behalf, they declared that the followers of Christ have taken on as their own the whole range of human experiences. The important thing here is the comprehensiveness of this undertaking. There is no question of the church leaders just picking out some joys and hopes and sorrows.

So we have here a standard or measuring-rod to see how thorough our sharing of the good news has been in any particular part of the world. In each country or area we have to ask whether we Christians have really integrated into our Christian vision and practice the whole gamut of joys, hopes, sorrows, and anxieties which the local people experience. If not, then our task of evangelisation remains an unfinished project.

There is no such thing as evangelisation in the abstract. It always has to be done in a given situation, within a particular culture and in a particular political and social context. It is always a matter of enabling the gospel to intersect with the way of life of a people or community. This is called *inculturation*. So evangelisation and inculturation are just two sides of the same process.

The best way to share the good news is by being interested in our own and others' experience of God or spiritual experiences. We can go about this in two stages. The first is to foster, nurture and deepen these spiritual experiences, ensuring that we ourselves and others recognise and value them, and where possible finding ways to evoke such experiences. The second aspect is interpreting these experiences in the light of Christian revelation. My aim in this chapter is to examine a wide range of common spiritual experiences and to explore to what extent we in the Western church have successfully integrated them into our Christian faith.

'Depth Experiences'

The Celts, the Greeks, and other peoples of ancient times took for granted that what we now call 'depth experiences' were caused by some god or divinity. And this way of interpreting life still holds sway among most Hindu people and in the primal cultures of Africa and elsewhere. For instance, in ancient Greece when the woman we now call Helen of Troy fell in love and left her husband Menelaus to elope with her lover, everybody took it for granted that this was the work of Aphrodite, the goddess of passionate love. Similarly, when an ancient Irish warrior got into a battle-frenzy, people would assume that the warrior goddess Mór-Ríogain (or Morrigan) was at work (Ó hÓgain 67).

It is quite difficult for us Western Christians to understand this way of thinking. The difficulty arises partly from the rather secular character of our Western world. But more fundamentally it arises from the success of the Judeo-Christian tradition in giving us a concept of a truly transcendent God. This transcendent God is radically different from the gods of the pre-Christian Celts, or of the ancient Greeks, or of most present-day Hindus, or of the African traditional religions. As Vincent Vycinas remarks (314): '... the name "god" for a Greek deity and the Christian God ... is used to a great extent equivocally'. He points out that the Greek gods are worldly, whereas the Christian God is above the world. I do not intend to be irreverent when I suggest that, whenever Christianity became fully accepted in a culture, our transcendent God tended to 'hoover up' all the gods, divinities, and quasi-divinities of the local culture, subsuming them as far as possible.

We have tended to assume that this was the right thing for Christianity to do. And in some spheres of life it worked well. So in these situations what took place was a successful evangelisation insofar as a particular aspect of the Christian faith was well integrated into the local culture. I believe, however, that this subsuming of the local divinities into the Christian God did not work in some situations – and could not work because many of the local divinities could not easily be subsumed into the transcendent God.

Consequently, many depth experiences were left on the margins of the new Christianised culture, or, worse still, were seriously misinterpreted. In these situations what took place was a quite inadequate form of evangelisation/inculturation. My intention is to look at different spheres of life where primal peoples had a sense of being in touch with the world of the gods, and in each case to see what happened when Christianity replaced the ancient religion.

Popular Devotions

I begin with some rather obvious examples where this kind of evangelisation was done successfully. I draw my examples first from my present Irish situation and then I shall comment on the different situations which prevail in Britain, in Latin America, North America, Australia, and to a lesser extent in New Zealand. Ancient Ireland had a multitude of local sacred shrines, each with its own local divinity. These were places where people came to make contact with powers from 'the beyond' – and frequently this involved a search for healing or for guidance in life. The strategy of the early Irish church was to 'baptise' these shrines and replace the divinities with local saints. It seems that at times the divinity was transposed into a saint – for instance, the Celtic goddess Brighid was subsumed into Saint Brighid (Ó hÓgain 112 and 203).

In general this seems to have worked well. But if this kind of inculturation is to be successful on an on-going basis it is not sufficient for succeeding generations to hold on to what was done in the past. Culture is constantly changing, so the process of inculturation has to be kept up to date, and at times it has to be re-thought in new and creative ways. In Ireland today there are some places which are excellent examples of this kind of successful on-going inculturation of the gospel.

For me, the most outstanding example is Lough Derg (also called St Patrick's Purgatory). There the full rigour of the ancient tradition of devotion has been retained – going barefoot, fasting, a lot of prayers, night vigil, etc. (cf. Turner 104-139). But the atmosphere there is now quite different from the harsh spirituality which prevailed there fifty years ago. The whole ambience at present is one of compassion, welcome, joy, hope, and reconciliation. The result is that Lough Derg responds very profoundly to the spiritual hunger of modern Irish people, as well as of the many pilgrims who come from abroad.

Glendalough is an ancient monastic site situated in a beautiful valley south of Dublin. It has been a place of pilgrimage for many centuries. It is encouraging to see the recent developments there – new centres for retreat, for reflection, for exploration of Celtic and ecological spirituality. It is especially helpful to find there a warm and sensitive welcome for spiritual 'searchers' who may have little or no connection with the church. On the other hand, it is a great pity that these new features came so late that for the great majority of visitors the place seems to be mainly just an interesting archaeological and geological site; the only spirituality which they pick up there is that which is imprinted on the stones themselves.

The holy mountain Croagh Patrick in the west of Ireland is another traditional place of pilgrimage, going back to pre-Christian times, long before St Patrick came there to fast and pray. On the last Sunday in July about 50,000 people climb this holy mountain. However, the pilgrimage aspect does not seem to have been updated as successfully as at Lough Derg. A generation ago the local church authorities decided that the climb should take place during the day rather than at night. No doubt there were sound practical reasons for this change, but the pilgrimage lost an important element when the mystery and danger of the night climb were removed. Nowadays, only a relatively small number of those who climb the mountain go through the traditional rituals of reciting prayers while circling the 'beds' or 'stations' on the route. And this time-honoured devotion has not been replaced by any appropriate alternative. Mass is celebrated in the little chapel on the summit of the mountain, but this is not accessible to the ordinary pilgrim.

It should not be too difficult to deepen the experience of pilgrimage for those who take part. It would, however, require an exercise of creative dramatic imagination, combined with exceptional managerial skills – exactly the combination which has already been shown by those who have developed the nearby Ballintubber Abbey and the ancient pilgrimage route from it to Croagh Patrick. The crucial point is that authentic evangelisation requires that the process of inculturation be constantly up-dated to take account of the way the culture is continually changing.

Britain

When we look at the challenge of inculturation in Britain, it soon becomes evident that ecumenism must play a central role. This is especially obvious in the case of England. Until quite recently, the Catholic Church there was a minority and largely immigrant church. Only a small number of 'native Catholics' had any significant roots in the English past. In England the Anglican Church has been the mainstream carrier of the Christian tradition over the past four hundred years. The Reformation led to the cutting off of some of the links with the past, and so the role of popular devotions was diminished. But the Church of England maintained a more organic continuity with the past than did the churches which adopted a more unequivocally Protestant and Calvinist theology. The ancient holy island of Lindisfarne is not merely a link with the Anglo-Saxon and Celtic past, but also a place where the different Christian churches come together to serve the large number of pilgrims. Walsingham is another holy site where Christians of the different churches draw more closely together, as they nurture their spirituality by linking it to the tradition of the past.

Present-day Anglicans have inherited a very rich tradition of prayers and Bible readings, rendered into a splendidly majestic style of English which has deep roots in the past. In seeking to re-connect with the ancient English tradition, the Catholic Church must come closer to the Anglicans. This is already taking place in so far as Catholics are gradually adopting many of the magnificent old hymns and in general are shaking off their 'foreign' baggage and taking on 'local colour'.

The situation in Scotland is rather different. There the dominant church is quite Protestant in tone, and has less connection than in England with the pre-Reformation past. On the other hand, the Celtic past is still very strong, and the link with the past is preserved above all in the holy island of Iona, which is a focus of unity between the churches. Some of the Scottish Isles have maintained an unbroken Catholic tradition. The main body of Scottish Catholics are descendents of Irish immigrants. So it should not be too difficult for them to make a closer connection with the indigenous Celtic Catholic tradition – which itself carries echoes and elements from the religion of pre-Christian times.

Wales is different again. It is a country whose Christians are strongly rooted in a very Protestant tradition, and where there are few indigenous Catholics. But there is a rich Celtic tradition which is now 'carried' to a considerable extent in the Protestant churches and chapels. The main carrier of the Celtic tradition is, of course, the Welsh language. There is a strong tradition of hymn-singing and a large corpus of hymns in Welsh, carrying on a devotional history which goes back for many generations. The Catholic Church must be very actively ecumenical if it wishes to become more deeply rooted in local culture.

Latin America

In Latin America, the liberation theologians have recently come to a new appreciation of popular devotions. They have succeeded fairly well in their efforts to adapt these devotions, replacing elements that seem rather superstitious or magical with a liberationist perspective. All this is admirable. But some awkward questions remain.

The fact is that the church in most of Latin America has still not faced up fully to the reality of the colonisation of that continent. Very many, if not most, of the present inhabitants are of mixed race, since the European settlers intermarried with both the indigenous inhabitants and with those who had been brought in as slaves from Africa. Despite this ethnic mixing, racial and ethnic prejudice and discrimination is still an on-going reality in much of Latin America.

It is true that the church has become a very powerful champion of 'non-white' people in many parts of the continent. But this commitment at the political level has not always been matched by a sufficient degree of cultural and religious sensitivity. Inculturation of the Christian faith should give more prominence to the valuable elements in the traditions of the indigenous peoples of Latin America. There is need also for a more serious inter-religious dialogue with the Brazilian spiritist cults of Umbanda and Candomblé which originally developed among the people of African ancestry. Furthermore, there is need for the leadership of the church at every level to include far more members of these 'people of colour' who up to now have largely been seen as second-class citizens.

North America and Australia

The situation in North America and Australia is different again. The great majority of people there are descendents of immigrants from Europe and elsewhere. Over two or three centuries the Native American and Aboriginal peoples were almost wiped out in a slow war of attrition, which many would now see as genocidal. (In New Zealand the Maori people still make up a sizable proportion of the total population so the situation is not quite the same.) In recent times many committed Christians have taken up some of spiritual practices of the Native American or Aboriginal peoples (e.g. sweat lodges, spiritual quests, 'walkabout', dream-time, etc). I have no doubt that many of these practices are spiritually valuable and truly compatible with the Christian faith. Nevertheless, some serious questions have to be asked about this approach.

It is obvious that what happened in the USA, in most of
Canada, and in Australia (and to a lesser extent in New Zealand)
is quite different from the pattern in, say, Western Europe,
where successive waves of immigrants became fairly well integrated with the earlier inhabitants and where each new ethnic
group brought in traditions which were modified and integrated
to a greater or lesser extent. The situation in USA and Australia
has more in common with what happened in Eastern Europe
after World War II. There, whole areas of eastern Poland were
'ethnically cleansed' and Russians moved in; and at the same
time Germans were pushed out of large areas near the old bor-
der between Germany and Poland, and that land was taken over
by Poles. In these cases the new migrants brought their own
traditions with them and made little or no link with the traditions of the previous inhabitants of the area.

In the USA, southern Canada, and Australia, does occupation
of the same territory provide an adequate basis of continuity
between the newly dominant 'white' people and the traditions of
the dispossessed peoples? The indigenous people could claim
that what is happening at present is rather like the victors sifting
through the spoils of the vanquished people and picking out the
bits which appeal to them. I think that there is only one condition on which Christians of European or Asian stock are entitled
to take on some of the spiritual practices of Native America or
Aboriginal Australia. That condition is, that they willingly identify with and support the indigenous peoples in their struggle for
survival, for justice, and for restitution. Then they can come into
real solidarity with them, supporting these peoples in their
efforts to preserve their cultural and spiritual identity.

If that takes place, then there can be a bridging of the otherwise unbridgeable gap between the descendents of the victors
and the tradition of the vanquished. And then the adoption of
some of the spiritual practices of the indigenous peoples will be
part of a process of reconciliation and healing rather than an act of
exploitation. (John May has an interesting account of the challenge
facing those Australians who wish to avoid '"appropriating"

Aboriginal culture and spirituality', and instead come to terms
with 'the atrocities perpetrated on the Aborigines and the land
that was their life' – May 34 and 39.)

The religious traditions of the African-American population
are gradually coming more into the mainstream of church life in
the USA. Gospel choirs now have a very respected place in the
churches. And, from within the African-American churches,
exceptionally talented and respected leaders, such as Martin
Luther King and Jesse Jackson, have emerged. However, the
Catholic Church in particular still has some way to go if the full
inculturation of the faith in the African-American culture is to be
achieved.

The immigrant inhabitants of North America and Australia
come from a very wide range of ethnic backgrounds – Italian,
Polish, English, Scottish, African, German, Irish, Hispanic, 'mes-
tizo' Latin American, Scandinavian, Greek, Croatian, Chinese,
Indian, Vietnamese, Japanese, etc. The immigrant groups have
their own spiritual traditions – most of them Christian – so there
is a rich historical legacy which each group can draw on. There
has, of course, been a great lot of inter-marriage. This means that
many people now have very mixed ancestry indeed. Given this
situation, it is neither possible nor advisable to suggest that the
different ethnic groups stick rigidly to their own traditions. The
existing pluralism can be seen as providing an extended 'menu'
from which people are free to choose. The result should be the
emergence of a new tradition which integrates elements from
many of the older sources.

The Prayer of Petition
The people of my parents' generation showed their faith in
God's loving care by their very firm belief in the power of the
prayer of petition. At times they addressed their prayers directly
to God; and at other times they invoked the intercession of the
Blessed Virgin Mary, or St Thérèse, or St Anthony or some other
saint. The choice of saint depended partly on personal devotion
and partly on whether the person was praying for the healing of

sickness, or for success in exams, or for finding something that had got lost. And of course St Jude was the patron of hopeless cases. Within the past generation there has been a sense that much of this is outdated devotionalism. It is an open question how much of this change of attitude is due to the new theology of Vatican II and how much is due to the increasing secularisation of Western society.

I make no apology for asserting my own firm belief in the prayer of petition and my conviction that it is a central aspect of authentic Christianity. Following from this, I believe that one of the key challenges of evangelisation / inculturation in the Western world today is to find ways in which the sense of the providence of God and the power of prayer can be experienced as vividly or even more vividly than in the past. People have a deep spiritual need for devotions or rituals which enable them to experience God's care. So when they do not find ways of meeting this need in any authentic way, what happens is that inappropriate and quasi-superstitious devotions tend to flourish. It is easy to think of examples of places where this is taking place – either by continuing old-style devotions that have long passed their 'sell-by' date, or by propagating bizarre new devotions which have a strong taint of superstition, and which distract people from the kernel of the Christian faith.

I refrain from giving examples of what I consider outdated or distorted devotions, because these cults often evoke profound religious devotion in their devotees. Even if a particular devotion is out of tune with the message of Jesus, church ministers need to show great sensitivity and respect in weaning people away from it. The best way to do so is by offering an alternative which meets the spiritual need of the devotees in a way that is closer to the heart of the gospel.

I want to focus instead on a more positive example. Two years ago I was invited by the Franciscan community in a town in the west of Ireland to be the preacher for the nine-day novena to St Anthony. Over a thousand people took part in the services each day, about half in the morning and the other half in the evening. These were not particularly pious people, but a cross-section of 'ordinary' people, ranging in age from teenagers to pensioners. Their faith and their devotion were palpable, and it was evident that the St Anthony devotion really spoke to them. Almost everybody had some favour they wanted to pray for. The devotion strengthened their faith in God's loving care and God's willingness to answer their prayers. And St Anthony brought God's care close to them, made it more 'real'. This kind of devotion, when properly organised as it was in this case, and when backed up by the availability of spiritual direction and counselling, is genuine evangelisation. It deepens people's understanding of what prayer is really about, it gives them a vivid sense of God's loving providence, and it also gives them a warm sense of community support.

Destiny or Fate

In looking at the different spheres of life which are to be evangelised, I started with traditional popular devotions, because this is the most obvious area, and the one which is perhaps easiest to deal with. I want now to look at several other spheres of life, where people have deeply spiritual experiences. In many of these situations the process of evangelisation/inculturation poses serious challenges.

I shall take my examples mainly from the ancient Greek world. One reason for doing so is that most Western cultures are profoundly rooted in ancient Greek culture. Indeed, the first missionary expansion of the church, starting with St Paul, involved recasting the Christian faith in terms of the Greek culture which more or less permeated the whole Roman Empire. In taking examples from the ancient Greek world we have the advantage that it is very well documented – whereas much of what we hear about the Celtic gods is based on conjecture or even on modern romanticised fancy. A further great advantage of choosing the ancient Greek culture as the basis of comparison with our present Christian worldview, is that the Greeks had a very comprehensive pantheon in which the whole set of

Olympian divinities (the 'sky gods') representing a patriarchal system were in constant dialectical relationship with the earth-divinities of the earlier matriarchal culture.

In the work of Homer there is a mysterious power called *Moira*, meaning Fate or Destiny. Moira belongs to the older matriarchal religious stratum; and in later Greek literature she often appears as threefold, namely, the three fates – the one who spins the thread of life, the one who measures out to each person his or her allotted span, and the one who cuts the thread of life. Moira is a power so fundamental that even the gods have to abide by her decrees. Her primary qualities seem to have been implacability and inscrutability: it is pointless to try to avoid one's destiny or to question it. For instance, nobody can begin to understand why Oedipus was destined to have such a tragic fate – it is just a 'given'.

This is one point where the Christian worldview offered a fundamental challenge to the Greek view (and of course to other primal cultures like that of the Celts which generally had a somewhat similar conception of fate or destiny). In many Christianised societies the concept of a loving provident God succeeded to a remarkable extent in replacing the inscrutable Moira or its equivalent. The Ireland in which I grew up was one where there was still a certain amount of fatalism. But for people of strong faith this was tempered and largely transformed by a very staunch belief in the providence of God.

I think it is important to reflect on how we handle death and funerals, since this is one place where the question of fate comes to the fore. In the past we had keening women, who helped to give public expression to the grief and the sense of horror which people often experience in the face of death. Furthermore, at the funeral Mass the priest wore black vestments and we sang the doleful *Dies Irae*. Now these have all been left behind. It is widely assumed that they are inappropriate in modern times.

The new version of our funeral service seems to put all the emphasis on the positive aspects of the death of a Christian. Some funeral homilies seem almost designed to prevent the

dead person's family and friends from experiencing or expressing their grief, their incomprehension, and their outrage against
God for allowing this death to take place. This can give an air of
unreality to the funeral service. Furthermore, it is psychologically
damaging to people to inhibit them from acknowledging the full
extent of their grief and anger as they mourn the dead person. I
think that, without denying our hope, we need to give expression
in our words, symbols, and rituals to the dark incomprehensible
mystery of death. Even in our Christian world, Moira has not
gone away entirely. If we try to shut her out totally from people's
mourning she may stay around to haunt them for the rest of
their lives.

Ecological Spirituality
I move on next to the question of ecological spirituality. Artemis
is the Greek goddess of nature in its untamed and mysterious
form. The Celts, too, had a sense of the mystery and sacredness
of nature. There are indications that early Celtic Christianity
retained the sense of the presence of God in nature. The ancient
prayers have a very strong ecological dimension, where God is
experienced in the 'flashing of lightening, wind in its swiftness,
deeps of the ocean, firmness of earth' (St Patrick's Breastplate).
As Seán Ó Duinn remarks, God was everywhere – in the trees,
the rivers, the woods, the animals, the people, and the sea:
'Advancement in holiness, according to the Celtic way, involves
an effort to develop an awareness of the presence of God in
everything and everybody – above us, below us and all around
us at the four points of the compass' (Ó Duinn 87).

   In recent centuries, however, Christians (as well as Jews and
Muslims) put a one-sided emphasis on the transcendent nature
of God. God seemed to become somewhat detached from nature.
The spiritual power which the ancient Greeks called Artemis
was played down, not given the important place which it
deserves. So the Christian theology and spirituality in which we
were brought up left little room for us to experience a sacred or
divine energy in nature.

In our own days, a lot of people – Christian and non-Christian – in the Western world have rediscovered nature as a powerful source of spiritual nourishment. Unfortunately, the 'message' of the present-day official church is quite 'thin' in this area. Church teaching today does not give sufficient emphasis to this aspect of spirituality. There is an imbalance, with undue prominence given to the other-worldly dimension of Christianity. (This is not to ignore the very valuable work done by Tom Berry, Sean McDonagh, and some other theologians; but the official church has not given their work the welcome it deserves.)

It is hardly surprising, then, that the development of what is called 'deep ecology' has taken place in an atmosphere which is at times positively anti-Christian. We have here an obvious need for inculturation, one which provides a counter-balance for our one-sided emphasis on the transcendence of God by giving a central role to nature mysticism and the immanence of God in our world.

Celebration and Dionysus

The next sphere of life I wish to look at is celebration. Here again I start from my experience of Irish culture. We Irish people are known worldwide for our ability to celebrate. Our football fans seem at times to become quite ecstatic, quite 'out of themselves' in their enthusiasm. That word 'enthusiasm' comes from the Greek words 'en theos' and the literal meaning is 'to be taken over by a god'. In the ancient Greek culture this god of celebration was Dionysus. It is he who evokes the ecstasy which breaks us out of the bounds of a stable and ordered society. Dionysus moves us into a 'world' which, from a rational point of view, is quite chaotic. But this is not necessarily an inhuman world. It is a state where we come alive and human in a quite different mode, namely by being 'taken out of ourselves' in exuberant enthusiastic celebration. This kind of wild celebration sometimes involves getting rather drunk – and in these cases the Greeks would see the god Bacchus at work.

It is clear that neither Dionysus nor Bacchus could easily be assimilated into the transcendent Judeo-Christian God. The result is that this very important area of human life – the sphere of celebration – has largely slipped out of our Christian world-view. No wonder, then, that Irish people are reluctant to sing and celebrate in church; and that Christian faith seems quite irrelevant to the wild celebrations which take place on the occasion of our major sporting events. It seems that we live in two radically different worlds: one where people celebrate and sing in bars and at pop concerts and football matches, and the other where we worship God with the utmost restraint.

Recently I realised that when I picture Jesus at the celebration of the wedding-feast in Cana I am inclined to imagine him sitting in a corner watching the scene while discretely sipping a little wine. But if I take seriously my belief that he took on human life to the full perhaps I should picture him as one of those who caused the wine to run short! Did he perhaps drink a few glasses of wine and then lead the wedding guests in an exuberant dance of celebration?

If we are to re-integrate celebration into our experience of Christian spirituality, the most important step is to take the incarnation seriously. We need to be aware that Jesus took on the whole of human life, not just its more serious and solemn aspects. In principle this should enable us to feel that celebrating a football victory or a party does not involve moving out of the Christian worldview. But to bring this into everyday pastoral practice will require a lot of creative imagination. The kind of creativity that is required will not be very common among elderly celibate priests. Church leaders will need the collaboration of young people if they undertake the task of restoring celebration to its rightful central place in the Christian experience.

In fact there is one outstanding place where Western Christians can find a spirit of joyful spiritual celebration. It is in the churches, chapels, and prayer-halls of the immigrants and asylum-seekers who have come to live among us – especially those from Africa and the Caribbean. Appalled at the dullness and the brevity of our liturgies, they have formed their own vibrant communities of worship. Furthermore, as the sociologist Grace Davie points out (85), they 'see themselves as missionaries in a secular continent'.

Passionate Love

In chapters 4 and 5 I treated the topic of sexual love at some length. So at this point I wish merely to look briefly at the way it was interpreted in ancient Greece. The Greek goddess of passionate love is Aphrodite and there is also the male love-god Eros. Anybody who has the experience of falling in love will understand why the Greeks would associate this kind of love with the gods. There is something overpowering and ecstatic – almost divine – about the experience.

When one reads the words of any of hundreds of popular love-songs, they may seem utterly banal and syrupy; yet lines such as 'all day long I seem to walk on air' do put words on the experience of being passionately in love. In the Song of Songs the Christian Bible gives us a vividly sensuous, even erotic, love poem. But the ambivalence with which Christians down the ages have regarded this book of the Bible is a good indication of our failure to integrate the experience of passionate love into our version of the Christian worldview.

How can we overcome this serious inadequacy in the way the gospel has been integrated into human life? It is obvious that once again the solution must lie in taking the incarnation more seriously. We must recognise that the body of Jesus was not made of marble but was one which could experience passionate love. This will help us to be more at ease with our own bodies and with sexual attraction and the experience of falling in love.

The God of War

Is there any relationship between the god of war and the Christian God? It is obvious that Ares, the ancient Greek god of war, cannot easily be subsumed into the transcendent Judeo-Christian God. Yet it is clear that there is a kind of 'enthusiasm' for war which sometimes takes over certain people. The mere fact that a person is a Christian, or that Christianity has been present within a particular culture for centuries, does not make one immune to the danger of being 'taken over' by a warlike spirit. The clear lesson of history, including the recent history of the war against Iraq, is that a frenzy for war can become the ruling power in a person's life – or in the life of a whole nation.

It has frequently happened that Christians, when taken over by such a war-frenzy, have turned the Christian God into an idol. They have assumed that God is on their side and is *their* God rather than the transcendent God who loves all peoples and has a particular care for the powerless. Some obvious instances are the way in which God was 'claimed' by the Spanish *conquistadores*, by the white South African apartheid government, and more recently by several of the top people in the present government of the USA.

The Old Testament provides some basis for this distortion. There is one strand in it where God is considered to be the God of the Jewish people in a privileged sense – and, at times, in a quite exclusive way. Furthermore, some of the psalms seem almost to envisage Yahweh as a war-god. So it is important to note that in general the progress in the Old Testament was away from this exclusive and warlike approach and towards an understanding of God as the God of all peoples, rather than just of the Jews. And, as we see very clearly in the Acts of the Apostles and the Epistles of St Paul, there is no doubt at all that the Christian God 'shows no partiality' towards one people over against another (cf. Acts 10:34-5). So it is vitally important that we who aim to be true to the Christian revelation should strongly oppose any tendency in ourselves or in our political leaders to claim, explicitly or implicitly, a kind of 'ownership' of God. In this way we will be defending the truly transcendent nature of God and correcting a serious distortion in the process of inculturating the gospel.

Healing

In each of the several cultures which I have experienced, healing is enormously important in the lives of most people. Indeed it is almost certain that there are or will be times in the lives of all of us when our major concern will be healing for ourselves or somebody dear to us. A very large part of traditional religion has to do with healing – and this applies not only to primal religions such as African Traditional Religions but also to the kind of traditional Christianity practised in the Ireland in which I grew up. Even still, in most parts of the Western world, one of the few times when one can be pretty sure of an overflow congregation in the local church is when somebody known as a healer is invited to lead a healing religious service there.

Up to about a hundred years ago traditional healers played a major role in Irish society. There were bone-setters, and herbalists, and individuals such as the seventh son of a seventh son, who practised a more spiritual or mysterious type of healing. In general these traditional forms of healing fitted quite comfortably into the Christian culture of the time.

In more recent times, with the rapid advancement and spread of modern scientific medicine, these traditional types of healing have been marginalised. They are practised only on the fringes of modern society, that is, in the areas which are seen as 'traditional' or even 'backward'. Furthermore, with the spread of the more rational post-Vatican II theology, the practice of spiritual healing has been pushed out to the margins of Christian spirituality. Those who practise it may still recite some prayers but they get very little encouragement from church authorities.

It is true that Lourdes, Knock, and Fatima are places of pilgrimage where many people come to find healing. But even there it seems that healing tends to be categorised under the general heading of 'miracles' rather than seen as a normal everyday aspect of our religion. So I think we are not doing a good job in integrating healing into people's everyday experience of being a Christian.

We can contrast this with the place of healing in ancient

Greek society. The medical practitioners of that society were people who were dedicated to continuing the work of the semi-divine figure of Asklepios (also spelt Asclepius). So, when one of them undertook the task of healing a sick or troubled person, both doctor and patient had a sense that something sacred was taking place. They believed they were invoking a divine power and felt that they had moved into the sphere of the divine.

For them, there was none of the sharp distinction we tend to make between 'normal' healing and miraculous healing – and this is still the case for primal peoples today. Furthermore, for them there was little or no basis for making the distinctions we make between bodily healing, healing of psychiatric illnesses, and healing from spiritual ailments. They were all aspects of the work of the divine or quasi-divine healing energy that was 'channelled' by Asklepios.

I am not suggesting that we try to return to that primal way of experiencing life. To do so would be an abandonment of our more scientific understanding of the causes and cures of sicknesses of various kinds. But should we not offer Christian affirmation and encouragement for a more integral conception of healing – including its spiritual aspect? In this way we could help people to re-discover and name the deeply spiritual dimension of healing. It could then become a normal part of Christian spirituality, as it was in the very early church. This whole sphere of healing is a very special gateway which leads us into the presence of God in our lives. Christian spirituality today should allow us to share the experience which the followers of Jesus had when he exercised his healing powers – and when they learned how to follow him in doing so.

On the topic of healing a valuable contribution has been made by Dr Michael Kearney (2000: 35-8) who points out that already in the Greek world there were two approaches to healing – Hippocratic medicine, which was more 'scientific' in the modern sense, and the more holistic Asklepian approach. He proposes an integration of modern scientific medicine with the holistic 'Asklepian' model of healing.

The Muses

An important role was played by the muses in the life of the ancient Greeks. It was the muses who inspired the poets, artists, and dramatists whose work commemorated, and celebrated the people's history – and who gave a quasi-sacred character to the deep experiences of their lives. I think a great opportunity for evangelisation was missed when the Christian faith was permeating the culture of Western countries. It would have been possible at that time to emphasise the inspiring power of the Holy Spirit and to see poets, dramatists, and artists of all kinds as privileged channels of the Spirit. But I do not see any evidence that this was done to any notable extent – even during the many centuries when the popes and the bishops were the main patrons of art. Presumably these churchmen were keenly aware of the faults and sins of many of the artists; and it may not have occurred to them that such 'sinners' could nevertheless be special instruments of the Spirit. Or perhaps this was just one more instance of the general lack of awareness of the extent and variety of the work of the Spirit in people's lives.

Whatever the explanation for the failure to attribute artistic inspiration to the Holy Spirit, the consequence was a widening of the gap between human endeavour and creativity on the one hand and Christian spirituality on the other. This may not have mattered so much in the Middle Ages when most of the art was explicitly religious. But the consequences are more evident in our modern world, where only a tiny proportion of art focuses on overtly religious themes. Nowadays, the whole realm of art, poetry, and imaginative creativity is given very little prominence in the Western Christian vision of life; for Christianity is now articulated mainly in terms of truths to be believed and moral rules to be obeyed.

It is true that at the present time we have a small but significant amount of fine religious art, architecture, and poetry. But the fact remains that the whole sphere of art and poetry seems to be experienced as too chaotic and anarchic to fit comfortably into mainstream Christian spirituality. This is a great loss. Why should we not follow the lead given by the well-known Irish poet Brendan Kennelly (1995) who did not hesitate to attribute his poetic inspiration to the Holy Spirit?

Divination and Oracles

A vitally important aspect of life for the Greeks (as well as for other people practising a primal form of religion) was divination. The oracle of Delphi (associated with the god Apollo) was just the most famous of the many oracles consulted by people to find guidance in their lives. Once again a wonderful opportunity was missed when Christians attempted to inculturate their beliefs and values into the local cultures. It would have been so easy to emphasise the role of the Holy Spirit as the utterly trustworthy source of practical wisdom and guidance for people's lives. And if church leaders did so, they would have been following the pattern of the very early church.

Unfortunately, however, this aspect of the life of the first Christians was almost completely neglected and forgotten in the later church. As Frederick Crowe (311) remarks, for the past nineteen centuries there has been 'a sort of suppression of the religious experience that fills the New Testament'. This experience, he says, is one where people looked for and received 'direct guidance' from the Holy Spirit, rather than just the merely 'negative assistance' that theologians would allow the Spirit to exercise at ecumenical councils.

I can only presume that the church authorities, the priests, and the theologians did not trust so-called 'ordinary people' – or perhaps they did not trust the Spirit – and so they failed to encourage people to consult the Spirit and ask for guidance in prayer. When Christians needed guidance they were encouraged to turn, not to the Spirit, but to the clergy; and when clergy needed guidance they turned to higher church authorities or to theological 'experts'. This gave a great deal of power to clergy, to Rome, and to theologians. And it gave security to those who relied on them for guidance.

The church is now paying a high price for this cult of power and security. For theologians now have little credibility; people no longer accept unquestioningly the guidance of priests; and the rigid control which church authorities exercised in the past can no longer be maintained. As a result, people have been left with a hunger for spiritual guidance. No wonder, then, that so many people have turned to astrology and a whole variety of other New Age practices in an attempt to assuage this spiritual hunger.

What might be involved in evangelisation and inculturation in this sphere of life? That is an issue which hasn't been given much prominence in Western Catholicism. The question is how to help people to have a vivid sense in their everyday working and social lives of the active inspiration and guidance of the Holy Spirit. The movement of Charismatic Renewal could have been a very effective instrument in this regard, for it put a good deal of emphasis on the guidance of the Spirit. But the opportunity seems to have been missed. I suspect that this was because those 'charismatics' who put most emphasis on the guiding role of the Spirit were, for the most part, the very ones who adopted a quite authoritarian and patriarchal model of governance – one which left little room for personal guidance by those who were not in a leadership role.

There is an important exception to what I have been saying about the inadequacy of contemporary Christian spirituality. It is the rediscovery and development of what St Ignatius Loyola had in mind when he worked out his theology of discernment. As understood today this is a highly sophisticated process in which Christians explore their affectivity or feelings in order to seek guidance from the Holy Spirit. (I have described this in more detail in Chapter 1.) Unfortunately, only a small minority of Christians have even heard of this process. My hope is that more church leaders and educators will come to know and practise it themselves and encourage others to use it in their daily lives.

I venture now to refer again to another way of seeking guidance from the Spirit – one to which I have devoted a lot of time and energy over the past seven years, and which I referred to in Chapter 1 above. During these years I have facilitated a large number of specialised spiritual workshops or retreats in which the specific focus is to get in touch with spiritual energy and inspiration. In these workshop-retreats the participants seek for a wisdom which comes from within, in the belief that the Spirit is at work in the depths of our spirit.

Having worked at some depth with perhaps 1,500 people in these retreats and workshops I have no doubt at all that a lot of people have a real spiritual hunger for this kind of experience. Some of these 'searchers' are committed Christians while others have little or no time any more for the church as they have experienced it. It only occurs to a very small proportion of these people that what they are searching for is the inspiration and guidance of the Holy Spirit. For the reality is that they heard little or nothing of the Spirit in their religious education. Very few of them even heard the basic Christian truth that the Spirit speaks to our spirit, guides us, comforts us, inspires us, challenges us, and prays in us. However, they are engaged in a genuine spiritual search and as a Christian I believe that the Holy Spirit is the source of that search and also its goal. When running these workshops and retreats, it is for me a matter of practical pastoral strategy whether or not I mention the Holy Spirit explicitly. For, in my opinion, it is a matter of secondary importance whether the Holy Spirit is named explicitly – since the Spirit is quite used to working anonymously and blowing where it will.

I must add that in my experience the particular spiritual hunger to which I am referring – primarily a sense of deep need for guidance in everyday life – is not at all so evident among priests. I think it is only in these dark times that we priests are beginning to question our assumption that we already had most of the spiritual answers that we need – and that our people need. There is, however, a relatively small but growing number of priests who are now willing to take time to engage in this kind of spiritual search, alongside other 'searchers'.

Reason

I have been looking at several areas of life which were associated with divinities by the Greeks, and which I think have, in varying degrees, been left out of the Christian world vision. I want now to refer to a sphere of human life which seems to me to have been given *too much* prominence in present-day Western Christianity. This is the sphere of the rational.

The Greeks had two divinities which were associated with being reasonable. There was the goddess Athena who was linked to practical wisdom, to being able to cope with situations of danger or crisis, and to prudent action in everyday life. On the other hand, there was Apollo who is to some extent connected with intellectual knowledge (though he is mainly associated with divination more than with reason). He is the god of higher knowledge who throws light on situations and brings calmness to a disordered world. Whereas Athena came close to people in giving them practical guidance, Apollo was seen as maintaining a certain distance from people, throwing light like the sun from afar; this is symbolised by his shooting arrows at people rather than touching them.

In looking at the role of reason among the ancient Greeks it is important also to take account of their great philosophical tradition. Of course, Greek philosophy developed several centuries later than Greek religion. But belief in the gods still persisted during the time of the great philosophers, Socrates, Plato, and Aristotle, who developed the power of reason to such a high degree.

Our present Christian worldview is one which is quite comfortable with reason, both in its practical aspects and in its more speculative form. So it would seem that the process of evangelisation/inculturation has been very successful in this regard. But I would like to argue that there is a serious inadequacy even here. This does not arise because the spheres of practical and intellectual reason are ignored or neglected in our present-day Christianity. It comes rather because, in neglecting the less rational spheres of life, we give undue importance to the rational sphere.

We find it hard to associate God with the 'madness' of falling in love or of a wild celebration – and so we are inclined to associate God too much with being reasonable.

The consequence of this imbalance, this one-sided emphasis on the rational, is that our conception of God has become diminished and 'thinned down'. I suspect that one major reason why many people seldom think of God is because for them God has been reduced to being the essence of reasonableness – and that seems rather dull and unattractive. Furthermore, many people in today's world are inclined to assume that they themselves are extremely reasonable, and so it doesn't occur to them that they need a God whose main characteristic is reasonableness!

'The Boss'

Finally I come to Zeus, the supreme god of the Greeks – or at least the one who was supreme among the Olympian sky-gods (as distinct from the earlier pantheon of earth-gods who continued to exist alongside the sky-gods and partly in opposition to them). Zeus can be seen as 'the boss' of the Greek gods. I am deliberately using this slang word 'boss' because the supremacy of Zeus was much closer to that of 'the boss' in a factory than to the supremacy of the Judeo-Christian God. When 'the boss' is absent or distracted, people can 'get away with' doing things which he would disapprove of if he knew about them. If he discovers that they have been 'cheating' in this way he is likely to punish them; and that is how we see Zeus behaving in the writings of Homer.

Furthermore, people take it for granted that 'the boss' will do things in his own way. His decisions may be arbitrary rather than reasonable. That too is how Zeus sometimes appears in the literature of the ancient Greeks. He comes across as one who exercises power and does not care much what mere humans think of his decisions and actions.

A Serious Mistake

I think the greatest failure of the evangelisation/inculturation which took place in the Western world is that, to a considerable

extent, our Christian God has simply taken over the position of
Zeus. What this means in practice was that for many people –
including many preachers and teachers – God was experienced
as 'the boss'. This 'boss' was often experienced as judgemental
and harsh. But at the root of the misconception was the notion
that God is arbitrary, even at times to a point of cruelty, imposing the divine will relentlessly and with little care for human
concerns or weaknesses. Of course people were frequently told
that God is loving, or even that God is love. But for much of the
time they could not experience this divine love; indeed some
people never experienced God as loving.

I suggest that in many cases when people heard that God is
loving, the effect was not to enrich their understanding of God
but rather to diminish their understanding of love. This may
help to explain how many nominally good Christian parents,
teachers, or priests could invoke their Christian faith to justify
the coldness, callousness, and cruelty of the way they treated
people.

An Unfinished Project

I have been suggesting that many important spheres of life were
left quite marginal in the Christian spirituality and worldview
which has been dominant in the Western world. Furthermore, in
the Christianity which we inherited, the transcendent God was
very largely reduced to playing the role of Zeus, 'the boss' –
modified with a strong element of reason as 'carried' by the two
divinities Athena and Apollo and by the philosophers.

The challenge of evangelisation/inculturation for us today is
to ensure that this diminished and distorted notion of God is
replaced by the transcendent God of the Jewish scriptures as
re-interpreted by Jesus and the New Testament. The loving
providence of this Christian God extends to the smallest details
of our lives. God's extraordinary love is the reason why God
sent – and continues to send – the Holy Spirit to animate the
whole of creation and to guide us on every step of our journey.
Furthermore, this excess of love impelled God to share our
human condition by sending Jesus to be one of us.

Conclusion

I have been giving a brief account of the differences between the religious experience of the ancient Greeks and the spirituality which is implicit in present-day Western Christianity. What emerges are some tentative pastoral suggestions, which can be related to the three persons of the Blessed Trinity.

I believe that our emphasis on the transcendence of God has been unduly one-sided. And so, I suggest that we need, firstly, to enrich our conception and our experience of the prodigal Abba God, by finding the Creator immanent in every aspect of the work of creation, and above all in our relationship with nature.

Secondly, we need to take the incarnation far more seriously. We need to accept that Jesus has shared fully in all the deepest experiences of our lives as human. We need to take seriously the fact that, in living out a fully human life, Jesus reveals his God and our God. The God whom Jesus reveals is Abba, the Provident One who cares for all the hairs on our heads, the forgiving Father who longs for our prodigal return, the one who always hears and answers our prayers, the One who can turn the defeat and shame of the cross into victory and new life.

Thirdly, we need to open ourselves to have a living experience of the Holy Spirit. This is the One who blows where it will and so is not confined by our rules or confined to our religion; the One who pours the love of God into our hearts moment by moment; the One who teaches us to pray and who prays in us in movements of the spirit which are too deep for words; and – not to be forgotten – the One who inspires us and who offers us continual guidance in our everyday activities and decisions. If we open ourselves to this guidance, then the heart of our spirituality becomes not a project of 'getting our act together' and taking control of our lives but much more a matter of listening and responding moment by moment to the inspirations of the Spirit.

To sum up: I believe that we need a God who is transcendent, rather than some scaled-down God who is too closely identified with any particular limited aspect of human experience. But I also believe that the only way in which we can hold on to the experience and understanding of such a fully *transcendent* God over the long haul is by balancing it with an experience and understanding of this same God as also *immanent*, a God who is intimately present and involved in every facet of our lives. That is the God revealed by Jesus and in Jesus. That is also the God whom the Spirit is constantly inviting us to allow into every moment of our lives. In chapter 1, I tried to spell out in some more detail what is involved in living out a Christian spirituality as a personal relationship with each of the three persons of the Trinity. In chapters 10, 11, and 12, I want to focus attention on how the church can become a more effective 'carrier' of such a Christian spirituality.

CHAPTER 10

Pastoral Priorities

Our call and our desire as followers of Jesus, led by the Holy Spirit, is to share in the work of Jesus in proclaiming and living out the good news which was the heart of his mission and purpose in life. In this chapter I intend to look at how we Christians can do this more effectively. The first stage is to spell out as clearly and simply as possible what *is* this good news of Jesus.

Good News
Humans live in different cultures, and these cultures develop and change as we move through history. For this reason the good news can never be fully expressed in one definitive and unchanging set of words. In each culture and at each new stage of history we have to find new ways of articulating the central elements of the Christian faith. There will be different emphases and different images, taking account of the way people think and feel, and responding to the crucial questions and issues that concern people in each particular culture and at each particular time. That does not mean that we abandon the older formulas, such as the Nicene Creed; but these have to be understood in the light of the background against which they were formulated.

I suggest that at the present time in the Western or westernised world, much of the central aspects of the good news can be summed up in four basic propositions, which I see as a partial summary for our time of the message of the gospel:

1. Our lives are not governed by chance, or by blind fate, or by malevolent powers, but by a loving Providence. This is a personal providence which Jesus called 'Abba'. This personal God loves each of us personally; and God's concern reaches

to every detail of our lives, since Jesus assures us: 'the very hairs of your head are all numbered' (Lk 12:7).

2. The Holy Spirit is God's active loving presence in our lives, guiding us, consoling us, challenging us, and praying within us.

3. We can get some understanding of the mystery of how Jesus brought us salvation by taking seriously the title he gave himself, namely, 'The Human One'; it indicates that he calls us to be fully human and reveals that the way to be in communion with God is by living a fully human life.

4. Jesus teaches that all humanity is one family, that each member of that family is equally a child of God, whether we be 'Jew or Greek, slave or free, male or female' (Gal 3:38; cf. Col 3:11); so each person's dignity and fundamental rights are to be respected; and all are to work together for the welfare of humanity and of the earth.

When we commit ourselves to following Jesus in proclaiming the good news, we are undertaking to live by these truths, to make them the touchstone by which we interpret everything that happens to us, and the standard by which we judge how we ought to act. Furthermore, we are undertaking to share these truths with others, while at the same time listening to *their* fundamental truths, and engaging in a mutually respectful dialogue with them. This dialogue is essential, because it is not sufficient to just 'live and let live', leaving everybody their own opinion, on the ground that there is really no way of reaching objective truth. We are committed not just to living out these truths in a purely private world but to applying them to the world we share with others – re-shaping our world in the light of these truths, insofar as we can do so while not simply imposing our beliefs on others.

In practice, of course, this cannot be done simply by *telling* people these truths but by a whole variety of practical *actions*. These activities can be summed up under three general headings, namely, liberation, reconciliation-healing, and community-building. I do not intend here to examine what is involved in these activities because I have written extensively elsewhere about them (see Dorr 2000). What I want to focus on here is the four truths I have just listed, because they express the meaning and purpose which underlies our commitment to liberation, reconciliation-healing, and community-building. They are the verbal aspect of the good news, which express in words the meaning and purpose of our Christian actions.

A brief word about the technical theological terms 'evangelisation' and 'inculturation'. 'Evangelisation' can be understood in a somewhat restricted sense where it refers to the verbal aspect of the good news – proclaiming the Christian message, in dialogue with others. 'Evangelisation' can also be understood in a much broader sense where it includes also the practical actions of liberation, reconciliation-healing, and community-building – once again in dialogue with others. Inculturation is working to ensure that Christian truths and values – in dialogue with the values already operating in the society – shape the various cultures and the social structures in which people live out their everyday lives. Evangelisation is inseparable from inculturation because we cannot proclaim and witness to Christian truths and values in the abstract; it always has to be done for real people and therefore in relation to some particular culture.

Co-Responsibility

Having tried to clarify what we are called to do as Christians, I now move on to look at how best we can do it. The first thing to say is that while each one of us needs to be involved in this work, we do not do it as isolated individuals. It is above all the work of the church, that is, of the Christian community as a whole. 'Ordinary' Christians are not being faithful to the gospel if they do not expect – and even demand – that Church ministers and authorities consult with them and enable them to be actively involved in shaping and carrying out the mission of the church. So a particular responsibility falls on those who have roles as leaders and ministers in the church.

If church authorities and ministers wish to be faithful to the gospel, they have to engage in serious dialogue with the rest of the Christian community. Their duty is to ensure that there is active participation in decision-making and co-responsibility in carrying out the decisions. This is not just a matter of clergy 'allowing' lay people to be involved. It is the right and duty of all Christians to be co-responsible, since we all share in the three-fold ministry of Christ as priest, as prophet, and as leader.

A Time of Crisis

The present is a time of crisis for the church in the Western world. This comes about through a convergence of several different problems. The one that is receiving the most media coverage at present is the scandal arising from the revelation of very many cases of sex-abuse by priests and members of religious orders, and the extremely inadequate way in which many of these cases were handled by church authorities. Behind that issue lie more fundamental issues. Many people are now questioning our present model of priesthood. The number of men training to be priests in the Western world has dropped very significantly; and there are serious questions to be asked about the type and quality of many of those who are applying. The Vatican has taken a very strong line on the questions of women priests and married priests. Many Catholics in the Western world are becoming more and more disappointed and disenchanted with the Vatican and with church authorities at the local level. There is an alarming drop in the numbers of practising Catholics in Ireland and a less dramatic drop in some other Western countries.

This crisis can become an opportunity for a major renewal of the church if we are prepared to cast a cold eye on our present pastoral priorities and our structures. In the present chapter and the following one, I want to look closely at our pastoral policies, while postponing to chapter 12 the question of the structures of the church. I will consider first of all our overall approach and then go on to make some suggestions about some particular pastoral strategies. In all of the comments and suggestions I make I shall keep in mind the fundamental task I mentioned at the beginning of the previous chapter – to help ourselves and others to foster spiritual experiences and to help people interpret them in the light of Christian revelation. That phrase 'in the light of Christian revelation' may have seemed rather vague when I used it there; but I hope that the four basic Christian truths I mentioned at the beginning of the present chapter will clarify the meaning of the phrase.

Our Overall Priority

I believe that this is a good time for the church in the Western world to change its overall priority – to change from an attitude of maintenance and servicing of our present practising communities, to what I would call 'frontier work'. By the phrase 'frontier work' I mean work on and beyond the regular boundaries of the church. This calls for a 'reaching out attitude' and an eagerness to enter what seem like foreign 'worlds', especially the world of the 'unchurched' and the world of those who are engaged in a spiritual search. The change of priorities also requires a broadened understanding of the mission of the church, and a new strategy of evangelisation. So in some respects this 'frontier work' has more in common with the work of the 'foreign missionary' than it has with the 'pastoral mission' of ministering to an existing Christian community.

Until recently it was generally assumed that the task of the priest and the religious educator was to minister to the present members of our congregation and as far as possible to expand the membership of the church. Within the past generation, however, theologians have come to distinguish more clearly between the church and the reign (or kingdom) of God. On this basis it is helpful to make a distinction between two different aspects of the church's mission:

–   The first focuses primarily on serving, nourishing, expanding, and developing the church both as a community and in its institutional aspects;

–   The second is primarily concerned not immediately about the church but about promoting certain key Christian values

– living these values, giving witness to them, and promoting
them in society.

Both of these are important. Each contributes to the other and
there is a considerable overlap between the two. The key point is
that the church is not an end in itself; it is called to serve the
world. Its purpose is to help people live out and share their
Christian values.

In the past, the first of these aspects was the main focus of
training in the seminaries and institutes of religious education.
Priests and religious educators were trained mainly for pastoral
ministry within the church rather than for the task of evangelisation or re-evangelisation on its frontiers. I suspect that most of
them feel that they haven't really been prepared very well for
what I am calling frontier work. So they don't feel as at home
with it as they do in ministering to the Catholic congregation.

But the situation in which we find ourselves today requires
that church leaders and ministers now give at least as much
emphasis to the second aspect as to the first. This does not at all
mean that they should play down their ministry to the present
practising members of the church. But it does mean helping the
whole Christian community to shift focus, to look outwards and
be more keenly aware of its mission to the wider world. We
follow Jesus by living by, and promoting, the values he stood for
in his life and death. As Christians we are called to continue the
mission of Jesus. So it is not enough for ministers and church
authorities to look after the practising Christians. The whole
Christian community must reach out and play an active part in
transforming society and saving the earth itself.

Sometimes more 'churchy' Christians are inclined to believe
that those who devote themselves to, say, the promotion of
human rights or reconciliation or ecological work, are doing
something that is not really evangelisation, not preaching the
good news of Jesus Christ. That is because this kind of work is
not specifically Christian, since secular humanists are involved
in it as well. So it is important to insist that those engaged in promoting and witnessing to these values of the reign of God can be

just as authentically sharing the good news as those instructing converts or preparing people for the sacraments. Christian values such as justice, reconciliation, and contemplation are worthwhile in themselves, even apart from any immediate connection they may have with the church. We become engaged in them in order to follow Jesus and to share in his mission to the world, and not merely as a means to achieve the end of building up the church.

Not All-or-Nothing

The Christian way of life is not an all-or-nothing package. The clear-cut boundaries of the institutional church are a very poor guide to determining who is living the Christian way of life and to what extent they are doing so. It is easy to count the numbers who are registered church members. But it is far more difficult to measure the numbers of people who, whatever their circumstances, live their lives partly or wholly on the basis of the Christian vision.

In order to illustrate what I mean let me note that in Japan and India there are many non-Christians who went through the Christian school system. There are clear indications that many of them were profoundly affected by their contact with Christianity. Many of them partly accept the truth of the Christian story, and find spiritual nourishment in Christian rituals and symbols. There are many more who have been deeply influenced by the Christian value-system and have largely adopted it, even though they do not call themselves Christians. Furthermore, there are many people who scarcely ever think of themselves as influenced by Christianity but who live according to values which are fundamental to the Christian vision and value system.

The situation of many people in the Western world (though not so much in the USA) has some similarities and some differences from that of Asian non-Christians who were educated in Christian schools. A significant number of people now engage in what the sociologist Grace Davie calls 'vicarious religion' (see Davie 19, 44, 138-9). What this means is that most of the time they allow others to practise Christianity on their behalf. They have gone a stage further than being non-practising Christians. They may not be baptised and are more or less 'unchurched'. However, they have not rejected Christianity, and in fact they generally see it as 'a good thing'. Then on special occasions, such as the time of national tragedy, or of a personal bereavement or a family celebration, they may attend a church service. It is probably not unfair to see them as 'passengers'. As Davie sees it, they allow the more active believers to 'carry' them and to hold the meaning of Christianity which the 'passengers' connect with when they are deeply touched by some spiritual experience.

In addition to these 'vicarious believers' or 'passengers' there is an ever-growing number of people who could be called 'spiritual searchers'. These are by no means passive, and they are not at all willing to have others carry a spiritual vision of life on their behalf. Quite the contrary. They are generally people who feel a deep need for a purpose and meaning in their lives, people who often have profound spiritual experiences of one kind or another. Many of them were brought up as Christians, or in some other organised religion, but they have become dissatisfied with the simplistic version of religion they were given as children. Consequently, a lot of them have more or less abandoned all formal religious practice – not because of indifference but more because of a healthy disillusionment. They may be disenchanted with the way they see Christianity being lived out around them, but they have not given up the search for a system of belief and spiritual practice which affirms and nourishes their own spiritual experiences.

Finally, there is a number of confirmed secular humanists. Generally, these are people who have little interest in religious beliefs or spiritual practices. But they are likely to have strong ethical principles and a commitment to making the world a better place.

I suggest that we in the Christian community should reach out to both the passive 'passengers', and the more active 'spiritual searchers' – and also to the secular humanists in so far as they are willing to engage with us. The kind of reaching out I have in mind here is not primarily one of trying to get them to become active members of the church – that is a long way down the road and may never happen. We reach out to them by joining with them in promoting and witnessing to certain key truths and values, which we believe to be central to Christianity; and also by allowing and inviting them to share with us the body of rich Christian symbols which may speak to their minds and touch their hearts. In this way we are promoting the 'reign of God'.

We should not feel that doing so is some kind of second-best activity, justified only on the ground that it prepares the way for 'real' evangelisation. Our work is authentic evangelisation in so far as it promotes values which we can name as Christian; or in so far as it enables people to be moved by authentically spiritual symbols. And this is true whether or not those who live by or are influenced by these values or symbols name them as Christian. What I am saying is not some far-out theology of 'anonymous Christianity'. It is simply an implication of our belief that the task of sharing the good news is not merely a matter of developing the church but also of promoting the reign of God.

A Wider Sphere of Influence

The success of this kind of frontier work cannot be measured in terms of the extent to which the official church is established. We may think of a wide penumbra around the church, a zone where Christian values, truths, rituals, and symbols have an impact on the lives of people who are not church members. A very important part of evangelisation – and especially of re-evangelisation – is to widen and deepen this sphere of influence since it is a key element in the embodying of the faith in the local culture and society. Ideally, of course, the founding, nourishing, and expanding of the church should go hand in hand with this broader and more intangible work of enabling the faith to permeate society, and each of these two aspects of the work of mission should support the other.

When Pope John Paul talks about re-evangelisation he is asking us to help people get in touch with the fundamental Christian values which lie buried deep in the culture of countries which in the past were deeply influenced by the Christian faith – values which are no longer very alive or effective for most of the population. His aim is to re-animate elements in the apparently secularised culture which have deep roots in the Christian heritage (e.g. *Redemptoris Missio* 33). This will lead to the transformation of society in the light of the gospel.

We can go further: we must recognise that in the Western world today there are many good people whose cultural roots are not Christian – for instance, most of the immigrants and asylum-seekers from Asian countries. We know that the Spirit of God blows where it will, and touches people who have had little or no contact with Christianity. Part of our task as evangelisers is to recognise, affirm, and help to nourish the good values which animate the lives of these people. In doing so we are carrying out our mission by promoting the reign of God.

If we do succeed in touching in to people's explicitly or implicitly Christian values and bringing these values to life in our society today, it does not necessarily mean that our Catholic Church will suddenly be thronged with new converts or newly practising Christians. The more likely outcome is that certain key values of Christianity will begin to seem more relevant to the non-church-going people. This may eventually lead to a trickle of new converts but the main benefit will be in expanding and deepening what I have been calling the penumbra of the church. This is a vital part of re-evangelisation – ensuring that these 'reign of God values' find a place in the apparently secul-arised world in which many of our people are living. By helping people to appreciate and live by these values we are ministering to the 'unchurched' people all around us.

What I'm saying may seem rather abstract and unreal so I want now to try to apply it to the situation of the church in the Western world today. I shall consider the topic under three headings, namely: spiritual leadership, moral leadership, and

community-building and solidarity values. In the remainder of
this chapter I shall examine the first two of these topics and in
the next chapter I shall give a more extended treatment of the
issue of community-building, linking it with questions about the
celebration of the eucharist.

Spiritual Leadership
The best way I can communicate what I mean by spiritual leadership is by recalling the kind of stature which Cardinal Hume
had in Britain and even in the wider world. People really listened
when he spoke – and even by his presence he somehow reminded
people of God. I think Rowen Williams, the new Archbishop of
Canterbury, has already become that kind of spiritual leader (at
least for a considerable number of people) and may in future
have a much higher profile in that regard. In the wider world, of
course, several outstanding Christians gave an example of
spiritual leadership in our time. One thinks of Dorothy Day,
Martin Luther King, John XXIII, Helder Camara, Mother Teresa
of Calcutta, John Paul II, Jean Vanier, and Oscar Romero.

All church authorities, priests, ministers, and religious educators are called in their own way to this kind of spiritual leadership. When people meet us they should in some degree be put in
touch with God – not by any false piety on our part but by a kind
of transparency and integrity, and by a type of contemplative
presence. Furthermore, our task is to ensure that the Christian
community – our local church – is also a model of spiritual leadership. This means that unchurched people will have a sense that
we are not just a cosy club or a moral pressure group pushing a
particular agenda but a beacon of light, of hope, of inner peace
and serenity.

How can we attain this role of giving spiritual leadership by
our lives and our words? I think there are two aspects. The first
and by far the most important is by being ourselves spiritual
people, by nourishing our own spirit and spirituality so that
when we speak about spiritual matters – or about everyday issues
– there's a depth to what we say. It is hard to put words on this,

but it has something to do with a simplicity which goes to the
heart of things. In this way we can show in our own lives, our
words, and our very presence something of God's care, compassion, gentleness, and vulnerability. And central to this is that it is
not just a matter of pastoral strategy – we don't do this in order
to give spiritual leadership. Spiritual leadership is a by-product
of this kind of spiritual integrity. It would be bordering on
hypocrisy if we were to set out to develop these attitudes with
the sole purpose of giving spiritual leadership.

The second crucial element in giving spiritual leadership is to
take very seriously the words and example of Jesus: 'The one
who wishes to be great ... and to be the leader among you must
become as one who serves' (Lk 22:26), and: 'If I your Lord and
Teacher has washed your feet, you also ought to wash one
another's feet' (Jn 13:14). There are many liturgical and non-
liturgical services which church authorities and ministers can
offer in order to build up the community sense in our neigh-
bourhoods. I shall spell this out in more detail in the next chapter.

However, it is important to note a danger here. What Jesus
asks of us is 'to be as one who serves'. He does not simply ask
that we provide a service. In providing various services, ministers of the church could unconsciously use them to emphasise
their role or their own importance. From my own experience as
a church minister, I know that we need to tread a very narrow
line between being unduly prominent and holding back unduly.
I don't think we can find this balance on our own. We need
friends who can give us 'feedback' and challenge us. We also
need some form of supervision where we can reflect on our style
and our motivation.

Moral Leadership
In regard to giving moral leadership, we can no longer assume
that people will pay much heed to condemnations by church
spokespersons. At the present time, the role of moral leadership
must be built up again almost from scratch. Indeed in some respects
we may have to begin from a long way behind the starting line,

because people have got used to clergymen 'sounding off' on various moral issues; they expect it and pay little heed.

Furthermore, we need to take seriously that we now live in a very pluralist world. If our voice is to be heard on moral issues we must try as far as possible to act jointly with others – leaders of the other churches, of the other religions, and also agencies such as Amnesty International, emigrants' support groups, Greenpeace, Friends of the Earth, and those who oppose cruelty to animals.

We have to be quite judicious in deciding which issues to emphasise. We cannot expect to be heard if we 'sound off' on everything we find unsatisfactory in our society. On the other hand, we have to avoid the danger of our church and ourselves becoming entirely focused on just a single agenda. If we give almost all our attention to one agenda item such as the anti-abortion campaign, we and our church are in danger of losing our role of giving overall moral leadership. So there has to be a delicate balance. On the one hand, we must not compromise on our basic belief in the right to life. But, on the other hand, we must also pay due attention to other urgent moral issues.

CHAPTER 11

Community-Building and Eucharist

In this chapter I want to make some comments and suggestions about the role of the church and its ministers in creating a sense of solidarity in the wider community. It is above all at the time of a local tragedy that the sense of community solidarity comes to the fore. Think of what happens after the tragic death of a young member of the community. When the funeral takes place, the church is quite likely to be full, mostly with people who would never otherwise think of coming to church.

This indicates first of all that both church-going and non-church-going people feel themselves to be part of one local community. But it also suggests that even the non-church-goers have a sense that the local church building is a place where this sense of community and solidarity can find expression. In this kind of situation one of the tasks of the priest or minister is to acknowledge and nourish that sense of community solidarity. If possible the minister should deepen it by reminding people that God welcomes and calls all of us into community with each other – and that God wants us to carry that solidarity and care for each other over into our everyday life. In this way we can help to counteract the privatisation of grief and mourning. We can also resist the breakdown of a sense of community solidarity which is typical of our Western society.

It is not a question of using this occasion to moralise or 'get at' people, but simply of letting them be in touch with the beautiful rituals and symbols which the church provides to 'carry' and deepen their sense of community and solidarity. We need to remember that one of the means of sharing the good news is the use of Christian rituals and symbols. So the very act

COMMUNITY-BUILDING AND EUCHARIST

of coming to church and of sharing in the ritual on these special occasions is already a nourishment of the spark of faith which lies half buried in people; and it enables them to express that faith in symbol and ritual if not in words.

I've spelled this out in relation to funerals but much the same applies to weddings. Here it may be helpful to stress that love is a very special gift which comes from God. Another point to stress is that the wedding creates solidarity and friendship between two families and extended families. Leading on from that, the priest or minister could ask family members and friends for a commitment to give support and practical help to the young couple – for instance to undertake to do baby-sitting for them occasionally.

Who Shares in the Eucharist?
In the previous chapter I identified three groups of people who are more or less outside the boundaries of the church as an organisation. They are the people whom I called 'passengers', those whom I named as 'spiritual searchers', and the secular humanists. I suggested that we in the church can reach out to them not only by promoting and witnessing to certain key Christian truths and values, but also by allowing and inviting those who are interested to share with us the body of rich Christian symbols which may speak to their minds and touch their hearts. I want now to focus attention on the most powerful of all our Christian symbols and rituals, namely, the eucharist.

On the occasion of funerals or weddings, many of those who are present are not practising Christians. Quite probably some of them are not even fully believing Christians, but are 'passengers', who allow the faith to be 'vicariously' carried for them by others, in the sense I described earlier. We do not – and could not – prevent these people from sharing in the Eucharist. I believe that this should be seen not just as a practical necessity but as a positive opportunity to awaken their dormant faith. Others in the congregation are likely to fit more into the category which I have called 'spiritual searchers'. But the question arises, how could any church authority decide who is a 'passenger' and who is a 'searcher'? So, in practice, such people are not excluded either. But why should we want to forbid them from taking part – even if we could conveniently do so? Once again, I believe that this is a wonderful opportunity for them to receive spiritual nourishment by sharing in this symbolic high-point of Christian faith.

The document on the church issued by Vatican II says that the eucharist is 'the source and summit of the whole Christian life' (*LG* 11). Largely on the basis of this statement, the Catholic Church authorities have drawn the conclusion that the eucharist in the Catholic Church may be shared only by those who accept the full Catholic faith, except in exceptional cases (*Directory for the Application of Principles and Norms on Ecumenism*, No 160). Furthermore, Catholics are forbidden to receive communion in Protestant or Anglican Churches. These rules have caused a great deal of tension between the Catholic Church and other Christian churches. They have also given rise to an exceptional amount of pain to many individuals – for instance, the partners in mixed marriages. Not just pain, but anger too. A lot of people are quite scandalised both by the rules and more particularly by the very rigid way in which they have been interpreted and applied by some regional and local church authorities – for instance, in the document *One Bread One Body* issued in 1998 by the Bishops of Britain and Ireland.

Many people have serious problems of conscience about obeying these strict rules. As a result, they have been left with mixed feelings of disloyalty, defiance, and guilt. What is perhaps even worse, the delicate process of the education of their consciences gets seriously distorted: some are likely to be pushed towards moral conformism (accepting the rules blindly), while others are likely to move towards moral individualism (ignoring church rules whenever it suits them). All this puts a very heavy onus of responsibility on church leaders to ensure as far as possible that any rules they propose do not put a burden on the consciences of their people. We recall the strong condemnation by Jesus of religious leaders who lay heavy burdens on those subject to their authority (Mt 23: 4).

There has been a lot of theological discussion about whether the Catholic rule, or its application, could be broadened to allow Catholics to share eucharist with other Christians. The usual arguments for and against such a change turn on the question of the degree to which these other Christians share our Catholic faith. I want to put forward a case for a much more radical approach, namely, that we should be far more open and welcoming and should not try to scrutinise to what extent those who share in the eucharist share our faith. My argument in favour of this change is quite different from the usual one, because it does not depend at all on an evaluation of the official eucharistic teaching of other Christian churches.

The Banquet

My starting-point is not the doctrinal formulations of different churches but the gospels. The parable of the banquet gives us a solid scriptural basis for an enriched theology of eucharist and communion. In this story told by Jesus, the man providing the feast insisted on bringing in the most unlikely guests, including the poor, the blind, and the lame from the highways and the hedgerows (Lk 14: 21-23). It is quite likely that some of those who were gathered in from the roadside for that feast had at first little or no sense of communion with the people who invited them to come, and perhaps not much idea of what was going on. But it was not their responsibility (at first) to define the purpose of the whole event or to generate a sense of communion. That was the task of the one who had organised the feast and his close friends. This inner group could then extend their community to embrace those who had been invited in from outside.

Why not use this as an image of the eucharist? At this Christian banquet, just as at the feast in Jesus' story, it is essential that there be a core-group who hold in place the full meaning of what is taking place. In a kind of penumbra around this inner group of firm believers there is room for others who may be less sure of one or other aspect of the meaning. And, outside them, there may be others who do not see themselves as sharing the same faith but come as respectful visitors, attracted by the sacredness of the event, willing to share in it to whatever extent their own faith allows. Finally, there may be on-lookers who come in idle curiosity, or who just happen to be present; their lack of faith and lack of communion with the group means that for them there is no eucharist, no holy communion.

'Visitors'

There is no reason to think that the full meaning of the Catholic eucharist would be eroded, or challenged, or dishonoured by the presence of 'visitors' from other churches, or of people who are less explicit or less sure of their faith in the mystery that is being celebrated – provided the central core-group do not water down their own faith in what the eucharist really means. Quite the contrary, in fact. The eucharistic faith of the core-group of believers would in this case take on a missionary character, inviting others to a firmer or more explicit faith and to a deeper communion with God, with Jesus, and with each other. Such eucharistic openness would in fact be a particularly good example of the process I mentioned earlier, namely, inviting people on the margins of the church to 'share with us the rich Christian symbols which may speak to their minds and touch their hearts'.

The eucharist represents the summit and source of Christian life; and it represents the unity of the Christian community of believers. That is true, but it may not be the whole truth. Should we not add two further equally important points? Firstly, the eucharist can also be a very powerful instrument of reconciliation, a means of promoting and deepening the unity of believers. And, secondly, it can be a very effective means by which the Christian community fulfills its missionary task of drawing others to have an experience of God and to be touched by the Spirit of Jesus.

The meaning of the eucharist is carried, not primarily in the doctrinal statements of any of the churches, but in the minds of those who take part in it – and in their hearts as well. To illustrate what I mean by this, I recall an occasion some years ago when I was one of an Irish group taking part in a dialogue in Geneva with Third World theologians. Feeling that the atmosphere was rather coldly academic, our small group began to celebrate eucharist together in a somewhat informal way in the evenings. Some other participants heard what was happening and began to join us, because they too felt the need for spiritual nourishment.

On the final night of the conference, a party was arranged for all the participants. We decided that if the atmosphere was right we would offer to celebrate a eucharist with the whole group. As it worked out, however, the opportunity to do so did not arise; so we let it go. Late that night, while sitting in a circle and drinking wine with the other forty participants, I felt hungry. I got a roll of bread and broke off some to eat. I passed on the rest of the roll to my neighbour who took some and then passed on the remainder to her neighbour, and so it went round the circle. As the bread was passed from hand to hand, an extraordinary thing happened: it began to dawn on us that we were eating bread and drinking wine at a celebration – and we began to recall the words of Jesus 'do it in memory of me'. The eucharistic meaning began to emerge into what had previously been a purely secular event.

Nothing was said; but one could see the whole atmosphere changing as the deep spiritual meaning came home to people and their faces lit up. Some of those present were too engrossed in conversation to notice what was happening. But it was evident that for many of the group this sharing had become eucharistic. Was it a eucharist in the full sense? I hesitate to say 'yes', but I am not sure that I can say 'no'. In any case, this event made me realise that the meaning of eucharist is carried in our minds rather than in some creedal formula.

My suggestion is that we should not use any doctrinal church statements as a standard for judging who is allowed to share in our eucharist. It may not be appropriate for Catholic church leaders to take on the onus of trying to weigh up the authenticity of the faith or goodwill of those who come as 'visitors' to share in our eucharist. I am not for a moment suggesting that the issue of the worthiness of the visitor is irrelevant. But is it our task to make the judgement? The parable of the wedding-feast seems to indicate that we may invite all and sundry to come and share the feast, and then leave it to God to judge whose wedding-garment is adequate.

A Matter of Prudence

In support of my suggestion, I note that no serious Catholic leader or theologian would now claim that it is wrong to allow Christians from other churches, or non-Christians, to be actively and prayerfully present at a Catholic eucharist (apart from receiving communion). Once we have conceded that such joint worship is a good thing, it is a matter not of doctrine or principle but rather of 'prudential wisdom' where we draw the line about the extent of such participation. Even at present that line is drawn in different places in different countries (and this re-inforces my contention that the issue is one of prudence rather than of principle).

What needs to be protected at all costs, is the fundamental meaning of the eucharist. At each and every Catholic eucharist this central meaning must be 'held' by an inner core of believers who are the church at this moment, because they are in commu-nion with each other in faith, in hope, and in love. If we were ever to reach a point where there was no such inner core of believers, then the meaning of the eucharist would have been eroded. That is 'the bottom line' – it is what ensures that the basic meaning is not lost or watered down. However, as I suggested above, the participation of 'visitors' does not necessarily erode or dishonour the meaning of our Catholic eucharist – provided the inner core group do not allow the presence of 'guests' to dilute their belief. I believe that, far from eroding their faith, the involvement of such 'visitors' may in fact enrich it enormously by giving it a vibrant missionary dimension.

A second key point to note is that the connection between the unity of the church and sharing in the eucharist is not a strictly logical one. It belongs rather to the symbolic sphere: the fact that we receive communion together symbolises the unity of Christians. But in fact, our unity within the Catholic Church is a very imperfect and fragile one – and this is true both at the global level and at the local level. Whenever the eucharist is celebrated, all of us who take part are people wounded by sin and prone to further sin. Apart from the exceptional case of excommunication, we are not forbidden to share in the mystery even though our communion with each other is far from perfect.

Furthermore, there is no rule which excludes those Catholics whose personal understanding of the meaning of the eucharist may seem vague or woolly. Why then should we exclude those whose church or religion may profess on their behalf an understanding of eucharist which is different (to a greater or lesser extent) from our official teaching? The non-Catholic individuals who come to our eucharist may have only a quite vague idea of the official eucharistic doctrine of their own church. Perhaps the parable of the banquet invites us to realise that the more crucial issue is the degree to which they and we open ourselves *here and now* to experience a real communion with each other, and the extent to which we together seek to deepen that communion. (I note here that James Mackey, using a different line of argument, comes to a similar conclusion – that eucharist should be open to all who wish to take part in it; see Mackey 2003a: 38).

The task of the authorities of the different churches, with the active participation of practising Christians, is to explore together how best to reflect both the fundamental unity of faith of Christians from different Christian traditions, and our lack of full institutional unity. What weight do we give to this lack of full institutional unity *vis-à-vis* the fact that there is grave disunity even within the Catholic Church? And how should we bear witness in our eucharist to our commitment to going out 'to the highways and the hedgerows' to invite the unlikely people to God's banquet? How can our eucharist make visible not just the present (imperfect) unity of Christians but also the fact that it is 'a pledge of future glory' including the glory of the perfect unity which Christ promised? Prudential issues of this kind cannot really be resolved by the imposition of a set of rules based on a theology which maintains that the eucharist can normally be shared only by those who share the full Catholic faith.

The Eucharist as Evoking Faith

I have been suggesting that we adopt in principle a far more open approach to the sharing of communion with other Christians, with 'passengers', and with 'spiritual searchers'. In putting forward this view I am relying on my experience as a missionary priest. I have found that among the most missionary actions I have undertaken have been occasional celebrations of the eucharist. I have in mind occasions when I took part in workshops or retreats, in which we sought guidance and direction in life, and at times had a palpable sense of the presence of the Spirit. Some of the participants were practising Christians and others were much more 'on the margins' – or perhaps outside them.

Quite frequently, the high point of these events was a eucharist in which the participants celebrated the gifts of God and came to appreciate the gracious and mysterious purposes of God at work in their own lives and in the wider world. In these situations it would have been quite invidious to have quizzed these people beforehand about the niceties of their eucharistic belief. And in any case I have no doubt that, if they had been asked, many of them would have given a quite different – and much more 'faith-full' – answer at the end of the whole event than they would have given beforehand. In other words, the celebration itself had brought to life a faith that had been somewhat dormant or latent.

In our Western world today there are many 'searchers' who may no longer have a strong affiliation to any institutional church but who are hungry for spiritual nourishment. The eucharist can provide that nourishment in full measure – provided it is celebrated in a truly 'meaningful' way. Let me spell out some elements which can help to make the celebration 'meaningful' for such people:

— Those who take part should really experience communion with each other; they should not normally be surrounded by strangers who neither know nor care who they are.

— As they partake in this great act of faith, they should not be left as mere onlookers in a purely passive role; they should have some opportunity to share their own faith, or their search for faith, at least to some minimal degree, depending on the size of the gathering.

— The scriptural Word of God should not only be spoken and heard but should also be related to their everyday world.

— The participants in this eucharist should be nourished not just by words and 'the Word', but also by the ritual aspects of the celebration, that is, the gestures and posture of the participants, and the manner in which they carry out the sharing of the Living Bread and the Cup of Salvation, as well as the music, the sacred vessels, the candles, the incense, and beautifully decorated surroundings. All of these should be experienced as having a venerable weight of tradition behind them; not, however, as lifeless relics of the past but as channels of divine grace and energy which bring here-and-now nourishment to the spirits of those who take part.

— The priest who wishes to preside over such a celebration needs to let go of the older clerical 'baggage' and learn to work in a very facilitative and participative style, again depending on the size of the group.

The easiest way to celebrate a 'meaningful' eucharist of this kind is with a smallish group of committed people. It is more difficult to achieve the same effect with a very large gathering. It requires careful planning and considerable liturgical skill and sensitivity; but the reward is worth the effort. When the eucharist is celebrated 'meaningfully' in either a large or a small group it becomes a very powerful means of sharing the good news. Not only does it nourish the faith of the inner core of firm believers but it also re-kindles the sparks of faith in the embers of those whose faith has almost died, and it may evoke faith in the hearts of those who up to then may have seen themselves as 'outsiders'.

Inter-Communion

I return now to the issue of the way forward in relation to inter-church communion. At present, the Catholic rule allows other Christians to receive communion at a Catholic eucharist 'in exceptional cases'. This provides a basis for local church author-ities to adopt a more lenient and flexible interpretation of the rule. There are various people who exist in an 'exceptional' situ-ation (for instance, people in a mixed marriage); so the word 'exceptional' need not necessarily be taken to mean 'rare'.

In the longer term (but not too long!) there is need for a seri-ous re-think of the whole theology of worshipping together and of communion. We have a precedent for such a re-think. After all it is not so long ago that our rules forbade Catholics to be present in Protestant or Anglican churches for any religious services. But, after Vatican II, theologians and church leaders abandoned the theology which said that this amounted to sinful participation in false worship.

Having conceded the general principle that it is acceptable for Catholics and non-Catholic to worship together, it seems to be a prudential matter how far we go in sharing in the worship of other churches as well as in allowing other Christians to share in ours. So it is not unthinkable that a fresh look at what the eucharist is about could lead to a change in the rules. None of us who live in the present painful situation can afford to imagine that we have a monopoly of the truth. After all, the original con-text of the parable of the banquet was one where all of us Gentiles were 'the outsiders' invited in from the highways and the hedgerows. Now that we see ourselves as 'the insiders', we should follow the example of Jesus in making the Banquet open to all.

Special Occasions

It would be a mistake to think of eucharistic sharing as the only way of creating and nurturing community. Other special occasions will arise naturally, or can be created by us; and our task is to make the most of each situation. I am making a number of suggestions, in the hope that some of them might strike a chord, or spark off some creative ideas, in those who read this book. Here are some possibilities:

— A special Earth Day where people are nourished by the spiritual resonance we find in nature. Such a day could provide an opportunity for reaching out beyond the boundaries of the Catholic community to others who are deeply committed to environmental issues. We could find common ground here with 'New Age' people. In sharing with them there can be mutual enrichment of our spirituality.

— A special children's event for Christmas with a Christmas angel, a pageant with the baby Jesus carried in by a child, and St Nicholas to give gifts – and to receive gifts for poor children at home or abroad.

— A welcoming of 'Wise People' from the East at Epiphany time, where people of Eastern religions would be welcomed and there could be some joint prayer and some dialogue between Christians and people of Eastern religions.

— A mid-summer or mid-winter solstice event, which again would draw in the environmental people and the 'New Age' people.

— A celebration of the Spirit around Pentecost; this could include some practical way of recognising that the Spirit blows freely among non-Christians as well as within the church.

— A celebration for Mothers' Day and Fathers' Day.

— A celebration for lovers on Valentine's Day; perhaps one for young lovers and one for older lovers.

— A healing celebration on St Blaise's feast and/or on other special occasions. (Based on my experience both in Ireland and in Africa, I'm inclined to think that healing services are one of the most effective ways to reach out to people.)

— A practical course on meditation, perhaps using the John Main approach, or Christian Yoga; this could answer the deep need which many people feel for a meditative or contemplative space in their lives.
— Festivals of various kinds designed specifically for young people.
— A service for people whose sexual orientation is gay or lesbian.
— Outings, expeditions, pilgrimages of all kinds. Some would be of the more traditional Christian kind, while others might be less overtly religious but with a spiritual-ecological dimension, for instance, hill-walking with a meditative space at the beginning and end or in the middle.
— A service for people with disabilities and their families and friends.
— Some events which would involve reaching out to people who are on the margins e.g. homeless people or 'druggies'.
— A service for those who have experienced miscarriage or stillbirth.
— Services for the families and friends of those who have committed suicide.
— A special service for people suffering from depression.
— Services for widows and widowers, and for divorced people.
— A Peace and Reconciliation service which might focus partly on local tensions (e.g. with immigrants or asylum seekers) and partly on world issues (e.g. Iraq, or Israel/Palestine).

Some aspects of the various events or celebrations I have listed would be overtly religious and could be carried out in the church. Priests have a recognised expertise and credibility in organising and presiding over explicitly religious celebrations and services carried out in our church buildings. But they must resist the temptation to take the easy option by just putting on a 'special Mass' for some of the occasions or situations I have listed above.

There is need also to think of ways of building up the community which are not church rituals or services. Obvious examples are Sports Clubs, Scouts, Music Societies, and dozens of similar activities. In the past it was fairly common for a local clergyman to be the patron or the chairman of many of these organisations. I'm inclined to think that it may be just as well that that day is gone. I think if priests or other church ministers get involved in any of these activities it should be out of personal interest; and if they play a big role it has to be on their own merits and not simply because they are clergy.

Common Interests
In making the above suggestions I have been thinking mainly of how to reach out to non-practising or 'unchurched' people (the 'passengers') and to the 'spiritual searchers'. But all this is relevant for practising Catholics as well. We need to take seriously the fact that local communities are no longer the only basis for church congregations. Increasingly in modern society – especially in urban areas – Christian congregations are composed on a 'voluntaristic' basis, that is, on the basis of common interests. Many people are willing to travel quite long distances to take part in a service which meets their particular needs or interests.

In fact Pete Ward, who has acted as the Archbishop of Canterbury's advisor on youth ministry, suggests that we adopt the model of 'a consumer oriented church'. This would mean that, instead of the traditional routine church services we would offer 'a varied and changing diet of worship, prayer, study and activity'. Each service would be designed to suit a particular group of 'consumers' or constituents (Ward 2002: 89). So, rather than thinking in terms of 'members' we would aim to attract people who would participate actively and become involved. Instead of seeking to build a sense of community on the basis of the local congregation, we would build on the basis of 'common cause, similar desires' (92). My own view is that we should still work to build up a sense of community at the local level, but we should also design services for particular 'interest groups'.

Let me summarise the main thrust of what I've been saying in the previous chapter and this one. In the present situation we are called to the missionary task of re-evangelisation. To a large extent this involves helping to bring to life in society certain fundamental Christians values which are latent in the culture. I've suggested three aspects of this work, namely, giving spiritual leadership, giving moral leadership, and nourishing the sense of community and solidarity. In attempting these daunting tasks one of the most effective means we have available to us is the use of rituals and church services. These can be tailored to respond to what Paulo Freire would call generative issues in society – that is, issues which respond to the deep unmet needs and hungers of the community or significant sectors of the community. If the church comes to be experienced by the mass of the people as responding to these needs, then its credibility is enhanced and it will nourish community solidarity. In this way it can recover its role as a beacon of hope in regard to spiritual issues and a beacon of guidance on moral issues.

CHAPTER 12

A Way Forward: Structural Changes

In the previous chapters I suggested a variety of ways in which the Catholic Church can become a more effective 'carrier' of spirituality for members of the church and for others who are on its fringes or even quite unconnected with it. But it must be admitted that there is need for more than just a change in policies and approaches. At present, people who look to the church for guidance in relation to spirituality find themselves frustrated, and at times scandalised, by structural aspects and practices in the church which give a counter-witness to some of the key values of a Christian spirituality. So, structural changes are an urgent necessity if the church is to play an effective role in promoting and modelling a spirituality which is authentic.

In this final chapter I want to address the issue of structural change in the Catholic Church – not in any detail but by giving a broad outline of some of the more obvious and more pressing elements which need to be changed. The three most striking aspects of the structural problems in the Catholic Church in our time are clericalism, a dysfunctional style of exercising authority, and excessive centralisation. I propose to look at each of these issues in turn.

1. Clericalism

Reviewing the way the present Catholic conception of priesthood developed over the centuries, James Mackey (2003a: 17-9) insists that it was only after two or three generations that the notion of a specialised priesthood emerged in the church. It was adopted because it was in accord with the thought categories of the cultures into which Christianity was spreading. Mackey considers that to have been the right way – provided 'this select and especially trained group were simply serving the whole people ...'. He goes on:

> But it would only be and remain true to Jesus and to what he did, as long as this special priesthood was understood, not as a cultic priesthood which stood as intermediary between a priestly people and God, but as a function or office that convened the priestly people for their priestly eucharistic function and led them in the exercise of that function. (19)

Sadly, it must be acknowledged that the way the priesthood developed was not at all in accord with the mind of Jesus and the style of the very early church. What emerged over the centuries, and what we still have today, is a privileged clerical caste.

Unlike most caste systems, and also unlike the priesthood of the Hebrew Bible, membership of the clerical cast is not based on birth. However, it is a very closed system, for there are rigid entry-qualifications. First of all, half of the human race is excluded because women are not eligible for membership. Secondly, entry to priesthood in the Western church is restricted, except in very rare circumstances, to those men who agree to commit themselves to live celibately. Thirdly, they must go through many years of training-and-formation; during this time, those who seriously challenge the system or its theological underpinning are 'filtered out', either by their own decision, or by the authorities. Fourthly, diocesan priests enter a tightly-structured system where advancement, and even survival, depend on conformity to the existing rules and practices. Fifthly, only priests can become bishops; and only bishops can become pope. Furthermore, one has to be a bishop to have a senior role at management level in the Vatican and even relatively low-level administrative roles there are held to a very large extent by priests.

It is worthwhile looking at how clericalism developed over many centuries. Within the community of Christians, there is one quite small group whose primary work concerns the institutional aspect of the church – for instance, organising and leading the celebration of sacraments, and the training of various church ministers. The bishops and priests, whose full-time role is concerned with

these institutional tasks, amount to less than 1% of the membership of the church. But because of their role, all the power in the
church tended to gravitate to them.

Over the past few centuries, up to quite recently, practically all
theologians were drawn from the ranks of the clergy. It is understandable – but quite unfortunate – that their theological interests
revolved mainly around their own relatively small sphere of
Christian activity. In their articulation of the nature and mission of
the church, they gave undue emphasis to its institutional aspect.

Clericalism arises from the concentration of ecclesiastical and
theological power in the hands of clergy. It is a situation in which
the area of clerical control has expanded to a point where it seems
to most people that 'the church' equals 'the institutional or clerical church'. Consequently the activity of lay Christians appears
to be marginal to what the church is about; and if it becomes significant it is almost immediately taken under clerical control.

This should not have happened. Think of how things might
have developed if there had been less emphasis on the inner organisational aspects of the church and more on its relationships
with the wider world of politics, economics, arts, culture, and
education. In that case much of the decision-making and power
could have stayed with lay Christians deeply involved in these
different sectors of society.

In recent centuries many outstanding lay Christians have
made an enormous contribution in bringing gospel values into
the spheres of education, health, and social welfare. I am thinking here of people like Nano Nagle, Louise de Marillac, Catherine
Macauley, Mary Ward, Edmund Rice, Mary McKillup, Margaret
Aylward, and Mary Martin. As soon as the work of these lay
people became significant, church authorities set out to control
their work, both at diocesan level (cf. Twomey 2003: 97) and
through the Vatican Congregation for Religious. Initiatives that
should have remained 'charismatic' and free-flowing were
taken into the sphere of the institutional church. There, the
Spirit-inspired initiatives of these lay people were subject to the
clergy who control that sphere. In this way the clericalisation of

the church has expanded to a point where it is quite damaging, because it inhibits lay Christians in following the call of the Holy Spirit.

In the church today there is a further reason why clericalism is problematic. It is that a great lot of ministerial and even priestly activity is in fact being done by people who are not ordained clerics. Nowadays we all know and admire many non-ordained people who are engaged in the kind of work that was carried out almost exclusively by priests a generation ago. For instance, my own spiritual director is a lay woman. I consider that the work she does for me and for others is in some respects truly priestly work. But women are not allowed to be ordained and neither are married people. So the distortion that is clericalism is made even worse by the fact that the clerical sphere is not co-terminus with the area of priestly or ministerial activity. It is obvious, then, that an essential step in the way forward must be the dismantling of clericalist structures and the clericalist mentality.

Contrast with the Gospel

The concentration of power in the hands of clerics was a more or less inevitable consequence of the fact that church leaders failed to take seriously the model of authority proposed by Jesus:

> You know that the rulers of the Gentiles lord it over them, and their great ones are tyrants over them. It will not be so among you: but whoever wishes to be great among you must be your servant, and whoever wishes to be first among you must be your slave. (Mt 20:25-7)

> If I your Lord and Teacher have washed your feet, you also ought to wash one another's feet. For I have set you an example, that you also should do as I have done to you. (Jn 13:14-6)

Instead of following these very clear guidelines, church leaders adopted the authoritarian styles of governance which prevailed in the secular world. They borrowed elements from the Roman Empire, and from the kings and nobles of the Middle Ages; they even took on aspects of the notion of the 'divine right of kings' which was prevalent about 300 years ago. They took over the grandiose titles of the secular world ('my lord', 'your eminence')

– and their status symbols, their pomp, and their luxurious style of life. What is worse, they held on to most of these trappings of power long after most secular authorities had given them up. We now have a situation where church authorities reject calls for a more collaborative style of governance, on the grounds that 'the church is not a democracy', while failing to acknowledge that much of the present model of authority in the church is an outdated borrowing from secular rulers of the past.

The concentration of power in the hands of clergy has continued even after Vatican II. The Council rightly insisted that the task of bringing Christian values into the social and political world belongs to lay people rather than to clergy. This injunction has been repeated again and again by church authorities. But the main practical conclusion they have drawn from it seems to be that priests should not get into politics – and particularly not into left-wing political activity. The far more important issue of working out guidelines for how lay people should inculturate the gospel in secular society has been left underdeveloped.

Think of the voluminous rules and instructions which have come from Rome about how the liturgy should be celebrated. Contrast that with the severe shortage of practical guidance on ecological issues, or issues about worker's participation in management, or on what would constitute an abuse of human rights when dealing with people suspected of terrorism. In the moral sphere, the only area where detailed guidance is offered to lay people is the one area in which clergy have least experience, namely, sexual relationships.

I am not suggesting that church authorities, relying on scripture and tradition, could lay down detailed guidelines on a whole range of moral and political issues. In fact I suggested, in an earlier chapter, that we need the guidance of the Holy Spirit in facing current ethical issues. But this guidance should normally be mediated through human agencies. Certain ethical issues are so pressing that church leaders have a duty to convene meetings of experts in different relevant fields – and to give full weight to their conclusions and recommendations. However, this would not work properly if the church authorities hand-picked experts whose views were in full accord with the views of the authorities. A good model might be the expanded commission on birth-control set up by Pope Paul VI in the 1960s. Of course, the subsequent rejection by the pope of the majority report and conclusions of that commission shows how impossible it is to move to a new model of authority while still clinging on to the old one.

2. The Exercise of Authority

The clerical-hierarchical church is dysfunctional in its exercise of authority at three distinct levels. Firstly, the laity in a parish have scarcely any real power *vis-à-vis* the priest(s). This disparity in power between priest and people in a parish has a solid legal base in the church's code of canon law. For the church law gives the parish council and the financial council only advisory power. In some parts of the world, genuine efforts have been made to minimise this disparity and ensure that there is participation in decision-making; but, even then, it is only rarely that there is a genuinely collaborative exercise of power at the parish level.

In other places, the reality 'on the ground' is far worse than the legal position: priests simply refuse to set up, or make use of, parish councils and committees. I know parishes where the priests do all the readings at the celebration of the eucharist. They say they cannot persuade any of the lay parishioners to take on this task. The most credible explanation for this reluctance of the laity is that the priests in these situations are looking for 'functionaries' rather than 'ministers'. In other words, they are willing to share the duties or 'jobs to be done' but are not willing to allow the parishioners any real 'say' in the running of the parish. The result is that the laity have no real sense of 'ownership' of the whole project and therefore are not willing to invest energy in it.

A second location where the structures of the church are dysfunctional is in the relationship between diocesan priests and their bishop. It is dangerous to generalise, since there are some dioceses where there is a good spirit of collaboration. But in many places the relationship is poor; and even where there are good relationships there may not be much active collaboration.

In the past, many bishops felt it was part of their role to be rather distant from their priests and to exercise authority unilaterally, for instance, in making clerical appointments. In some countries there has been a change to a more modern style. But, unfortunately, the new model of authority tends to be a bureaucratic one, at times marked by some of the worst features of the business world.

In some situations (and quite frequently in the young churches) the bishop has almost all the power and is the legal owner of almost all church property. In other situations priests in parishes have gained a lot of power *vis-à-vis* their bishop. Indeed the bishop may well be left rather powerless when it comes to making the radical changes that are required. It is very seldom that there is a truly effective collaborative sharing of power between bishop and priests and among the priests themselves.

There is a third location where the current structures of the Catholic Church are dysfunctional. This is in the relationship between bishops and Rome. One of the important contributions of Vatican II was its emphasis on what was called 'collegiality'. This means that all the bishops, together with the pope, have a collective responsibility for the church all over the world. Unfortunately the Roman authorities have made no serious attempt to put appropriate structures and consultative processes in place to make this a practical reality. They have not developed a collaborative model for sharing power between the Vatican and the bishops as a whole, or between Rome and the bishops of a particular country or region.

Quite the contrary, in fact. The Synod of Bishops has been deprived of real authority and independence by a whole series of restrictions imposed by the Vatican. Furthermore, loyalty to Rome was taken as the most important criterion in the selection of bishops. This has resulted in the appointment of many extremely cautious bishops, especially in areas where liberation theology had flourished. In addition to that, there has been a

serious effort to undermine the importance and authority of
National Episcopal Conferences. And, in recent decades, the
Vatican has increasingly taken over more and more of the power
of individual bishops, who have lost much of the autonomy they
used to have. This centralisation of power in Rome has been ac-
celerated by the use of modern means of communication. It is so
much a feature of the church today, that I suggested in an earlier
chapter that it can be seen as a part of the process of globalisation which is typical of our world.

Theology and Authority
One of the areas in which the church today is most dysfunctional
is in relation to theology. Traditionally two kinds of authority
were recognised in the church. Firstly, there was a pastoral type
of authority or leadership exercised by church ministers at every
level. It was concerned with managing the Christian community
and its various services in a way that was effective and fruitful.
But it was not just a managerial type of authority. It involved
also having the final 'say' in resolving disputes about the fundamental meaning of the Christian message. Secondly, there was a
theological authority which was one of expertise. It was exercised by theologians who had devoted much of their lives to
study and reflection on the sources of our faith.

If the church is to be faithful to its mission it is essential that
there be a good balance between these two kinds of authority.
Each needs the other and each must respect the competence of
the other. There is bound to be a certain tension between the
two, since the task of theologians is to push out the boundaries
of knowledge and faith, while church ministers and leaders
have to be more aware of the pastoral implications of new ideas
and approaches. But this is a healthy tension – one which is
mirrored in a lesser degree in the mind and heart of every
Christian.

Over the past 150 years the balance between these two types
of authority has been seriously disturbed in the Catholic
Church. To explain how this took place would require a long
historical study; and one could locate many faults on either side

which contributed to the breakdown of trust between the two sides. My concern here is simply with the resulting situation, which is that in recent years the Vatican has seriously undermined the authority of theologians. It appears that the Roman authorities wish to restrict the role of theologians to that of apologists for the theological views which are acceptable to Rome.

There are many well-known instances of mishandling of theologians by the Vatican. I shall mention just one of them here – that of the Sri Lankan Oblate theologian, Father Tissa Balasuriya. It illustrates how badly the theologian can be treated, but also how the problem can be resolved. The Vatican was unhappy with some of his writings and not satisfied with his response to their criticism. They excommunicated him in 1997. There was widespread strong protest about this harsh treatment. After two years, a meeting was arranged, facilitated by one of his Oblate confrères who is very skilled in this kind of conflict management. The outcome, after much dialogue, was an agreed statement which both sides felt was satisfactory; then the excommunication was lifted.

The point I wish to emphasise is that the problem was resolved through intense dialogue over six days, under the direction of somebody who was trusted by both sides, and who specialises in this kind of work. This is in sharp contrast to the usual Roman practice – one where the theologians feel that their judges are also their accusers, and where they feel very unsafe and at a serious disadvantage. What a pity that the facilitative and dialogical mode of exercising authority is not always practised by Rome. If it were, there would be a lot less tension between the Vatican and theologians of good will.

James Mackey distinguishes between the kind of theology which has its proper location in the academy 'where it can pursue its critical and creative service to the transmitted culture of any society' (2003b: 47); and, on the other hand, what he calls 'seminary theology' which 'is taught, text-book like, to future preachers, ministers and leaders of [the] church' (49). It is a helpful distinction, since ministers and church leaders may not have the interest, or the ability, or the time, to devote themselves to the kind of theological exploration which is the task of the professional theologian.

But it would be a serious mistake to push this distinction very far. For church leaders and preachers need to have some familiarity with what might be called the frontier issues of theology at any given time – and a good deal of empathy with the theologians who are working on these frontiers. (One such frontier at present is the relationship between Christianity and the other religions, including not just the world religions but also primal religion.) Indeed most of the difficulties which theologians are having with church authorities at present spring from the failure of church leaders to keep up to date with recent theological advances; this leads them to rely on theologians of an older school whom they consider to be orthodox.

Intransigence

At the present time the Vatican has taken an extremely 'hard line' on such issues as the ordination of women, birth control, the use of condoms by the marriage partners of people infected with HIV/AIDS, and the whole question of homosexuality. Why is it that the Vatican forbids discussion about these issues? The most fundamental reason seems to be a fear that a change from the norms of the past would undermine the authority of 'tradition' and of church leaders. But the practical effect of this 'hard line' is a much more serious undermining of the credibility of the church authorities. As González Faus (25) points out: 'Authority, wishing to save its credibility, lost it.' On this issue the analysis of James Alison (2003: 78-99) is both enlightening and challenging.

Church leaders should be supporting Christians in their efforts to listen to what the Spirit is saying to them. They should be articulating the spirituality which is emerging from the struggle of the faithful to read the signs of the times. What we have instead is the sad spectacle of the leadership at the highest level of the church being pitted against an emerging consensus of Christians 'on the ground', supported by some open-minded and courageous theologians. The result is that in attempting to work out an appropriate spirituality of sexuality, Christians have largely been deprived of the support of the pope and most of the bishops. They have also been forced to develop a practical spirituality of passive resistance to what many experience as an oppressive use of authority.

There is need for an open and serious dialogue between church authorities and theologians on these and similar issues. The most fundamental requirement is the creation of an atmosphere of openness and trust, instead of the present atmosphere of suspicion and repression. We need a situation where issues can be explored by theologians and other scholars without the threat of being condemned by the Vatican. And we need to find ways of drawing on the immense body of data and of experience which is now available. The dialogue must be inclusive. There is a particular need to take account of the experiences and the thinking of those whose voices have been largely unheeded until now, for instance, women in general, gays and lesbians, young Christians who live in a world where many of their friends practise 're-creational sex', active Christians who practice contraception, as well as Christian women and men who are divorced.

We need also to hear the voice of more 'traditional' Christians who are living alongside those whom the present disciplines leave on the margins. Many church leaders resist change for fear that such change would cause people to lose faith in the church. But this may be just a rationalisation, a refusal to face up to the fact that these leaders' primary concern is a preservation of their own power and privileged role. There are indications that the majority of 'the faithful' are more open to change than are the leaders themselves.

It Could Be Different

Some people may say that one is being unrealistic and 'starry-eyed' in looking for a truly respectful dialogue between church leaders, academic theologians, and the wider Christian community – and for a real sharing of responsibility and authority in parishes, in dioceses, and between Rome and the dioceses all over the world. But it is not at all unrealistic, if those who have leadership roles at all levels are willing to work for a change in the structures. What I find sad and disturbing is the very sharp contrast that now exists between the hierarchically structured church on the one hand and most of the religious congregations on the other. In the years since Vatican II, most religious congregations – especially the international congregations of women – have committed themselves wholeheartedly to a major project of developing collaborative leadership; and they have succeeded to a remarkable extent.

It is now more or less taken for granted in religious orders and congregations that there will be a high level of involvement by almost all the members both in developing policies and in choosing leaders. After a lot of exploration and experimentation – some of which has been difficult and painful – most groups have made two major changes. Firstly, they have adopted a system of team leadership; this means that, in practice, though not strictly in church law, the members of the council are no longer just advisors but really share responsibility for making and implementing policies and decisions. Secondly, most leadership teams are deeply committed to a maximum degree of consultation and participation with the membership as a whole in the on-going governance of the congregation. Furthermore, this model of team leadership and group participation is operative at every level, from the international right down to the local level.

The leadership teams of religious congregations frequently employ skilled facilitators to help them bond together as a team and to help them in their visioning and planning. They also employ facilitators to ensure that they get maximum participation from their members. Furthermore, many, if not most, of the leaders are themselves very familiar with the use of facilitative skills.

All this is in sharp contrast to the situation which prevails in most of the clerical and hierarchical side of the church. Here we still find a 'top down' style of exercising authority. The appointment of bishops by Rome is shrouded in secrecy; and, quite frequently, those who make the appointment take little or no account of opinion 'on the ground'. In the appointment of priests to parishes there is generally a certain amount of prior consultation with the priests concerned. But this seems to be mainly in the interests of good management, and to ensure that there is no trouble, rather than out of a commitment to collaborative leadership; and there is seldom any consultation with the lay members of the parishes.

In quite a number of dioceses, there have been diocesan assemblies in which important issues were identified and suggestions put forward. Both in England and in Scotland there have been national gatherings of representatives from all sections of the Catholic Church, out of which came new energy and hope, as well as many practical proposals. But, in general, this institutional side of the church has a very long way to go in the whole matter of developing a participative and collaborative style of leadership.

Why the difference between the way authority is exercised in the religious congregations and how it operates in the hierarchical-clerical side of the church? I think the 'clerical culture' is a very serious obstacle to change. One element in this 'culture' is a distrust of those who are not part of the 'in group'. Consequently, those who are in positions of authority are reluctant to relinquish their power and privilege. A second reason why things have been so slow to change is that there is no encouragement 'from the top' to do so. There have, of course, been some new church laws which stress the importance of parish councils and committees. But Rome itself has not set an example of collaborative ministry; by and large it has, in recent years, moved in the opposite direction.

Bishops and priests have much to learn from the religious congregations in regard to the exercise of authority. The church could also look judiciously – but critically – at some of the better aspects of how authority is exercised in business organisations. It would also be helpful for them to see how the principle of subsidiarity is applied in the European Union, some matters being left to the national governments and others dealt with centrally; and it is also interesting to see how power is shared out between the Commission, the Council of Ministers, and the European Parliament.

Practical Proposals

What we should look for at present is that the pope would commit himself to exercising his authority collaboratively with a team which would include people from different backgrounds. These could include men and women, priests and lay people and members of religious orders. The team might be made up of, say, a liturgist, a theologian, a management consultant, a sociologist, an expert in world religions, an artist, and a couple of people from pastoral and contemplative backgrounds. Bishops and parish priests could make a similar commitment to work collaboratively with a team – though obviously local teams would not be so 'high-powered'.

If all this worked out, then at some future time an interesting theological question might arise: does the role of the bishop nec-essarily have to be exercised by just one individual or could it be exercised by a team of people? And then, of course, the same question might arise about the papacy. Could the role of the pope be exercised by a team? Needless to say this is just a specul-ative question at present. But it would arise as a real theological issue once there was visible evidence that team leadership works well in practice.

It is quite obvious that there is always the danger of abuse of power when a great lot of authority is given to one man for the rest of his working life. So, one change which would to help this new style of participatory and team leadership to work would be that bishops should no longer be appointed for life. Why not have them appointed for a ten-year period? After that time they should move out of leadership of the diocese. And of course the same should apply to the pope. Ten-year appointments could help the dream of a collegial and participatory church become a reality within a generation.

Disengagement from the Church?

The upshot of the very wide gap between the ethos of the

hierarchical-diocesan aspect of the church and the ethos which now prevails in most religious congregations is that many members of the congregations are distancing themselves from the institutional church. One of their main reasons for doing so is their anger and disillusionment about the way authority is exercised by official church leaders; they find it non-participative, and at times repressive. (Another common reason for this distancing is the failure of church leaders to take a sufficiently radical stance on issues of justice and poverty.)

This tendency towards disengagement from the clerical church is being supported by serious theological arguments. Diarmuid O'Murchu says:

> ... we have been conformed and domesticated to a degree that has all but usurped our potential for liminal witness and prophetic contestation (1998: 134)

So he offers support to those who consider the option of adopting a non-canonical status (61); in other words they would no longer seek to be recognised by the official church authorities as a religious congregation.

> There may be ... something deeply prophetic in the desire among increasing numbers of religious to adopt a non-canonical status. In many cases it is neither a comfortable nor irresponsible cop-out, but a positive and courageous option to safeguard and foster what is truly unique about the vowed life ... (1998: 138-9)

The fundamental point is that the primary commitment of those who have taken vows is not to the institutional church but to the values of the new reign of God (e.g. 1998: 135 and 74).

This desire to dissociate oneself from the institutional church is evident not just in members of religious congregations but even more so among lay Christians, particularly in the Western world. Of course, when lay people disengage, few people even notice what has taken place. So the witness value of their action is minimal. Church authorities are more likely to interpret their action as a loss of faith or of interest, rather than as a prophetic act of protest. Furthermore, those who distance themselves from

the church generally do not even have the support of a community or group in doing so. Without such support there is a real
danger that they will drift away not just from the church but
from the gospel values which inspired them to distance themselves from the church.

My reason for writing this book is because I too have a strong
sense of disenchantment in relation to the way authority is being
exercised by many of the leaders of the institutional church.
However, I am a member of a missionary society of priests
rather than of a religious congregation. As an ordained minister
of the church I am passionately committed to helping the church
to be faithful to the gospel and sensitive to the promptings of the
Spirit in our time. Furthermore, I have learned from the liberation theologians of Latin America that it is not enough to work
for change in the church. One must also *love* the church; and I do
love it, despite my disappointment, irritation, and occasional
outright anger with the Vatican and some of the bishops. For
these reasons, I am hesitant to encourage either lay people or
members of religious congregations to distance themselves from
the church in order to be more true to the values of the reign of
God. I do not think it is necessary or useful to choose between
church and reign of God. We are not normally faced with a
choice of 'either-or'; in most situations I think it is still possible
to opt for 'both-and'.

Distancing oneself from the church is not a very effective
prophetic gesture. If the person who disengages from the institutional church does so as a lay person he or she is labelled as just
one more individual who has joined the ranks of non-practising
Christians. If an individual or a group of vowed religious do so,
they are very likely to be dismissed by church authorities as
'cranks' or malcontents. In fact there are indications that some of
the Vatican authorities no longer take much account of the voice
of vowed religious in the Western world. They have put their
hope on the more compliant religious congregations of the
young churches.

It is better, normally, to stay within the church in working for change. However, it is important to be quite strategic. We should take very seriously the words of the gospel 'let the dead bury their dead' (Mt 8: 22). For me this means not wasting time in speculating about who will be the next pope, or in working for minor changes in out-dated structures. It means living and acting as far as possible in accordance with the values of the reign of God. This involves stretching the rules at times.

Working effectively for change may even mean applying the principle which moralists call *epikeia*. My understanding of this principle is that, where an authority is unwilling to change a grossly unjust or unreasonable law, or rule, or practice, a person is entitled to act on the basis of what would have been a reasonable response by the authority. This is an extraordinarily helpful principle which effectively liberates the Christian from being morally bound by unreasonable laws and unjust authorities.

By recognising this principle of *epikeia*, moralists are saying that what is paramount in the church can never be imperfect human laws or the arbitrary use of authority. For the church, the law of God is superior to every human law and authority. In this regard the church differs radically from the state, where individuals may at times be unfairly bound and restricted by laws which were not designed to cover their situation. In the last analysis, membership of the church is not just a legal reality but is a matter of being in communion with the community of Christian believers.

If we take the principle of *epikeia* seriously, we need never experience a radical conflict between fidelity to the church and fidelity to the values of the reign of God. It is not surprising, then, that church authorities seldom refer to this principle; for it puts a very severe limit to their use of power. Those of us who work for change in the church may have to invoke this principle at times – and perhaps encourage others to do so as well.

Of course, this puts a great onus on one to ensure that one's conscience is not misguided. The principle should be invoked only in exceptional circumstances; and one should normally trust the authorities and give them 'the benefit of the doubt'. But the principle enables one to live in our imperfect church with a fairly good conscience and with a fair amount of spiritual freedom. By working this way within the church, one can contribute to a loosening up of outdated structures and one can gradually widen the 'space' for prophetic witness in the church.

3. Decentralisation

Closely linked to the need to overcome clericalism and the issue of the way authority is exercised, is the need for the church to be far more decentralised than it is at present. Most of the organisational aspects that are required could be carried out at the local or national level. If this sounds unrealistic it is only because we have become used to a very highly centralised model of church, forgetting that this structure developed only in recent centuries.

Why should the church not be structured in a way similar to that of the major religious orders and congregations, where each province has a very high degree of autonomy? The church's central leadership in Rome should get out of administration and focus instead on exercising an animating and monitoring role, such as is exercised by the central leadership of, say, the Dominican Order or the Mercy Sisters. In their case the number of people working at the central level is quite small, because their role is not administrative but primarily one of animation. Within the past few years I have run workshops for the leadership teams of several international congregations of both women and men. In all these cases I was very struck by how well they have learned to define their role as one of animating leadership, while leaving administrative autonomy to their various provinces.

The worldwide church organisation Caritas is another striking example of decentralisation, combined with co-ordination from the centre. Caritas has hundreds of thousands of employees working in various dioceses around the world. Yet Caritas Internationalis, which is its highly efficient international headquarters in Rome, has only 20 or 30 employees. Why should not the Catholic Church be organised along these lines? Would it not be a very good example of the principle of subsidiarity which has been such an important element in the church's social teaching, over the past seventy years? (cf. Dorr 1992: 18, 128, and 353)

This principle of subsidiarity has now become an embarrassment to the Vatican. At the Synod of Bishops in 2001, there were repeated requests, by bishops from many parts of the world, that the principle be taken seriously by Rome. The formal response of Pope John Paul II to these requests came in the post-synodal document *Pastores Gregis* dated 16 October 2003, which stated: 'The concept of subsidiarity has proved ambiguous' (Pope John Paul II 2003: No 56). This response is itself remarkably vague and ambiguous. But the document makes it is clear that the Vatican is unwilling to accept that the principle of subsidiarity is applicable to the church. It insists instead on the concept of 'communion' which it uses as a justification for the present highly centralised approach. González Faus (4-5) is trenchantly critical of this 'distorted' understanding of the word 'communion', describing it as 'a manipulation of communion in favour of power'.

Some church-people might argue that the quite radical application of the principle which I am advocating may be alright for church organisations or religious congregations, but not for the hierarchical church itself. But in fact this approach is used nowadays in every country of the world. There is a National Episcopal Conference in each area where bishops come together to decide on policy issues; and there are various church agencies which are organs of the conference as a whole, dealing with such issues as justice and peace, overseas aid and development, emigrants, and immigrants. But, though the National Conference exercises central leadership and animation, administrative autonomy is left to individual dioceses. As I have already mentioned, some senior Vatican figures have recently sought to play down the importance of these National Episcopal Conferences. Perhaps one reason for this is precisely because they offer an alternative model to the present one where power has become more and more centralised in the hands of Roman officials.

There is a further aspect of the issue of decentralisation

which is well expressed by Enda McDonagh (2003: 62), who
links it closely to putting an end to clericalism. It is that bishops
and priests should 'be chosen ... by the believing community
they are to serve, while confirmed in the unity of the whole
church by local bishops and by the church's traditional symbol
of universal unity, the Bishop of Rome'. It is true that this could
give rise to difficulties. There is a danger that these roles would
become politicised, or that there would be a kind of popularity
contest to see who would become bishop. But the fact is that the
appointment of bishops has already become 'politicised', in the
sense that only those are appointed who are likely to stick closely
to the very rigid and narrow theology and spirituality which
Rome imposes at present. The problem at present is an imbalance of power between the centre and the periphery. It should
not be too difficult to design a system of checks and balances
which would leave more of the decision-making authority at
local and national level, while still leaving an oversight role to
Rome.

The Church as a Movement

I am inclined to go one stage further and suggest that the church
should see itself more as a *movement* than as an *organisation*. This
would make it much more like the early church – and, I think,
more close to the mind of Jesus. What would this involve?
Primarily it would be a change of outlook and mentality. There
would be less emphasis on a legal understanding of membership. When we use the word 'member' we tend to think in terms
of certain rules. Perhaps a more fluid word like 'belonging'
should partly replace the more all-or-nothing concept of being a
'member'.

   If the church saw itself primarily as a movement, it is likely that
it would not burden itself with so much canon law. At present,
canon law provides people with some protection against flagrant
abuses of power by those in authority. But, in fact, even a very
good legal system is a rather inadequate protection, where
power is being abused. There would be far less need for the
safeguards of a complex legal system if we had a really effective

participative style of leadership in the church at every level. I shall give just two examples of areas where it might be helpful to dismantle aspects of the church's heavy legal system.

First, do we really need the legal processes involved in canonisation of saints and beatification? Why should we not just leave it to the body of Christian believers to decide who is a saint – as happened in the first thousand years of the church's existence? This issue was not particularly significant until recently, since the number of canonisations and beatifications each year was quite small, and the decisions of the Vatican about who should be beatified or canonised were fairly closely in line with popular devotion. At that time, the main aspect of these processes which caused raised eyebrows was the sheer cost of getting anybody canonised.

In very recent times, however, a certain 'politicisation' of the whole process has crept in. Take, for instance, the resistance in the Vatican to considering Archbishop Romero for beatification. Does this not indicate a deplorable prejudice against the whole liberationist current in the church? More shocking, however, was the decision to link the beatification of Pope John XXIII with that of Pope Pius IX. There can be no doubt that there was, and is, widespread devotion to John XXIII, and no doubt about his sanctity – or that his brand of sanctity is particularly relevant in the modern world. But I doubt very much whether the same can be said of Pius IX. One does not have to have a very Machiavellian mind to suspect that there was a 'political' motivation behind the linking of these two popes. Apparently Rome was afraid that John XXIII would be seen as the model of the ideal pope, or the ideal Christian. So there had to be a balance. But it is difficult to see how Pius IX can be a model of the right use of authority, or even a model of sanctity, for us today.

A second example: a good case can be made for having the church largely disengage from the legal formalities connected with marriage, leaving that to the State. This does not mean that the church would no longer present and promote the Christian ideal of marriage. The issue is simply whether it should try to enforce that ideal by means of a complex legal system. For many centuries the church did not feel the need to have its own code of laws governing marriage; it simply went along with whatever system was current in the different parts of the world. A few hundred years ago, church authorities felt that the current pastoral difficulties could best be handled by establishing strict legal controls over marriage. But in the present situation it may perhaps be more appropriate for the official church to step back from this legal approach. There may be more suitable and effective ways of promoting the high Christian ideal of marriage than trying to legislate it into existence.

Conclusion

I deliberately held over to this final chapter my more severe criticisms of some aspects of the church which I love. That was because I felt that before making these criticisms it was important to show that things could be different – that an alternative approach is quite realistic, provided a sufficient number of people are willing to make and support the necessary changes. Our church at present is seen as a very authoritarian, patriarchal, clericalist, and over-centralised institution. Church leaders still have a fair amount of spiritual power – especially when they articulate Christian teaching which puts words on what the Spirit has been saying in the hearts of the Christian community, and in the wider human society. They now have a clear choice.

On the one hand, they can cling on to the remaining vestiges of their privileges and spiritual power, while being excessively cautious about admitting mistakes or making changes. If they do so, the official church teaching – and the church leaders themselves – will seem more and more irrelevant to those who are trying to listen to the Spirit and live out a truly Christian spirituality in our time. On the other hand, they can take the radical steps needed to enable the church to be more faithful to the call of Jesus in the present-day world.

If they choose the more courageous course, it will involve a serious and urgent effort to dismantle clericalism and patriarchal attitudes and structures. It will require a decentralising of decision-making, in the interests of respect for local cultures, practices, and competencies. It will also involve the adoption of a much more participative and collaborative model of leadership and authority. Finally, it will lead to putting in place prayerful consultative processes through which the guidance of the Spirit is sought, not just by the pope and the bishops in isolation, but by them with the help of theologians, committed Catholics, members of other Christian churches, members of other religions, and of spiritual searchers and ordinary people of goodwill who may not be members of any institutional religion.

I have found it difficult to put forward my criticisms of Vatican policies and attitudes, and of dysfunctional structures and practices in the church. This is partly because I love this church in spite of all its inadequacies, and partly because I am afraid of the possible consequences for myself. There is a further reason why I find it hard to write in this way. It is simply because I cannot at all be certain that my criticism is justified. My judgements may be distorted or unbalanced. Despite my reservations, I am taking the risk of making these criticisms because I think it is 'time for a change', as I say in the title of my book. Or at least it is time for serious and respectful dialogue about these issues – a dialogue which should lead to some consensus about whether, or to what extent, changes are needed.

But what if I am wrong? In that case I adopt as my own the moving words of James Alison (79-80):

I am delighted to rest in the certainty that the One who loves us ... will not allow [me] ... to lead you too far astray without providing the means to lead us into all truth. And I am also sure that if my attempt ... be conducted with appropriate courtesy and tentativeness, then the One who makes the truth resplendent will have no difficulty in turning even my falsehoods into paths by which we may be called to live in the truth.

Bibliography

Alison, James (2003) *On Being Liked*, London, DLT

Armstrong, Karen (2000, 2002) *Islam: A Short History*, (revised and updated edition 2002), New York, Random House, Modern Library Paperbacks (earlier ed. 2000, London, Phoenix Press)

Baum, Gregory (2000) 'Management in God' *The Furrow*, May 2000: 267-278

Berry, Thomas (1988) *The Dream of the Earth*, San Francisco, Sierra Club Books

Bircham, Emma and Charlton, John (2001) *Anti-Capitalism: a Guide to the Movement*, London and Sydney, Bookmarks Publications

Black, Peter (2003) 'The Broken Wings of Eros: Christian Ethics and the Denial of Desire' 106-126 of *Theological Studies*, Vol. 64 (2003)

Bolman, Lee G. and Deal, Terrence E. (2001) *Leading with Soul: An Uncommon Journey of Spirit*, (new and revised edition) San Francisco, Jossey-Bass

Brown, Raymond E. (1994) *An Introduction to New Testament Christology*, New York, Paulist; and London, Chapman

Cardenal, Ernesto (1982) *The Gospel in Solentiname*, Maryknoll, Orbis

Catholic Bishops' Conferences of England and Wales, Ireland, and Scotland (1998) *One Bread One Body*, London, CTS; and Dublin, Veritas

Caux Round Table (1986) see www.cauxroundtable.org/

Coates, Barry (2001) *'GATS'* 27-40 of Bircham and Charlton

Coelho, Paulo (1995) *The Alchemist*, London, Harper Collins

Cozzens, Donald B. (2000) *The Changing Face of the Priesthood*, Collegeville, Liturgical Press

Crowe, Frederick E. (1989) 'Son and Spirit: Tension in the Divine Missions', 297-314 of *Appropriating the Lonergan Idea* (edited by Michael Vertin), Washington DC, CUA

Davie, Grace (2002) *Europe: The Exceptional Case: Parameters of Faith in the Modern World*, London, DLT

D'Arcy, Martin (1956) *The Mind and Heart of Love*, New York, Meridian

Dollard, Kit, and Marett-Crosby, Anthony, and Wright, Abbot Timothy (2002) *Doing Business with Benedict: The Rule of St Benedict and business management: a conversation*, London and New York, Continuum

Donnelly, Dody H. (1984, 1992) *Radical Love: An Approach to Sexual Spirituality*, Fremont , Dharma Cloud Publishers

Dorr, Donal (1984) *Spirituality and Justice*, Dublin, Gill and Macmillan; and Maryknoll, Orbis

Dorr, Donal (1990) *Integral Spirituality: Resources for Community, Justice, Peace, and the Earth*, Dublin, Gill and Macmillan; and Maryknoll, Orbis

Dorr, Donal (1992) *Option for the Poor: A Hundred Years of Catholic Social Teaching* (revised edition), Maryknoll, Orbis; and Dublin, Gill and Macmillan

Dorr, Donal (2000) *Mission in Today's World*, Dublin, Columba Press; and Maryknoll, Orbis

Dorr, Donal (2002) 'Bringing Ethics and Spirituality into Business' 195-213 of Pontifical Council for Justice and Peace, *Work as the Key to the Social Question*, Vatican City, Libreria Editrice Vaticana

Fox, Matthew (1995) *The Reinvention of Work: A New Vision of Livelihood for Our Time*, San Francisco, HarperSanFrancisco pb.

Fox, Matthew (2000) *Passion for Creation: The Earth-honouring Spirituality of Meister Eckhart*, Rochester, Vermont, Inner Traditions International

Freire, Paulo (1985) *Education for Critical Consciousness* (revised ed.), London, Sheed and Ward

Freire, Paulo (1996) *Pedagogy of the Oppressed*, Harmondsworth, Penguin

Frey, Bruno (1998) *Not Just for the Money: An Economic Theory of Personal Motivation*, Cheltenham UK, Edward Elgar; Northampton MA, USA

Galilea, Segundo (1984) *The Beatitudes: To Evangelize as Jesus Did*, Maryknoll, Orbis

George, Susan (2001) 'Corporate Globalisation' 11-24 of Bircham and Charlton

González Faus, José I. (2003) *Why the Church?*, Barcelona: Cristianisme i Justicia Booklets No 112

Grant, Michael, and Hazel, John (1993) *Routledge Who's Who in Classical Mythology*, London, Routledge

Gray, John (1992) *Men Are from Mars, Women Are from Venus: A Practical Guide for Improving Communication and Getting What You Want in Your Relationships*, New York, Harper Collins

Gray, John (Professor) (2003) *Al Qaeda and What it Means to be Modern*, London, Faber and Faber

Gui, Benedetto (2000) 'Beyond Transactions: On the Interpersonal Dimension of Economic Reality', *Annals of Public and Cooperative Economics* 71:2, 139-170.

Hay, David (2002) 'The Spirituality of the Unchurched' 11-26 of Mellor and Yeates

Hederman, Mark Patrick (1999) *Kissing the Dark: Connecting with the Unconscious*, Dublin, Veritas

Hederman, Mark Patrick (2000) *Manikon Eros: Mad Crazy Love*, Dublin, Veritas

Hederman, Mark Patrick (2003) *Tarot: Talisman or Taboo? Reading the World as Symbol*, Dublin, Currach Press

Hertz, Noreena (2001) *The Silent Takeover: Global Capitalism and the Death of Democracy*, London, Heinemann

Higgins, Patricia (2003) 'Social Justice, Why Bother?' 121-130 of Jesuit Centre for Faith and Justice, *Windows on Social Spirituality*, Dublin, Columba Press

Hogan, Linda, and FitzGerald, Barbara (eds.) (2003) *Between Poetry and Politics: Essays in Honour of Enda McDonagh*, Dublin, Columba Press

Hope, Anne, and Timmel, Sally (1995) *Training for Transformation: A Handbook for Community Workers* (2nd revised ed.) 3 Volumes, Gweru, Zimbabwe, Mambo Press:

Hope, Anne and Timmel, Sally (1999) *Training for Transformation: A Handbook for Community Workers*, Volume 4, Kleinmond, South Africa, Training for Transformation Institute

Jaworski, Joseph (1996) *Synchronicity: The Inner Path of Leadership*, San Francisco, Berrett-Koehler Publishers

Jung, Carl Gustav (1973) *Synchronicity: an Acausal Connecting Principle*, Princeton, Princeton University Press

Kavanagh, Patrick (1984) *The Complete Poems*, Newbridge, Goldsmith Press

Kavunkal, Jacob (2001) 'Mission in Asia' 163-175 of Stephen Bevans and Roger Schroeder (editors), *Mission for the 21st Century*, Chicago Il, CCGM Publications,

Kearney, Michael (2000) *A Place of Healing: Working with Suffering in Living and Dying*, New York and Oxford, OUP

Keenan, Marjorie (2000) *Care for Creation: Human Activity and the Environment*, (Pontifical Council for Justice and Peace), Vatican City, Libreria Editrice Vaticana

Kennelly, Brendan (1995) 'Spirituality and Prayer' (radio interview, 1995/05/24 tape), Dublin, 3R Productions

Kimmerling, Ben (1986) 'Sexual Love and the Love of God: A Spirituality of Sexuality' (a series of three articles) in *Doctrine and Life* 1986: 300-8; 363-7; 454-465

Kimmerling, Ben (1993) 'Celibacy and Intimacy' in *The Way: Supplement* No 77 (Summer 1993), 87-96

Laabs, Jennifer J. (1995) 'Balancing Spirituality and Work' in *Personnel Journal*, Vol. 74, No 9 (September 1995) 60-75

Mackey, James P., and McDonagh, Enda (eds.) (2003) *Religion and Politics in Ireland at the Turn of the Millennium*, Dublin, Columba Press

Mackey, James P. (2003a) 'The Internal Politics and Policies of the Roman Catholic Church at the turn of the millennium' 13-40 of Mackey and McDonagh.

Mackey, James P. (2003b) 'The Social Role of the Theologian from the Dawn of Western Civilisation to the Present Day' 32-50 of Hogan and FitzGerald

McDonagh, Enda (2003) 'Church-State Relations in Independent Ireland' 41-63 of Mackey and McDonagh.

McDonagh, Sean (2003a) *Dying for Water*, Dublin, Veritas

McDonagh, Sean (2003b) *Patenting Life? Stop! Is Corporate Greed Forcing Us to Eat Genetically Engineered Food?* Dublin, Dominican Publications

McGeachy, Catherine (2001) *Spiritual Intelligence in the Workplace*, Dublin, Veritas

MacNamara, Vincent (1994) 'Moral Life, Christian' 635-650 of Dwyer, Judith A., (ed.) *The New Dictionary of Catholic Social Thought*, Collegeville, Glazier, Liturgical Press

MacNamara, Vincent (1998) 'The Distinctiveness of Christian Morality' 149-160 of Hoose, Bernard, (ed.) *Christian Ethics: An Introduction*, London, Cassell

McVerry, Peter (2003) 'Mary's Vision of Justice outlined in the Magnificat' 39-48 of Jesuit Centre for Faith and Justice, *Windows on Social Spirituality*, Dublin, Columba Press

Main, John (1980, 1981) *Word Into Silence*, London, DLT; and New York, Paulist

Main, John (1998) *Moment of Christ: The Path of Meditation*, New York, Continuum

May, John D'Arcy (2003) *Transcendence and Violence: The Encounter of Buddhist, Christian and Primal Traditions*, New York, Continuum

Mellor, Howard, and Yeates, Timothy (eds.) (2002), *Mission and Spirituality: Creative Ways of Being Church*, Calver, Cliff College Publishing

Mitroff, Ian I., and Denton, Elizabeth A. (1999) 'A Study of Spirituality in the Workplace', in, *Sloan Management Review*, Summer 1999: 83ff.

Nathanson, Donald L. (1992, 1994) *Shame and Pride: Affect, Sex, and the Birth of the Self*, New York and London, W. W. Norton & Company

Ó Duinn, Seán (2000) *Where Three Streams Meet: Celtic Spirituality*, Dublin, Columba Press

Ó hÓgain, Dáithi (1999) *The Sacred Isle: Belief and Religion in Pre-Christian Ireland*, Cork, Collins Press

O'Murchu, Diarmuid (1998) *Reframing Religious Life: An Expanded Vision for the Future*, (revised edition) London and Maynooth, St Pauls

O'Murchu, Diarmuid (1999) *Poverty, Celibacy, and Obedience: A Radical Option for Life*, New York, Crossroad

O'Shea, Kevin (1975) 'Enigma and Tenderness' in *Spiritual Life* 21 (Spring 1975): 11ff.

O'Toole, Fintan (2003) *After the Ball*, Dublin, New Island

Pontifical Council for Justice and Peace (2002) *Work as the Key to the Social Question: The Great Social and Economic Transformations and the Subjective Dimension of Work*, Vatican City, Libreria Editrice Vaticana

Pontifical Council for Culture, and Pontifical Council for Interreligious Dialogue (2003) 'Jesus Christ the Bearer of the Water of Life: A Christian Reflection on The "New Age"', in www.vatican.va

Pope John Paul II (1990) *Message for World Day of Peace 1990: 'Peace with God the Creator: Peace with All of Creation'*, Vatican City, AAS 82: 147–56

Pope John Paul II (1990) *Redemptoris Missio*, Vatican City, Libreria Editrice Vaticana

Pope John Paul II (1991) *Centesimus Annus*, Vatican City, Libreria Editrice Vaticana

Pope John Paul II (2003) *Pastores Gregis* (Post-Synodal Apostolic Exhortation) 16 October 2003, www.vatican.va

Porpora, Douglas V. (2001) *Landscapes of the Soul: The Loss of Moral Meaning in American Life*, Oxford and New York, OUP

Rolheiser, Ronald (1998) *Seeking Spirituality: Guidelines for a Christian Spirituality for the Twenty-First Century*, London, Hodder & Stoughton. (A US edition of this book was published in 1999 by Doubleday, New York, under the title, *The Holy Longing: the Search for a Christian Spirituality*; the pagination in this US edition is slightly different.)

Schüssler Fiorenza, Elizabeth (1983) *In Memory of Her: A Feminist Theological Reconstruction of Christian Origins*, New York, Crossroad; and London, SCM

Schumacher, E.F. (1980) *Good Work*, London, Abacus/Sphere (original ed. 1979, London, Jonathan Cape)

Schumacher, E. F. (1999) *Small is Beautiful: a Study of Economics as if People Mattered: 25 Years Later ... With Commentaries*, Point Roberts WA and Vancouver BC, Hartley and Marks (original ed. 1973, London, Blond and Briggs)

Senge, Peter M. (1994) *The Fifth Discipline: The Art and Practice of the Learning Organisation*, Bantam Doubleday Dell

Serrano, Josep F. Mària i (2001) *Globalisation*, Barcelona: Cristianisme i Justicia Booklets No 100

Sipe, A. W. Richard (1996) *Celibacy: A Way of Living, Loving, and Serving*, Dublin, Gill and Macmillan

Smyth, Geraldine O.P. (2003) 'In the Middle Ground and Meantime: A Call to the Churches in Northern Ireland to Find Themselves on the Edge' 84-106 of Mackey and McDonagh.

Sparkes, Russell (2002) *Socially Responsible Investments: a global revolution*, Chichester UK, Wiley

Stiglitz, Joseph (2002) *Globalization and its Discontents*, London, Allen Lane

Swinson, Antonia (2003) *Root of All Evil?: Making Spiritual Values Count*, Edinburgh, St Andrew Press

Tuomioja, Erkki (2001) 'Europe Must Face Globalisation' in www.OpenDemocracy.net, 18 July 2001

Turner, Victor, and Turner, Edith (1978) *Image and Pilgrimage in Christian Culture: Anthropological Perspectives*, New York, Columbia University Press

Twomey, D. Vincent (2003) *The End of Irish Catholicism?* Dublin, Veritas
Vycinas, Vincent (1961) *Earth and Gods: An Introduction to the Philosophy of Martin Heidegger,* The Hague, Nijhoff
Ward, Pete (2002) 'Liquid Church' 83-92 of Mellor and Yeates
Wink, Walter (1992) *Engaging the Powers: Discernment and Resistance in a World of Domination,* Minneapolis, Fortress Press
World Faiths Development Dialogue (2001) *Occasional Paper* no. 3, 'A New Direction for World Development?'
Zohar, Danah, and Marshall, Ian (2001) *Spiritual Intelligence: the Ultimate Intelligence,* London, Bloomsbury

Index

Williams, Rowen 211
Wink, Walter 21
withdrawal 101, 107-112 *passim*,
    113, 125, 130, 131, 136
women's movement 47, 116
workaholic 103
working conditions 156, 159
workshops 25, 33, 195, 222, 246

World Day of Peace document 70
World Faiths Development
    Dialogue 152
Wuthering Heights 83
Yoga 51, 226
Zeus 197-8
Zohar, Danah 163
Zoroastrian religion 45